THE NEW CLARENDON BIBLE
(NEW TESTAMENT)
General Editor: THE REV. H. F. D. SPARKS, D.D., F.B.A.

THE ACTS

Head of the Emperor Claudius, from the River Alde, Rendham, Suffolk

THE ACTS

IN THE
REVISED STANDARD VERSION

With introduction and commentary

by

R. P. C. HANSON, M.A., D.D.
PROFESSOR OF CHRISTIAN THEOLOGY
UNIVERSITY OF NOTTINGHAM

OXFORD

AT THE CLARENDON PRESS

1967

Oxford University Press, Ely House, London W. 1

GLASGOW NEW YORK TORONTO MELBOURNE WELLINGTON
CAPE TOWN SALISBURY IBADAN NAIROBI LUSAKA ADDIS ABABA
BOMBAY CALCUTTA MADRAS KARACHI LAHORE DACCA
KUALA LUMPUR HONG KONG TOKYO

GENERAL EDITOR'S PREFACE

THIS volume replaces the old Clarendon Bible Acts, based on the Revised Version, which was edited by the late Bishop Blunt and first published in 1923. It has set out to embody the developments in scholarship which have taken place since then. In level and purpose this volume follows its predecessor, but its publication at this time has faced editor and publishers with a dilemma in deciding on which version of the Bible it could most usefully be based. After taking the best available advice they have chosen the Revised Standard Version, believing that this is the version which in the foreseeable future is most likely to be found suitable for examination purposes in schools and colleges. They hope also that the publication of a Catholic edition of the R.S.V., which differs only slightly from the original edition, will enable commentaries based on the R.S.V. to be more generally useful.

The editor and publishers wish to express their warm gratitude to the National Council of Churches of Christ in the United States of America for the permission, so readily given, to make use of the R.S.V. in this way.

The design of the new volume follows that of the old, except that it has been thought more practical to print both text and notes on the same page: subjects requiring more comprehensive treatment than the scope of the notes allows will be found as before in the Introduction and in appendixes at the end of each volume. It is hoped that the illustrations will be found as valuable a feature of the new series as of the old.

CONTENTS

ILLUSTRATIONS

AUTHOR'S NOTE

I would like to express warm thanks to the General Editor of this series, Professor H. F. D. Sparks, D.D., F.B.A., for very considerable help in revising this work, and to acknowledge gratefully the assistance which my daughter Catherine gave me in compiling the Index.

R. P. C. H.

ABBREVIATIONS

AV RV RSV	Authorized Version Revised Version Revised Standard Version
ET	English Translation
Gk.	Greek
LXX	Septuagint, i.e. the ancient Greek translation of the Old Testament
NEB	New English Bible
N.T.	New Testament
O.T.	Old Testament

[1] Those who wish to study the subject of the 'Western' text more closely are advised to begin with J. Rendel Harris, *Four Lectures on the Western Text of the New Testament* (1894); J. H. Ropes, *The Text of Acts*, in the series 'The Beginnings of Christianity'; A. C. Clark, *The Acts of the Apostles* (1933); and A. F. J. Klijn, *A Survey of the Researches into the Western Text of the Gospels and Acts* (1949).

LITERATURE ON ACTS

(A) COMMENTARIES[1]

The Beginnings of Christianity, ed. by K. LAKE and F. J. FOAKES JACKSON, especially Vol. iii, *The Text of Acts*, by J. H. Ropes; Vol. iv, *Text and Commentary*, by K. Lake and H. J. Cadbury; and Vol. v, *Additional Notes*, 1920–33.

The Moffatt Commentary on Acts, by F. J. FOAKES JACKSON, 1931.

The Acts of the Apostles, by F. F. BRUCE, 1951.

'The Book of Acts' in *The Interpreter's Bible*, by G. H. C. MACGREGOR, 1954.

The Acts of the Apostles, by C. S. C. WILLIAMS, 1957.

And for those who can read German:

Die Apostelgeschichte, by E. HAENCHEN, 1956.

Die Apostelgeschichte, by H. CONZELMANN, 1963.

(B) OTHER BOOKS ON OR RELEVANT TO ACTS

H. J. CADBURY, *The Making of Luke-Acts*, 1927 (reprinted 1958); *The Book of Acts in History*, 1955.

M. DIBELIUS, *Studies in the Acts of the Apostles*, 1956.

H. CONZELMANN, *The Theology of Saint Luke*, 1960.

C. K. BARRETT, *Luke the Historian in Recent Study*, 1961.

J. C. O'NEILL, *The Theology of Acts in its Historical Setting*, 1961.

J. DUPONT, *The Sources of Acts*, 1964.

A. H. M. JONES, *The Greek City*, 1940; *Studies in Roman Government and Law*, 1960.

A. N. SHERWIN-WHITE, *Roman Society and Roman Law in the New Testament*, 1963.

JOSEPHUS, *The Jewish War*, tr. by G. A. Williamson, 1959.

B. M. METZGER, *The Text of the New Testament*, 1964.[1]

[1] Where an author of a Commentary is referred to in this book and no reference given, it is to be understood that the reader is expected to supply the words 'in loc.', i.e. at the point where the Commentary handles the particular chapter and verse of Acts referred to. Otherwise references are usually given, both to the pages of the Introductions of Commentaries and to the pages of books on or relevant to Acts.

INTRODUCTION

I. *The Date and Authorship of Acts*

1. *Attestation*

IT is difficult to determine when precisely we can first observe quotations from or references to the Book of Acts in later writers. Some have imagined that they could detect quotations in Christian literature of the late first or early second century, in *1 Clement*, in the *Didache*, in *The Epistle of Barnabas*, and in the letters of Ignatius. Even closer are resemblances between some words in *The Epistle of Polycarp to the Philippians* (A.D. 130–40). But all such resemblances can be reasonably explained on the supposition that these works were quoting sayings and fragments of tradition wh:ch were at the time circulating in an oral form, and were not deliberately reproducing a single book, like Acts.

The question whether the author of the Pastoral Epistles (1 and 2 Timothy and Titus), who probably was not Paul but a later figure, writing perhaps in the early second century, knew Acts, is a more complex one. The saying 'the labourer deserves his wages' occurs at Luke 10⁷ and 1 Timothy 5¹⁸; this, however, need not represent a knowledge of Luke's Gospel (and presumably therefore of Acts) on the part of the writer of the Pastorals, but only the use of a common proverb by both writers. Again, 2 Timothy 3¹¹, where Paul is supposed to be writing to Timothy, mentions 'what befell me at Antioch, at Iconium, and at Lystra', and Acts certainly records painful experiences by Paul at the last two towns at least. It is possible that the author of the Pastorals had gained his knowledge of Paul's movements from Acts. There is, however, some information in the Pastorals about Paul and his companions which is not found in Acts (e.g. the names of Timothy's mother and grandmother, and the mention of Onesiphorus (2 Tim. 1⁵, ¹⁶)), and therefore it is possible that the author was drawing on sources of information other than Acts. He could of course have been using other information *as well as* Acts.

It is likely that the Gnostic work *The Gospel of Truth*, which many (but not all) scholars are inclined to date 145–7, knew Acts. It is very likely that Justin Martyr in his two *Apologies* (about 150) betrays knowledge of Acts. An ingenious presbyter of the Church in Asia some time early in the second half of the second century forged a romantic story called *The Acts of Paul and Thekla*; he probably, therefore, knew our Acts, and Irenaeus, writing between 170 and 180, quite certainly knew Acts.

In short, we cannot be absolutely certain that Acts was recognized and used widely by Christians before about 170; but there is strong probable evidence of its being known before that, possibly quite early in the second century, and in this discussion of the book's attestation there is nothing to prevent our assigning it a date either early in the second century or late in the first.

2. *References to External Events*

There is an abundance of historical references in the text of Acts which will, if they are handled in an orderly way, make it possible for us to date the writing of Acts with reasonable confidence.

To begin with, a number of facts suggest very strongly that Acts must have been written in the first century and could not have been written in the second, and there is some evidence which may enable us to be even more definite than this. We can first observe that the author of Acts is remarkably accurate about some of the titles of officials whom he mentions, both municipal officials and Roman imperial officials. Inscriptions have confirmed that the magistrates at Thessalonica in the first century A.D. were called *politarchs* (Acts 17[6]), and excavation has confirmed that the chief executive officer of the city administration of Ephesus was called a *grammateus* (Acts 19[35], translated 'town clerk' in the RSV), and *asiarchs* (Acts 19[31]) can be substantiated from other sources. The title 'proconsul' (Gk. ἀνθύπατος) is correctly attributed to the two governors of senatorial provinces named in Acts, Sergius Paulus and Gallio, governors of Cyprus and of Achaea respectively. In his double work, Luke–Acts, the author mentions several emperors (Augustus, Tiberius, Claudius) at appropriate times, and also three procurators of Judaea, Pontius Pilate, Felix, and Festus. He also refers in correct terms to Roman soldiers of various sorts, two centurions (Cornelius and Julius) with the names of their cohorts (Italian and Augustan), and one tribune, Claudius Lysias (Acts 21[31], etc.), *chiliarch* in Greek. The author has detailed knowledge of the unusual Roman administrative division of Macedonia. Unlike other provinces, Macedonia was divided into four administratively separate parts, and Acts 16[12] seems to reflect this. Other examples of accuracy in referring to the details of the life and society of people in the Roman Empire could be adduced. These details cannot, however, be regarded as convincing proof, because many of them hold true for the second century as well.

It could also be pointed out that the veracity of Acts is in many points confirmed by the Epistles of Paul himself, which are undoubtedly first-century documents; for instance, in Acts 20[4] we are told that Paul travelled from Greece to Jerusalem accompanied by a large party, Sopater, Aristarchus, Secundus, Gaius, Timothy, Tychicus, and Trophimus. In Romans 16 we find mention of Timothy, Jason, Sosipater, Tertius, Gaius, Erastus, and Quartus. Erastus and Jason appear elsewhere in Acts (19[22]; 17[5-7, 9]), and Aristarchus and Tychicus are mentioned in other Epistles (Col. 4[7, 10]; Philem. 24; Eph. 6[21]). Crispus is mentioned in Acts (18[8]) as the ruler of a synagogue, and in 1 Corinthians 1[14] Paul says that he baptized Crispus. Sosthenes is also mentioned in Acts as the ruler of a synagogue, beaten up by the Greeks after Gallio's judgement (18[17]), and 1 Corinthians is sent from Paul and 'our brother Sosthenes' (1[1]). But it must be admitted that as well as agreements between Acts and Paul's Epistles there are also disagreements. These will be examined later.[1]

So far, then, we have found only suggestions that Acts does not contradict a first-century dating, but nothing decisive. Decisive evidence, however, is not wanting.

All scholars are agreed that the author of Acts is anxious to present the Roman Government as treating Christians fairly, no matter how others may treat them. 'In the end it is confidence in the justice of the Emperor that forms the great climax of the narrative', says Conzelmann.[2] The author wanted

---

[1] See below, pp. 15 ff.
[2] *The Theology of Luke*, p. 144; cp. *Die Apostelgeschichte*, p. 10.

to represent Christianity as not contrary to Roman law, indeed as appealing to people who appreciate and admire and obey Roman law. The first convert from paganism is a Roman centurion (Acts 10). Sergius Paulus, the Roman official, behaves in exemplary fashion towards Christians (13[6ff.]). Paul's Roman citizenship is mentioned with pride (Acts 16[37], etc.). The incident before Gallio is an acted parable showing that the Roman Government can have no prejudice against Christians (18[12ff.]). In Acts 25[8] Paul says, 'Neither against the law of the Jews, nor against the Temple, nor against Caesar have I offended at all', and his subsequent trial before Festus vindicates this claim.[1] Gärtner points out that one of the aims of Acts is to show that officials of all types (and behind all officials, even behind King Agrippa II, stood the authority of Rome) regard Christian doctrine as harmless, in spite of the machinations of its enemies. Christianity is accused before Gallio (Acts 18[14f.]), by Demetrius the silversmith (19[23-24]), and by Tertullus (24[1-9]), but all these accusations are carefully answered. The Jews stir up trouble against Christianity in Pisidian Antioch (Acts 13[14ff.]) and in Lystra (Acts 14), and nearly lynch Paul in the Temple (21[27ff.,]); the mob rages against the Christian religion in Ephesus (Acts 19); the philosophers sneer at it in Athens (Acts 17). Paul is accused of introducing customs not lawful to Roman citizens (16[21]; 17[20]; 19[23f.]) and of turning the world upside down, acting contrary to the decrees of Caesar, and preaching another Emperor, one Jesus (17[6, 7]). But wherever Christians meet officials they are found innocent. The town clerk at Ephesus urges the mob to act according to due legal form, in fear that the Romans will punish rioting (19[38-39]). Festus declares that Romans insist upon a fair trial for accused persons (25[15f.]) and later pronounces Paul innocent (26[31]). A whole series of officials hear Paul's case—magistrates and *duumviri* (16[19]), *politarchs* (17[6]), a town clerk (19[35]), proconsuls (Sergius Paulus and Gallio), procurators (Felix and Festus), and King Agrippa (26[32]). None of them condemns him. Some openly declare him innocent.

It is virtually impossible to reconcile this attitude to the Roman Government with what we know about the relations between Church and State in the second century, even early in the second century. About the year 115 Pliny's letters to

[1] *The Theology of Luke*, pp. 141–4.

the Emperor Trajan, which he wrote to his emperor as governor of Bithynia, give us some idea of the situation, and so do the letters of Ignatius, written at about the same time as he travelled under escort from Antioch to Rome, where he was to be thrown to the beasts in the arena for professing Christianity. It is clear that by this time simply to profess the name of Christian was a grave offence which often entailed capital punishment, and that once a Roman magistrate was satisfied by the evidence brought before him that accused persons were Christians, he had no alternative but to condemn them. Pliny himself refers to similar prosecutions, like those which were brought before him in Bithynia, as having occurred twenty years earlier.[1] The evidence for persecution in the reign of Domitian (A.D. 81–96) is uncertain and indirect. But the violent language of the book of Revelation, which regards Emperor-worship as the last act of the Devil and the Roman imperial Government as the embodiment of Antichrist, can hardly be referring only to Nero, whose persecution was confined to a single year (64), a single city (Rome), and a single charge (arson). It is highly likely that the Church–State relationship reflected in the affairs of Ignatius and of Pliny had developed by A.D. 90. This is not one that is compatible with the language of Acts about the Roman Government. To say of this situation that the Roman Government is carefully neutral towards Christianity and, once it is apprised of the facts, regards it as harmless, would be grotesque.

We can, moreover, form a clear and reliable picture of the line taken by Christian apologists in the second century; we have the works of Aristides, of Justin, of Tatian, of Athenagoras, of Tertullian, of Minucius Felix, and of the anonymous author of *The Epistle to Diognetus*, as well as fragments from Quadratus and Melito. Their arguments are fairly consistent. They remonstrate with the Roman authority for the attitude it takes to Christianity and for tolerating the legal situation under which Christians suffer; they refute the gross popular rumours which attributed to Christians such enormities as child-murder, cannibalism, and unnatural orgies. There is nothing whatever of this visible anywhere in Acts. The exact position of Christians under the Roman Government, once they had become distinct in the eyes of the law from Jews, is

[1] Pliny, *Letters*, x. xcvi. 6.

admittedly uncertain,[1] but one thing is quite clear, that the later we place Acts in the first century the more difficult it becomes to reconcile its language about the Roman Government with the contemporary situation; and that if we place it in the second century (and as late as 130), we cannot reconcile the two at all.

The next piece of evidence to be adduced is that provided by the appeal to Caesar. There is no doubt whatever that the possibility of such an appeal had been open to Roman citizens from the second half of the first century B.C., and was in fact the development of an already existing, earlier, right. But the evidence for its precise form in the reigns of Claudius (A.D. 41–54), Nero (54–68), and the next few emperors is scanty. In fact, the case of Paul's appeal is one of the best attested in the period. But A. H. M. Jones[2] and A. N. Sherwin-White[3] are both satisfied that there is enough evidence apart from Paul's case for us to be sure that the type of appeal process reflected in Acts is an example of the process as it obtained in the first century, up till perhaps A.D. 89–90, and that by the time of Pliny's rule in Bithynia (c. 115) a rather different process was in operation. In the first century the accused person appealed *before* the magistrate trying him pronounced the verdict or the sentence, and thereby caused the case to be taken out of that magistrate's hands and put into the hands of the court of the Emperor himself at Rome. By Pliny's time, apparently, capital or serious cases involving Roman citizens in the provinces were automatically remitted to Rome, whether the accused appealed to Caesar or not.[4] Later still, the process of appeal took place only after verdict and sentence locally given, and did not involve anyone's going to Rome. It will be clear to the reader of Acts that the circumstances of Paul's case fit the earliest, first-century, situation better than either of the later two.

Another piece of evidence is the activity of the town

[1] See A. N. Sherwin-White, 'The Early Persecutions and Roman Law Again', *Journal of Theological Studies* N.S., iii (Oct. 1952), pp. 99–113), for an admirable treatment of the question. Also S. L. Gutermann, *Religious Toleration and Persecution in Ancient Rome*.

[2] *Studies in Roman Government and Law*, Ch. IV, pp. 53–65.

[3] *Roman Society and Roman Law in the New Testament*, pp. 68–70.

[4] Pliny, *Letters*, x. xcvi. 4. For a further discussion of this subject see below, Commentary, pp. 225–7.

assemblies of Ephesus and Thessalonica reflected in Acts (17^5 and 19^{29-41}). In the second century the functioning of these town assemblies (parliaments, as it were, of relatively self-governing cities) became rarer and rarer, as the town councils (the cabinets of the parliaments, so to speak) took over all their powers, and tended to dispense with them altogether. Clearly Acts does not envisage such a situation; so much so that Sherwin-White can say that the activity of the assembly in Ephesus as described in Acts 'not only agrees in general with the civic situation in Asia Minor in the first and early second centuries A.D., but falls into place in the earlier rather than the later phase of development'.[1] He makes much the same remark about the attitude towards Roman citizenship reflected in Acts. When there were not many Roman citizens, in the Eastern parts of the Roman Empire at any rate, the privilege was valued for the *political* rights it conferred (such as Cicero dwells on in his *In Verrem*). After the end of the reign of Claudius (A.D. 54) Roman citizenship becomes a much more common phenomenon, and it is the *social* advantages of citizenship that come to the fore. Pliny, for instance, inveighing against the ill-treatment by a cruel proconsul of a provincial Roman citizen about A.D. 95, emphasizes his social position rather than his political rights. But Acts 'breathes the climate of the earlier phase'.[2] Neither Paul the Jew nor Claudius Lysias the tribune enjoys high social standing, but both value their Roman citizenship.

Then there is the fact that Acts evinces no acquaintance at all with Gnosticism, that strange mixture of esoteric beliefs and ideas and speculations whose existence in the second century is unmistakable, but whose presence in the first century is a matter of considerable debate. Many scholars observe that it is a remarkable fact that Luke in Acts deliberately conceals all knowledge of this type of thought, though none of them produces a convincing reason why he should avoid this subject. Much the simplest, not to say the most scientific, explanation is that he wrote at a period in the first century before this phenomenon had appeared.

Finally, there is the embarrassment raised by the 'Western' text of Acts for those who wish to place the book in the second century. This type of text is now agreed by almost all scholars

[1] *Roman Society and Roman Law*, p. 85.   [2] Ibid., pp. 172–3.

to have been in existence in the middle of the second century, and some would place it as early as A.D. 150.[1] W. G. Kümmel conjectures that one type of the text of Acts, the 'Caesarean' type, existed in Egypt early in the second century; if we accept this view it becomes impossible to place the original composition of Acts in the same century.[2] This cumulative evidence ought to suggest that the attempt to place the writing of the book of Acts in the second century, and not in the first, is an impossible task, quite apart from the content of its thought, even if there were no further facts to consider.

But there are further facts. There are several small but significant points of historical detail incidentally retailed by Luke which suggest that he must have lived at a time not far removed from some of the events he was narrating. He tells us that Paul encountered the high priest Ananias shortly before he met the procurator Felix (Acts 23[2, 33], 24[2, 3]); that Felix was at that time married to Drusilla (24[24]); that some time afterwards (whether as long as two years or not is uncertain) Felix was superseded by Festus, who shortly after reaching Palestine attended to Paul's case and gave him, among other measures, a hearing before King Agrippa II, with whom the King's sister Berenice was at that time living (25[1-27]). This is a very remarkable piece of synchronization on the part of the author. We can gather from Josephus that Ananias was High Priest from some time before the year 48 until some point in the procuratorship of Felix, when he was deposed; in 66 he was murdered by terrorists (*Antiquities*, xx. 103, 104, 173–8, 179; *Jewish War*, ii. 441). It would have taken a very considerable amount of research for a later historian to discover that Ananias must have been the high priest contemporary with Paul at that point, that this took place in the period when Felix was married to Drusilla (who had been born in 38 and had had one husband already before Felix), and that not long afterwards Berenice (who had already had two husbands) was living for a period (a limited period) with her brother, during the procuratorship of Festus.

---

[1] For information about the 'Western' text, see below, pp. 55–56.
[2] Note the 'Western' reading at Acts 11[17] implying that the original reading did not necessarily associate the giving of the Spirit with baptism, a view corrected by the 'Western' reading. See also E. Haenchen, *Die Apostelgeschichte*, pp. 41–50, and especially on p. 41.

Then there is the interesting question, why did Felix ask Paul from what province he came, but then refrain from sending him back to it for trial (Acts 24[34-35])? The answer given by Sherwin-White is: because at that particular juncture, and only at that particular juncture, Cilicia, in whose territory Tarsus lay, was merely a dependency of the province of Syria, and the legate of Syria would not want to be burdened with a relatively minor case from an outlying part of his territory.[1] Cilicia had this status only for a limited period; there is some evidence that it had it in A.D. 52, but by the Flavian period (69–96) it had become a full province in its own right. It is likely that this state of affairs held good during the period of Paul's trial before Felix, but that twenty or thirty years later, when we may conjecture that Acts was being written, this state of affairs no longer obtained. A similar case is that of Gallio. Gallio was Proconsul of Achaea, it is known, during the year A.D. 52, which means that he must have held office either in 51–52 or 52–53.[2] Luke tells us that Paul was prosecuted unsuccessfully before him (Acts 18[12-17]), and this date offers no serious difficulty to a reconstruction of the dates and the order of Paul's career. But it would have been very difficult indeed for Luke to have discovered long after the event the fact that Gallio was Proconsul of Achaea when Paul was there at that point in his career. In the first century proconsuls certainly did not keep public records on the spot where they held rule; the only way to discover the dates and places of proconsuls' periods of office would be to go to the Senate-house at Rome and there search the archives until a record of the decree of the Senate appointing the proconsul in question was found; and access to the archives of the Senate was open only to persons of high rank.

Another example of the same remarkable accuracy in relating his narrative to contemporary history on the author's part is his reference to the Egyptian fanatic who started a revolt and led a band of terrorists into the desert (Acts 21[38]). Josephus, the Jewish historian of the late first century, mentions this very minor incident,[3] and tells us that the

---

[1] *Roman Society and Roman Law*, pp. 55–56.
[2] See Commentary, in loc., p. 186.
[3] *Jewish War*, i. 261–3. But Josephus assesses the terrorists at 30,000 men, with much less probability than Luke, who restricts them to 4,000. The old

procurator Felix chased the man away. Luke represents the tribune as referring to this as a recent occurrence, and he places the tribune's remark in the procuratorship of Felix, to whom the tribune shortly afterwards dispatches Paul. This would be an extraordinarily lucky piece of accuracy on the part of an author writing in 130, or even at the end of the first century! Another interesting point is the substance of the charges made by the orator Tertullus against Paul (Acts 23⁵). 'We have found this man', he says, 'a pestilent fellow, an agitator among all the Jews throughout the world.' A close parallel to this language can be found in the words of the Emperor Claudius in a letter he wrote to the people of Alexandria early in his reign on the subject of riots between Jews and Greeks in that city. He describes the Jews as by their actions 'producing a universal plague all over the world'. The comment of Sherwin-White on this point is: 'It is evident that the narrative of Acts is using contemporary language. The charge was precisely the one to bring against a Jew during the Principate of Claudius or during the early years of Nero.'[1]

Again, when Claudius Lysias said 'I bought this citizenship for a large sum' (Acts 22²⁸), he was not referring to any formal fee which he had to pay for the privilege, for there was none, but to the money he had to expend on bribes to clerks and officials in order to get his name on the appropriate list of those who were to receive citizenship. It is known that under the Emperor Claudius many people obtained Roman citizenship by means of bribing the relevant officials. In the time of his successor, Nero, this scandal was discovered, the people responsible for it were punished, and, as far as is known, it did not recur. Now Claudius Lysias must have obtained his citizenship under the Emperor Claudius, for he took his name; and he is supposed to be speaking just at the end of Claudius' reign (or, less probably, at the beginning of Nero's). 'The historical atmosphere of the Lysias incident', says Sherwin-White, 'is exactly right for the time of Claudius.'[2] Either the author of Acts has a surprising capacity for historical research

view that Luke had read Josephus' works is now, I believe, abandoned by everybody.

[1] *Roman Society and Roman Law*, p. 51. Cp. also H. J. Cadbury, *The Making of Luke-Acts*, p. 240, for further evidence of the same sort.

[2] *Roman Society and Roman Law*, p. 156.

and an historical imagination equalling that of Walter Scott and Robert Graves, or he lived near to the events he is relating, or he is using sources which derive from a time near to those events. Finally, there is the fact that the two centurions mentioned in Acts (10¹ and 27¹) are denoted by a single name, the *nomen* only, Cornelius and Julius.[1] This brief form, lacking the *cognomen* or third member, was an old-fashioned type of name, not found outside the conservative Roman army by the middle of the first century. The last example datable from an inscription is that of a Roman soldier killed on active service in the year 54 or some time after it. It surely is no coincidence that the only two people who have this type of name in Acts are both soldiers, at precisely the period when only soldiers are likely to be still using it.[2] Is this the sort of detail which somebody writing in the second century, or at the very end of the first, when this custom must have for some considerable time lapsed, is likely to have invented, imagined, or guessed?

This accumulation of facts, then, suggests very strongly that in the author of Acts we are dealing with somebody who lived during the first century, and not the second; but more than this, that parts at least of his narrative correspond closely to a particular period of history, roughly from A.D. 41 to 70, which may even be limited to the end of Claudius' reign and the beginning of Nero's. It seems likely that he has some close connexion with that period, either of sources or of personal experience; we are driven by the facts of the case to this conclusion. It should be noted that in reaching it we have not once referred to the 'we' passages.[3]

3. *Internal Chronology and Consistency*

The recognition that Acts was probably written in the first century, and at a period not far from the middle of that century, must not blind us to the fact that it is possible to detect several examples of confusion, inconsistency, and inaccuracy in the narrative of Acts. It has recently been suggested, for instance, that Luke betrays ignorance of the geography of

[1] The three proper names which usually composed the name of Roman citizens of the time of Paul were called the *praenomen*, the *nomen*, and the *cognomen* respectively.
[2] *Roman Society and Roman Law*, p. 161.   [3] See below, pp. 21–28.

Palestine; the sentence 'So the church throughout all Judaea, and Galilee and Samaria had peace and was built up' (Acts 9[31]) has been taken to betray a belief in the author's mind that Judaea and Galilee were next to each other and had a common frontier.[1] But a consideration of Acts 15[3], where Paul and Barnabas are described as traversing in a journey from Antioch to Jerusalem the territories of Phoenicia and Samaria, in correct order, should make one pause before accepting this theory. It is noteworthy, however, that the Ascension is described as taking place at Bethany in Luke 24[50], but in Acts 1[12] the Mount of Olives is the scene of this event. It has been suggested[2] that Luke wrongly supposed that Bethany was a village on the Mount of Olives, misled by Mark 11[1]. Again, in the account of the healing of the lame man in the third chapter of Acts, Luke appears to betray ignorance of the plan of the Temple, for if the man was healed at the 'gate . . . called Beautiful' (v. 2), and Peter and John then entered the Temple with him (v. 8), it would have been impossible for all the people who ran towards them in astonishment to meet them in Solomon's portico (v. 11), for this covered walk was not inside the Temple enclosure but built on to its outside.[3] It may be that Luke had little first-hand knowledge of Jerusalem.

There are several inconsistencies or improbabilities in the narrative of the early chapters of Acts. The release of the apostles from jail by the action of an angel (5[19]) is related in a very casual way, and the accusation of the High Priest and Gamaliel's reply make no reference to this highly unusual occurrence (5[2 ff.]), so that we may suspect its veracity. In this reply of Gamaliel one of the clearest examples of error on the author's part occurs. Gamaliel refers (vv. 35 ff.) to the abortive revolts, first of Theudas, and then of Judas of Galilee as following that of Theudas. But it is quite clear from Josephus that the rebellion of Judas took place in A.D. 6 and that of Theudas long after, about A.D. 44, a period later, indeed, than the point at which Gamaliel is supposed to be making this speech! Incidentally, this betrays the facts not only that the

---

[1] Conzelmann, *The Theology of Luke*, p. 69. See also Bartsch, *Wachet aber zu Jeder Zeit*, pp. 20–26. Bartsch further suggests that Luke 9[22] and 24[6] imply that Bethsaida was in Galilee, whereas in fact it was not.

[2] Bartsch, op. cit., pp. 20–26.

[3] The 'Western' text tries to correct this. See Commentary.

author can make mistakes, but that he himself must have composed the speech attributed to Gamaliel (it is, anyway, unlikely from the circumstances that he could have had access to reliable information about what exactly Gamaliel said at that point). Again we are told that Stephen was among the seven persons chosen to 'serve tables' (which presumably would include administrative work of various sorts, Acts 6²⁻⁵), yet instead of this he proceeds to perform wonders and engage in disputations (6⁸ᶠᶠ·). Luke places the death of Herod Agrippa I (related in Acts 12) during the Passover Festival (12³, 'This was during the days of Unleavened Bread' can only mean this); but we know from the evidence of Josephus, and from the fact that Agrippa's death came just after the official celebrations in connexion with the Emperor Claudius' return from Britain, that Herod must have died before the Passover in that year (to be precise, on 5 March A.D. 44). Further, Luke places the relief mission of Paul and Barnabas to Judaea during what he calls 'a great famine over all the world', before the martyrdom of James the brother of John and the death of Herod Agrippa (11²⁷⁻³⁰). But there is no other evidence of a world-wide famine during the reign of Claudius (i.e. one that affected the whole Roman Empire), and though Josephus does mention a severe famine in Judaea during Claudius' reign,[1] much the most probable time for it is A.D. 46–48, that is after Herod's death. It is, therefore, preferable to place this relief mission of Paul and Barnabas in 46.

The fact is that a careful study of the first half of Acts will suggest to the discerning reader that for this earliest stage of the Christian Church's existence, until the narrative reaches that period with which we have already had reason to think that our author is well acquainted, Luke is compelled to manage his account as best as he can with very scanty materials to aid him. The earliest chapters relating the birth of the Church and the first years of its existence are enveloped in a certain vagueness. The Ascension and the Coming of the Holy Spirit are indeed described, but the 'feel' of the narratives leaves the impression that these descriptions are literary reconstructions based on fact, but a minimum of fact. After all, both Matthew's Gospel and John's appear to give us an

[1] *Antiquities*, xx. 101. Haenchen, *Apostelgeschichte*, pp. 50–69, is most useful upon all points of chronology.

account of the same events (Matt. 28$^{16-20}$; John 20$^{10-29}$), and they reconstruct them in quite different ways. This 'literary reconstruction' is a recurring characteristic of the method of the author of Acts (cp. Luke 4$^{16-30}$, 24$^{10-35}$). As we continue to

Shops grouped round an open court at Ostia. The remains of the shop-keepers' living-quarters on the first floor are visible.

read the narrative of Acts, and encounter stories such as the description of the early 'communism' practised in the Church, the exemplary deaths of Ananias and Sapphira, the first healing miracles, the early trials before the Sanhedrin, the appointment of the Seven, and the martyrdom of Stephen, we gain the impression that for the composition of his history the author was able to discover a number of pieces of information but that they were detached, separate items with no connexion between them indicated anywhere, and that he did not know their original order or relationship to each other, if they had any. As his narrative proceeds his material becomes fuller, facts come thicker, and the early impression of vagueness fades away, though he still may have to use his powers of conjecture to determine the order and relationship of the events with which he is dealing.

The greatest crux of all for those who are trying to assess the chronology and the internal consistency of the narrative in Acts is provided by the 'Apostolic Council' described in Acts 15. This is probably the thorniest question facing historical investigation in the whole New Testament, and a vast amount of labour and ingenuity has been expended upon attempts to solve it, with very few solid results.[1] The difficulty appears when we compare Paul's account in Galatians 1¹⁵–2¹⁴ of his movements for many years after his conversion with the data given in Acts. We need not be troubled by Luke's omission of Paul's journey into Arabia and return to Damascus immediately after his conversion (cp. Acts 9²⁵, ²⁶ with Gal. 1¹⁷, ¹⁸), even though Paul says that three years had elapsed between his conversion and his first visit to Jerusalem after being converted, whereas Luke describes the interval in the words 'when many days had passed' (9²³). Much more serious is the fact that the consultation between Paul and Barnabas, on the one hand, and the senior leaders in Jerusalem, such as Peter and James the Lord's brother, on the other, described in Acts 15, is certainly represented by the author as Paul's *third* visit to Jerusalem since his conversion. The other two, alluded to in Acts 9²⁶ and 11²⁷–³⁰, were his visit after the conversion to accredit himself with the leaders of the Church in Jerusalem, and his famine-relief visit with Barnabas. The third visit Luke represents as a consultation on the subject of the application of the Jewish Law to Gentile Christians. But in Galatians Paul is most emphatic that the first two visits he paid to Jerusalem after his conversion were only the visit to accredit himself (three years after his conversion, Gal. 1¹⁸–²²) and the visit which resulted in a consultation with the senior apostles about how far Gentile converts were to be bound by the Jewish Law (fourteen years after either his

[1] C. S. C. Williams in *The Acts of the Apostles*, pp. 22–32, gives a very clear and concise summary of these attempts.

conversion or his previous visit, Gal. 2$^{1\text{ff.}}$). This last, by his account, can only have been his *second* visit to Jerusalem after his conversion. Here there appears to be an absolute contradiction.

It has been suggested that Paul did not mention the visit which he and Barnabas paid to Jerusalem in connexion with famine relief because it had nothing to do with the question of how far the Jewish Law applied to Gentile Christians. But not only would this make Paul's strong asseveration that what he wrote in Galatians was true look odd (Gal. 1^{20}), but it would mean placing the first entry of Paul into Europe on an evangelizing mission (which must on this view have taken place after the famine visit and after the Council) so late as to make the reconstruction of the chronology of Paul's career very awkward. It has been suggested that Galatians was written before the events described in Acts 15, and that the consultation narrated in Galatians took place at the time of the famine visit, but that Luke omitted the consultation from his account. In favour of this is the fact that if the 'apostolic decree', described in Acts 15 as framed to put an end to the controversy (vv. 28 and 29), was in existence when Galatians was written, then indeed it answered all the controversial points raised in that Epistle, and Paul could have ended the controversy by referring to it; furthermore, the words in Galatians (2^{10}) 'only they would have us remember the poor, which very thing I was eager to do' certainly suggest that something like famine relief was not absent from the minds of those who took part in the consultation described here. But there are two fatal objections to this solution: in the first place, it suffers, just as the first theory did, from the chronological difficulty of placing the consultation described in Acts 15 (which must, on this theory have taken place after the consultation of Gal. 2$^{1-10}$), embarrassingly late. In the second place, this theory would mean that Galatians was by far the earliest of Paul's Epistles, earlier by several years than I Thessalonians, which is usually reckoned his earliest, and much earlier than Romans, which must have been written relatively late in his career, not long before he took his final journey to Jerusalem to encounter arrest and imprisonment. But Galatians bears a most striking resemblance in matter and argument to Romans, so as to appear almost a summary presentation of parts of the argument of Romans, and appears therefore to be an example of Paul's thought at its most mature.

This difficulty cannot, in the present state of knowledge and opinion, be resolved. But certain points can be made which may put the subject in a clearer light and render the contradiction a little less acute. The first point is to observe a coincidence of date. If we grant that Paul was converted between A.D. 32 and 35 (which are the most usual limits assigned to the dating of this event), then fourteen years later would bring us to 46–49.[1] Because the ancients were always liable to reckon their dates inclusively, counting portions of years as whole years, we can give a little more elasticity to our counting and allow that fourteen years after 32 could mean 44 or 45, and after 33 could mean 46 or 47. This period coincides roughly with the most probable dating for the famine, which according to the narrative in Acts 11 caused Paul and Barnabas to come to Jerusalem. Luke does not attach to this visit any consultation about the treatment of Gentile Christians. But he has recorded that some people had already on occasion preached the word to Gentiles: Peter to Cornelius and his companions (Acts 10^1–11^{17}); and some Jewish Christians from Cyprus and Cyrene to Gentiles at Antioch, an action approved by Barnabas, who was sent by the Jerusalem Church to investigate it (11^{19-24}). Paul does not mention famine relief in his account of his second visit to Jerusalem (unless the phrase about keeping the poor in mind (Gal. 2^{10}), which we have already noted, refers to it), but he does say that he went up for this visit 'by revelation' (Gk. ἀποκάλυψις, Gal. 2^2). Now Paul uses this same word *apocalypse* in 1 Corinthians $14^{6, 26}$, in a list of contributions which Christians may make in the Spirit to a prayer meeting. It has been suggested by many scholars that by his reference to an *apocalypse* in Galatians 2^2 Paul means the incident recorded in Acts $11^{27, 28}$, when a prophet Agabus predicted a famine. If Paul, with Barnabas, was sent to Jerusalem as a result of this inspired prediction, he could well say that he went up 'as a result of an apocalypse'. It looks, therefore, as if there are some grounds for identifying the second visit according to Paul with the second visit according to Luke, and that this accords best with considerations of chronology.

[1] The Conversion must have taken place before the death of King Aretas in 39. See the Commentary, p. 116.

What then are we to say about the famous 'Apostolic
Council' recorded in Acts 15? This is probably one of Luke's
'literary reconstructions', the basis for which was the 'decree'
(15²⁸⁻²⁹) that was doubtless issued at some point, whose date
we cannot determine, by the Jewish Christian church in
Jerusalem, to define the minimum conditions to be imposed
on Gentile converts to Christianity, but not in the presence of
Paul and Barnabas. Even in Luke's account Paul takes very
little part in the proceedings of the Council, and later on,
in Acts 21²⁵, Luke seems almost to betray the fact that Paul
was not present when the 'decree' was decided on. There
is some considerable evidence that the conditions of this
decree were observed in the second century.[1] It is not impossible that Paul may have known of the existence of these
rules as conditions drawn up by the leaders of the Church at
Jerusalem, but may have chosen to ignore them as far as the
churches founded by him and under his care were concerned.
He was intensely sensitive about the independence of his
churches from control by any other apostles (Gal. 2⁶⁻¹¹; 1 Cor.
9¹⁻⁵; 2 Cor. 11⁵⁻12¹⁰). His attitude to these leaders of the
Jerusalem Church was indeed a complex one. He by no means
disowned them altogether. He admitted that if they did not
approve of his gospel he had 'run in vain' (Gal. 2²); he
acknowledged that it was from those who had been Christian
before him that he received the Christian tradition (1 Cor.
15¹⁻³). He declared that he had become a Jew for the sake of
the Jews in order to gain them (1 Cor. 9²⁰). We need not disbelieve the author of Acts when he tells us that Paul circumcised Timothy (Acts 16³), whose mother was a Jewess, even
though Paul himself insists that he did not circumcise Titus
(Gal. 2³), who had no Jewish blood. But on the subject of his
authority over his own churches he was adamant.

We need not assume that the occasion of the formulating
of this 'decree' was the first time that the question of how to
treat Gentile Christians had come into the foreground. On
the contrary, Paul in Galatians speaks as if bringing the gospel
to the Gentiles had been in his mind from the earliest moment
that he began to consider what God wanted him to do after
his conversion, certainly less than three years after that event;
and the author of Acts, as we have seen, represents the question

[1] See Commentary, in loc., p. 155.

as one which arose early in the Church's history, with the incident of Cornelius. It is true that the narrative in Acts 15 makes no overt mention of circumcision; but circumcision is inseparably involved in the question of table-fellowship, of the terms on which Christian Jews can associate familiarly with Gentiles, just because it was an association with the uncircumcised that Jews found so hard to envisage; and indeed 'lay upon you no greater burden' (Acts 15[28]) may be an oblique reference to circumcision. Both Paul and the author of Acts, being realists, associated these two questions together.[1]

Finally, we must note that it is not entirely clear who are the people to whom Paul's letter to the Galatians is addressed, and whom he had evangelized before he wrote that letter. The description 'Galatians' was a fluid one. It originally applied to people of Celtic race who had first invaded Asia Minor and settled in various parts of it in the fourth and third centuries B.C. There had been a kingdom of Galatia ruled by a client-king of the Roman government from 40 to 25 B.C., and this kingdom had latterly included not only the rather remote towns in the highlands of Anatolia such as Ancyra, Pessinus, and Tavium (the North Galatian towns), but also such towns as Pisidian Antioch, Iconium, Lystra, and Derbe much further south (the South Galatian towns). By Paul's day most of the South Galatian towns were included in the Roman province of Galatia as well as the North Galatian towns, even though the inhabitants of the South Galatian towns were not Celtic (and so not strictly Galatian) by race or language. They could therefore have been called 'the Galatians'. If Paul wrote his letter to the North Galatian towns, then we have no evidence at all as to when he evangelized them; they are not mentioned anywhere in Acts and, except for the fact that the 'Decree' was presumably applicable to them if Paul agreed to it, as he is represented as doing in Acts 15, they are not affected by the problems discussed here. But it is difficult to imagine when precisely Paul could have penetrated as far north as these North Galatian towns, accessible only by roads passing through quite high mountains; far less when he could have brought Barnabas with him (for Gal. 2[1, 9, 13] reveals that Barnabas was known to the Galatian churches). Most

---

[1] For a further discussion of this question, see the Commentary on Acts 15 below, pp. 153–9.

scholars therefore incline to the view that Paul in Galatians was addressing the four churches of Pisidian Antioch, Iconium, Lystra, and Derbe, churches he had evangelized in the journey described in Acts 13 and 14.

We must remind ourselves again that the author of Acts did not possess a consecutive account of the earlier career of Paul, nor of the careers of any others of the apostles. He had not read Paul's letters; Paul, even supposing that our writer was his companion at one time or at some times, did not carry around with him a filing-cabinet containing copies of his letters, nor did he pause at intervals to give lectures on 'My Career as a Writer'. The author of Acts had to decide for himself what were the order and relationship of the events about which he could get information. There are some events and movements of Paul implied in his letters to the Corinthians, during the last few years of his ministry in the Aegean littoral, which are unrecorded in Acts; just as there are some incidents in which Paul figured during the same period, such as his appearance before Gallio, that are not referred to in his letters but are recorded in Acts. The state of the sources for his history which were available to the author means that it is misleading to speak, as is often done, of Paul's 'First' or 'Second' or 'Third Missionary Journey', as if we were sure that he only made three missionary journeys, and that we have an exhaustive account of all his movements from his conversion to his arrest.[1] The author gives us only what he knows or what he has been able to discover. He does not give us a complete reconstruction of Paul's career. He was the first historian of the early Church on the scene, and he had few or no continuous records to guide him.

In fact, after Chapter 15 the narrative of Acts presents us with no serious difficulties. It is even possible to construct a very tentative chronology covering ten years of Paul's later life, based upon the proconsulship of Gallio, upon the year (whose dating is a complex but not impossible task) in which Festus succeeded Felix as procurator, upon the chronological indications given us in Acts itself, and upon some indications in Paul's own letters.

A.D. 51–52: Paul leaves Corinth and goes to Caesarea via Ephesus (Acts 18[21 f.]); then he returns to Antioch.

[1] Cp. O'Neill, *The Theology of Acts*, pp. 62–63.

52 autumn: he goes to Corinth via Troas and remains there for three months (during the winter 54–55).

55 early: he journeys via Macedonia to Jerusalem, where at Pentecost he is arrested in the Temple.

55–57: he remains in custody at Caesarea.

57 late summer: he begins his journey to Rome, which he reaches in 58.

58–60: he is kept in custody in Rome.

These dates could well be inaccurate by a few years in one direction or the other, but the events hang together as a connected series. It is significant that it is possible to construct this series for the later part of Paul's career, covered by the second half of Acts.

4. The 'We' Passages

We have hitherto refrained from examining one important piece of evidence, which has often in the past been thought to be decisive in determining the date and authorship of Acts, and that is the 'we' passages. These occur at points, from the 16th chapter onwards, where the writer, without explanation, changes from the third person plural ('they' passages) to the first person plural ('we' passages). They can be set out as in the following table, which also gives some idea of their content and their relation to each other in the chronology of the narrative:

16^{9-17}: *'we' passage: Troas to Philippi.*
    $16^{18}–20^4$: 'they' passage.

20^{5-16}: *'we' passage: Philippi to Miletus (some years later).*
    20^{17-38}: 'they' passage.

21^{1-18}: *'we' passage: Miletus to Jerusalem (on the same voyage as in the last 'we' passage).*
    $21^{19}–26^{32}$: 'they' passage.

$27^1–28^{16}$: *'we' passage: Caesarea to Rome (two years later).*
    28^{17-31}: 'they' passage.

It is important to realize that these 'we' passages do not differ in style or in vocabulary from the sections in which they are embedded; nor do they differ very markedly in subject-matter.

The same sort of material is found in them as is found in the 'they' passages, 'where Paul lived and where he preached, how long he worked and what success he achieved'.[1] Indeed it is noticeable that all through Chapters 16–28 there occur all sorts of small, apparently unimportant details—of persons, of places, and of events which Dibelius justly describes as 'too dull to be legend, too detailed to be fiction';[2] and they occur in the 'they' passages as well as in the 'we' passages. There are no very obvious reasons why, for instance, Attalia should be mentioned[3] in 14²⁵, or Samothrace and Neapolis in 16¹¹, or Amphipolis and Apollonia in 17¹, or why the incident narrated in 20¹³, ¹⁴ should be included, or why the name of Mnason should be mentioned in 21¹⁶. If we confined ourselves to the 'we' passages alone we might conclude that the author of them was not a fellow-worker with Paul but a companion of some of his journeys; the coastal areas seem to be the limit of his narrative.[4] Some (such as Dibelius) have thought that the account of the shipwreck in Acts 27 is a separate narrative from a separate source. Many have been anxious to see, behind Chapters 16–28 at least, a written source, which might be called an 'itinerary', worked skilfully into his narrative by the author. There are precedents for such a measure,[5] and there are several parallels in ancient historians for the author's lapsing without notice into the first person. But it is difficult to envisage exactly where the limits of a written itinerary used as a source by the author can be traced in his work. The complete consistency of his style and the fact that the signs of an 'itinerary' are not confined to the 'we' passages make this theory improbable.

The hypothesis which would explain most simply all the facts concerning the 'we' passages and the signs of an 'itinerary' in the second half of Acts, unless there are found to be

---

[1] M. Dibelius, *Studies in the Acts of the Apostles*, p. 70.

[2] Ibid., p. 78; cp. p. 197. See also J. Dupont, *The Sources of Acts*, Chs. VII and VIII.

[3] Indeed the interpolator in the 'Western' text seems to feel this, because he adds 'in order to bring them the gospel' at this point.

[4] See Conzelmann, *Die Apostelgeschichte*, pp. 5 and 6.

[5] A companion and disciple of Apollonius of Tyana, in the first century A.D., for instance, is said to have kept a 'diary' or 'scrapbook' embodying his notes made while travelling with Apollonius; see Philostratus, *Life of Apollonius of Tyana*, ii. 19.

insurmountable objections to it, is that the author of Acts, who is responsible for the style and vocabulary of the work, was a companion of Paul during the periods covered by the 'we' passages. He therefore lived close enough in time and space to Paul during the period of his life embraced by these passages to gain the pieces of information in the 'they' passages which have impressed so many scholars with their appearance of authenticity. This hypothesis would explain the consistency of style which continues during the 'we' passages, and the appearances of an 'itinerary' even during the 'they' passages; and it would obviate the necessity of assuming a written base for these passages, for they could then be based on personal reminiscences, or even on notes written by the author after Paul's arrival at Rome. Again, in all other cases where an ancient author lapses into the first person he intends that this should signify that he was present at the events narrated in the first person. It is almost impossible to avoid the conclusion that this is what the author of Acts intended the reader to think when he wrote the 'we' passages.

H. J. Cadbury, who takes this view, makes two interesting points in this connexion. He suggests that the wording of the last portions of three of the 'we' passages is intended to indicate that at that point in each case Paul and 'we' separated (Acts 16[17], 21[18], 28[16]), a suggestion which strengthens the view that the author meant to indicate by lapsing into the first person that he was present at the events narrated in the first person. Cadbury also calls attention to a phrase found in the first few verses of Luke's Gospel, in that very carefully constructed Preface, which may well be intended to refer to the double work, Luke–Acts. The phrase is 'having followed all things closely for some time past' (Luke 1[3]). Cadbury insists that this cannot mean simply that the author has investigated the events carefully, for he says that there is no single example anywhere of the word translated 'having followed' (Gk. παρηκολουθηκότι) meaning 'investigate'; it must mean 'follow with attention' or 'follow as a witness', and he produces a striking parallel from Josephus, who writes of one who 'has either followed the events as a witness (παρηκολουθηκότα) or has learned them from eyewitnesses'.[1] He thinks that there is a contrast in this Preface of Luke between *'from the beginning'*

---

[1] Josephus, *Against Apion*, i. 53.

(Luke 1²; Gk. ἀπ' ἀρχῆς) applied to the 'eyewitnesses and ministers of the word' and 'for some time past' (Luke 1³; Gk. ἄνωθεν). The author means that he had followed the course of events, not from the beginning, but from an early period, that he had come in later, but then had himself been present. Exactly this contrast occurs in Acts 26⁴, where Paul speaks of his life 'from the beginning' (Gk. ἀπ' ἀρχῆς), and shortly afterwards says that the Jews have known him 'for a long time' (26⁵: Gk. ἄνωθεν), i.e. from an early period.[1] This is significant evidence in support of the view that the author of Acts himself is in Chapters 16–28 reproducing partly his own reminiscences and partly events and details which happened within his knowledge though not actually when he was present. The fact that most of the striking examples of knowledge of contemporary secular events and situations that we have surveyed come from the second half of Acts adds additional support to this view.

But some scholars have thought that there are insurmountable objections to this view. They are connected with the author's presentation of Paul. Nobody, it has been urged, who knew Paul at all well, nobody who knew his convictions and his teaching, could draw the picture of Paul that Acts draws. In the first place, the author takes no account of Paul's passionately held conviction that he was an apostle, as much an apostle as Peter and James and John; Acts 1²¹ff. and 10³⁹ do not include him in the category of original witnesses nor number him along with the Twelve. In the second place, the writer wholly fails to reproduce the attitude of tension in regard to the admission of Gentiles without circumcision to the Church which constantly followed Paul's steps. He represents the Pharisees as on the whole siding with Paul (Acts 23⁶⁻⁹), whereas they were his bitterest enemies and unalterably opposed to him. He represents the question of circumcision and table-fellowship between Jewish and Gentile Christians as having been solved at the 'Apostolic Council' described in Acts 15 once and for all, whereas in fact Paul had to fight for his principles on these subjects throughout the whole of his

---

[1] These interesting suggestions of Cadbury's are contained in an article entitled 'We and I Passages in Luke-Acts' in *New Testament Studies*, iii (1956/7), pp. 128–32. J. Dupont, *The Sources*, pp. 103–8, summarizes them. Cp. Cadbury, *The Making of Luke-Acts*, pp. 345–7.

career. Again, he evinces no real knowledge of Paul's profound and subtle thought on the subject of the Jewish Law. In short, his ignorance of Paul's real opinions is so marked that he could not have been Paul's companion at any point, and therefore the author of Acts could not have been the author of the details which impress us in the second half of the book.

These are weighty objections, but they are not decisive. The question of Paul's claim to apostolic authority cannot constitute a fatal objection. Paul distinguishes himself from 'the Twelve' (1 Cor. 15⁵); he himself admits that he derived his knowledge of Christianity from others (1 Cor. 15³), and that if his gospel had not been approved by the apostles at Jerusalem his activity as an evangelist would have been futile (Gal. 2²). The author of Acts himself calls Paul and Barnabas, coupled together, 'the apostles' (Acts 14¹⁴). Paul too links Barnabas with himself as an apostle (1 Cor. 9⁵, ⁶), just as he similarly links Apollos (1 Cor. 4⁶⁻⁹). Of course the author of Acts, writing probably after Paul's death, does not feel the importance of Paul's claim to enjoy apostolic authority along with the original apostles as intensely as Paul did. But he represents Paul as founding churches, as looking after his converts there with apostolic zeal and care, and as feeling himself responsible for them before God (see especially Acts 20¹⁷⁻³⁵).

His representation of the conflict over the admission of Gentiles to the Church without circumcision is a graver matter. It is hard to acquit him of seeing the whole struggle through rose-coloured spectacles, and in retrospect blurring its sharp edges. But it is necessary to see this problem in its proper perspective. We mostly view the conflict from the point of view provided for us in Galatians, a letter of violent protest, written quickly, in a moment of intense anger and disgust. It is possible, but by no means certain, that the same problem lies behind the altercation reflected in the last chapters of 2 Corinthians. There may be a reference in Philippians (3²ᶠᶠ·), and possibly, but not even probably, in Colossians (2⁸⁻²³). But we cannot claim to know exactly who are Paul's enemies on each occasion. There is simply no evidence whether they were Pharisees or not, and no serious reason to contradict the account in Acts of Paul on one occasion gaining a temporary advantage by appealing to Pharisaic sentiments. When in one of his letters Paul is comparing himself with his opponents, he reveals that they are 'Hebrews, Israelites, the descendants of Abraham', and 'servants of Christ', and he claims as much for himself (2 Cor. 11[22, 23]). He does not suggest that they are Pharisees, though we know that he could have matched them in this claim too (Phil. 3[6]). J. Munck has argued persuasively that the leaders of the Jerusalem Church maintained no regular or serious opposition to Paul at all.[1] If the main opposition to Paul came, not from the 'pillars', as Paul calls them, in Jerusalem, but from quite different groups, then Acts has not seriously misrepresented Paul's position.

The book of Acts certainly records Paul as encountering opposition from Jews, wherever he goes, in Iconium and Lystra, in Philippi and Thessalonica and Corinth and Jerusalem and Rome. And it does represent the Jewish Christians as nursing suspicions about Paul long after the 'Apostolic Council' (Acts 21[20, 21]). The author shows himself to some degree acquainted with Pauline thought. There are 'Pauline' touches in some speeches.[2] The Areopagus speech reflects faithfully the fundamental position of Paul as set out in the early chapters of Romans.[3] It is notorious that we remember what interests us. It is possible that the author, by the time he came to write Acts, was not greatly interested in the question of whether Gentiles should be admitted uncircumcised to the Church. It is even possible that towards the end of his career Paul himself had begun to be less intensely concerned about this. It is indeed true that the author of Acts does not appreciate the depth and subtlety of Paul's teaching about the Law. But then who, until Augustine, who lived three hundred years later, *did* appreciate it? Shortly after Paul's death we find many deeply respectful references to Paul in Christian literature, but virtually no understanding of his thought. The author of Acts does not strike the reader as one likely to appreciate profound and subtle doctrine, even when he heard it: but he would appreciate self-sacrifice, devotion, learning, and energy expended in Christ's cause; and these Paul displayed in full measure.

We know Paul from his letters. This does not necessarily mean that we know all sides of him, or that what appeals to

[1] See his book, *Paul and the Salvation of Mankind*.
[2] See below, pp. 144–5, 203–4, 205.   [3] See below, pp. 177–83.

us, who know him in this intimate but limited way, would necessarily have greatly impressed one who was his travelling-companion. We may take an analogy from a figure who in his genius and in the complexity of his character is almost comparable to Paul, Samuel Taylor Coleridge. Hazlitt describes him when he was a young Unitarian minister preaching a sermon in 1798 as like 'an eagle dallying with the wind'. Thomas Love Peacock derisively sketches him in his middle period, in 1816, as Mr. Flossky in *Nightmare Abbey*, the muddled, pretentious, unintelligible transcendentalist philosopher. Charles Lamb later uses of him the unforgettable phrase 'a damaged archangel'. Carlyle, in his *Life of John Sterling*, describing Coleridge in his old age, says: 'The whole figure and air, good and amiable otherwise, might be called flabby and irresolute, expressive of weakness under possibility of strength. . . . I have heard that Coleridge talk, with eager musical energy, two stricken hours, his face radiant and moist, and communicate no meaning whatsoever to any individual of his hearers.' If we read Coleridge's letters, his *Biographia Literaria*, and his more personal works, even of his old age, we gain a quite different impression, one of vivid strength of intellect and bright, penetrating insight. We do not know enough about Paul to assume that the author of Acts could not have known him. The objections to the view that he was acquainted with Paul are not strong enough to outweigh the considerable evidence that he was.

We have so far called the author of Acts 'Luke' as a useful convention. There is no definite proof that if the author accompanied Paul on some of his journeys he was called Luke. Colossians 4¹⁴ tells us that somebody called *Lucas* is with Paul when he writes the letter (probably, but not certainly, in Rome). Somebody called *Lucius* is greeted by Paul in Romans 16²¹; he would presumably then be in Rome. But it is not clear that Lucas and Lucius are identical, and anyway it is not even certain that the people greeted in Romans 16 were in Rome; this might be a greeting list from another provenance, which has somehow become attached to Romans. Lucas is mentioned again in 2 Timothy 4¹¹ ('Luke alone is with me'). This may represent Church tradition in the first century and might be trustworthy.¹ If the author of Acts was the Lucas of

¹ So H. W. Bartsch, *Wachet aber zu Jeder Zeit*, p. 14.

Colossians 4¹⁴, then he was a physician. The tradition that Luke was a painter is very late and wholly worthless. Irenaeus (170–80) is the first to attribute the third Gospel and the Acts to Luke (and, incidentally, he notes the 'we' passages). Most

Reconstruction of a wine shop at Ostia. Liquor could be consumed on the premises.

commentators have been content to observe the convention of calling the author of Acts 'Luke'. We know so little about Luke otherwise that no harm can come by following this convention.

5. *The End of Acts*

The question of why Acts ends where it does is one which appears more puzzling the more it is considered. We are left with Paul under house-arrest in Rome. We are not told what happened to him later; we are not even told whether he was acquitted or condemned at his trial before the court of the Emperor himself. We today want to know the answers to these questions very much. Did the readers for whom Acts was written want to know them also? Several answers to the question, Why does Acts end where it does? have been given. In the ancient world, historians of the third or fourth century (such as Eusebius and Jerome) generally gave the answer that Acts was written by Luke shortly after the last event recorded in it. We are not told the outcome of Paul's trial, because it had not yet taken place. A few modern scholars have suggested this solution also. But it is one which encounters overwhelming difficulties. It is generally agreed that Luke used Mark's Gospel, and that Mark's Gospel was written in 65 at the earliest. Further, there are fairly strong grounds for thinking that the apocalyptic passages in Luke 21 were written with the taking of Jerusalem by the Romans in A.D. 70 in mind. If Acts was written later than Luke's Gospel, then it must have been written after 65 and probably after A.D. 70, and therefore after Paul's death. It is certain that Acts 1¹⁻³ at least was written after Luke's Gospel, for it refers the same Theophilus who is mentioned at the beginning of the Gospel (Luke 1³) to the Gospel itself. It is just conceivable, but wholly unlikely, that this Preface to Acts was written long after the rest of Acts had been composed. If it was, why did not Luke add an Epilogue, telling us about Paul's later adventures, as well as a Preface? This solution is a desperate one.

More recently, several scholars have maintained that even though Acts appears to us to end at an unsuitable place, this would not have seemed so to its original readers.[1] Ancient students of Acts, it is said, did not have the 'biographical' interest in Paul that we have today, and what they wanted to know was the difference between Christianity and Judaism, and how Christianity became free from Judaism, and how the gospel was proclaimed to the whole world. These questions are all answered by the point at which Acts ends, on the note sounded by the last words of the book—'quite openly and unhindered' (Acts 28³¹). The gospel now has free course. That is all the readers of Acts want to know. Compared with this, details of the lives and adventures of individuals are unimportant. After all, at least two other apostolic figures who were martyred are mentioned in Acts—Peter and James the brother of John; but in the case of Peter we are told nothing

[1] Haenchen, O'Neill, and C. F. Evans, 'The Kerygma' (*Journal of Theological Studies*, N.S. vii (1956), pp. 25–41) have put forward this view.

whatever about his end, and in the case of James only the barest minimum (Acts 12$^{1-2}$). Again parallels can be adduced in ancient literature for endings as uninformative as that of Acts.[1] Perhaps, then, readers of Acts would have felt no sense of unsatisfied curiosity after reading Acts 28^{31}.

The traditional account of Paul's later career has always been that Paul was acquitted in his trial before Caesar's court, and spent a few years in missionary activity in Spain and in a return visit to the Aegean littoral before being martyred in Rome during the persecution which Nero initiated in 64, when he endeavoured to throw the blame for the outbreak of the Great Fire of Rome on the Christians. The chief source of this story is the Pastoral Epistles, which not only speak of a first trial at which Paul was acquitted as well as a later trial at the end of which he expects to be put to death (2 Tim. 4$^{6, 11, 16, 17, 18}$), but also throughout seem to assume that Paul returned from Rome to revisit the scenes of his former labours round the coasts of the Aegean sea. In Romans (15$^{24, 28}$) Paul expresses the desire and intention to visit Spain. The author of *The First Epistle of Clement*, writing in Rome, probably in A.D. 96, refers to Paul's martyrdom in Rome, but in language so vague that little can be inferred from it. He does, however, say that Paul came to 'the terminus of the west'.[2] This could mean 'the end of his course, that is the west', and refer to Rome, or 'the extreme boundary of the west', and refer to Spain. On the whole it is rather more likely that the second meaning is intended and not the first. The author of the Muratorian Canon (a list of books of the Bible, written perhaps as early as 200) clearly believes that Paul visited Spain after his first imprisonment, but he may be merely reproducing the information given in Romans and in the Pastoral Epistles. Local tradition in Rome held that Paul had been martyred on the Ostian Way, a mile or so outside the city boundary, and Peter on the Vatican hill. Archaeology has established that the tradition concerning Peter was known as early as 160, when a small memorial shrine in Peter's memory was in existence on the Vatican hill; and a writer called Gaius, quoted by the historian Eusebius, writing about 200, declares that he has seen the memorial shrines of Peter and Paul on the

---

[1] Cadbury produces some from Philostratus and 2 Maccabees, in *The Making of Luke-Acts*, pp. 322–3.   [2] *1 Clem.* i. 5.

Vatican hill and the Ostian Way respectively. It is therefore very likely indeed that Peter was, as tradition says, crucified upside down on the Vatican hill (a story perhaps confirmed by John 21[18]), and Paul beheaded on the Ostian Way (beheading was a customary form of capital punishment for Roman citizens).

Since the Pauline authorship of the Pastoral Epistles has been widely questioned, however, most scholars have rejected the traditional view of Paul's experiences in Rome. It has been thought much more probable that Paul did not undergo two trials, but that he was condemned at his trial in the Emperor's court, and was executed immediately afterwards. If the Pastoral Epistles are not by Paul, then the evidence that he was acquitted in his first trial collapses, and except for the verses in Romans (which only express Paul's intention) there is no evidence that Paul ever went to Spain (unless we interpret the passage in *1 Clement* to mean that he did reach Spain). Instead of trying to fit a very conjectural visit to Spain and an equally uncertain return to the Aegean area into Paul's career, it is much simpler to assume that he was executed as a result of his trial, about two years after reaching Rome. This has now become an almost universally accepted opinion. It is further pointed out that Acts clearly expects Paul's death in the Christian cause (20[24, 25, 38], 21[10-14]).

But to this view there is a very serious objection, one to which not enough attention has been given. It is admitted by everybody that Luke wants to represent the Roman government as neutral, and as just, towards Christianity.[1] Is it conceivable that Luke knew, while he was writing to this effect, that Paul had been condemned by Caesar's court and executed, and that his audience knew? All Luke's protestations that Roman authorities do not regard Christianity as dangerous and subversive would be thus exposed as hollow, and it would not have been worth making the protestations. No, if anything is clear it is that the author of Acts believed that Paul was acquitted by Caesar's court. Such an event would not have been an extraordinary one. It is very likely indeed that not Nero himself but somebody delegated by him would have tried Paul's case in Rome.[2] Not many years later Apollonius of

---

[1] See above, pp. 3–4.
[2] See Sherwin-White, *Roman Society and Roman Law*, pp. 110–12.

Tyana was acquitted by the suspicious and tyrannical Domitian, presiding himself, on graver charges than those which Paul faced.[1] It is entirely possible that Paul should have been acquitted of the charges originally made against him by the Jews. And, if it is considered carefully, this theory that Paul was condemned by the Emperor's court at the end of his first two years in Rome is very brittle. There is no single piece of concrete evidence in its favour; it rests upon pure conjecture, and it has against it the strong objection that it would make nonsense of much of Acts if it were true. For the traditional view, that Paul was acquitted at his first trial, there are at least two pieces of definite historical evidence—the statements of 2 Timothy 4 and the words of the author of 1 Clement. The evidence of the Pastoral Epistles represents at least what was believed about Paul early in the second century. 1 Clement speaks of Paul as having been martyred. It is hard to interpret execution after a fair trial on the charge of raising a riot in the precincts of the Temple at Jerusalem, as martyrdom.[2] In Rome at the end of the first century the tradition about Paul was that he had been martyred; it is highly likely that the tradition was that he had been martyred at about the same time as Peter and as a result of the same incident, Nero's incrimination of the Christians for the burning of Rome, having been acquitted by a Roman court some years earlier of charges made against him by Jews. 1 Clement links together the deaths of Peter and Paul. Memories in the first century were not so fallible that we can dismiss evidence like this out of hand, as sheer legend. If we conclude that Paul was acquitted, this does not necessarily involve believing that Paul then went to Spain (though this is not impossible), nor that he returned to the Aegean littoral (which is wholly improbable). The Pastoral Epistles may have been filling in a gap in Paul's career which was known to have occurred.

But the view that Paul was acquitted at his first trial has to meet two difficulties. Why did Luke not mention this fact in Acts? for it would have been a strong argument for his view of the justice and impartiality of the Roman government. And would not Paul's execution under Nero as a result of the

---

[1] Philostratus, *Life of Apollonius of Tyana*, viii. 5.
[2] Perhaps we should add the words of Ignatius, referred to below, p. 34, as another piece of evidence.

persecution of A.D. 64 ruin the argument of Acts about the impartiality of the Roman government towards Christianity anyway? We shall deal with the second one first. The answer must be that a death under a trumped-up accusation of arson as the result of a despotic emperor's cruelty is very different from a death at the end of a trial provoked by the appeal of the accused himself on a perfectly serious charge of provoking a riot. By the time that Luke was writing Acts, Nero had died an ignominious death, outlawed by the Roman Senate. He had become the subject of wild popular rumours, like the rumours which circulated after Hitler's death. Even Tacitus the Roman historian, who was grossly prejudiced against Christianity, admitted that there was widespread sympathy for the Christians cruelly put to death by Nero, as the victims of an unscrupulous plot to make them scapegoats for the Fire of Rome. To have been put to death by Nero in such circumstances would have seemed no disgrace to many of the educated and sophisticated people, even non-Christians, for whom Luke was writing. Many honourable and eminent men, such as Seneca and Burrus, had been put to death by the capricious and suspicious Nero. Luke could therefore without inconsistency represent a number of different officials of the Roman government as impartial towards Christianity and claim that they found it harmless; he could lead up in his narrative to a point just before Paul's acquittal at his first trial, while knowing perfectly well that Paul had been executed a few years later by Nero. He may even have meant to make the point that in normal circumstances, when angry tyrants do not interfere with the course of justice, Christianity expects, and receives, fair treatment at the hands of the Roman Government.

But why did Luke not mention the outcome of this first trial? Why did he throw away the opportunity of clinching his argument about Rome's attitude to the Christian Church, if Paul was acquitted? This is a hard question which every theory about Acts has to face. It cannot be solved by denying that the readers of Acts had any 'biographical' interest in Paul. There is no evidence to support the theory that the Christians of the second half of the first century were not eager for 'biographical' details about their heroes and famous men. The Gospels were partly written to meet this 'biographical' interest. The Pastoral Epistles no doubt were intended to feed this interest. Late in the first century and all the way through the second there flows a constant stream of apocryphal Gospels and Acts and Epistles evoked by precisely this 'biographical' interest in Jesus and his apostles and disciples. In the secular world of the first and second centuries there was plenty of demand for biographies. The biography (*Bios*) was indeed a recognized literary form, whether the biographies were of philosophers or of emperors. Tacitus, Suetonius, Plutarch, Philostratus, all wrote biographies, to choose only a few out of many. No: there can be little doubt that by the time Luke was writing people wanted to know about Paul, as they wanted to know about Jesus.

Only one answer to this very puzzling question comes near to being satisfactory, and that is that Luke did not describe Paul's acquittal, and his subsequent career, because he knew that the people for whom he was writing were acquainted with these facts already. If Luke was writing the book of Acts for an audience in Rome, then indeed he had no need to extend his narrative beyond Paul's arrival there. The Christians of Rome, and probably many non-Christians too, would know about Paul's acquittal and his subsequent death as a martyr. What they would want to know is how Paul reached Rome, what started Paul on his career as a missionary, and what were the origins of the religion that Paul brought with him. This is exactly what Acts supplies. It might, of course, be asked why Luke did not also trace for his readers the career of Peter, up to his arrival in Rome, for Peter was always linked with Paul in the memory of Roman Christians, as, for instance, he clearly is in the mind of the author of *I Clement*, and in the mind of Ignatius when he writes to the Christians of Rome early in the second century.[1] The answer to this probably is that Luke does not follow Peter's career because he had no information about it after its early stages. Luke's path lay alongside the path of Paul, and so he brings Paul to Rome, and leaves him there, preaching the gospel openly and unhindered, confident that the Roman Christians know the rest. This theory gains a certain support from the observation made by one or two scholars that, though from Chapter 15 onwards Luke generally gives an abundance of details of names and places and even buildings, this interest in personal and

[1] Ignatius, *Romans*, iv. 3.

geographical details tails off towards the end of Acts.[1] He mentions, for instance, Syracuse, Rhegium, Puteoli, Appii Forum, and Tres Tabernae, all of them within reasonable reach of Rome, without explaining what or where they are. Contrast 'a city of Galilee named Nazareth', 'Capernaum a city of Galilee', and the locating of Emmaus, the country of the Gerasenes, Philippi, Fair Havens, and several other places distant from Rome. It is possible that he does not see the necessity of locating places whose location will, he is aware, be known to his public. Similarly, there is no reference in Acts to forums or temples, or even synagogues, in Italy or in Rome. The best reason (and even this does not quite satisfy) that we can give for Acts ending where it does is that the readers for whom the book was intended knew the rest of the story.

II. *The Theology of Acts*

I. *The Speeches in Acts*

All those who have attempted to examine the thought of Acts have necessarily found their primary material in the speeches embedded in the text of the book, for here more than anywhere else the description of the Christian faith and of its significance is to be found. These speeches vary greatly in length and language and context and subject. They vary from the early preaching of Peter to the Jews in Jerusalem to the adaptation by Paul of the Christian message to the ears of the philosophically minded Athenians; and from the short but flowery utterance of Tertullus (Acts 24²⁻⁸) to the much longer piece of biblical exegesis uttered by Paul for the benefit of the Jews of Pisidian Antioch (13¹⁶⁻⁴¹). They are given in such stirring circumstances as those provided by a riot in a Greek theatre, on the aftermath of an attempted lynching in the Temple area, at a farewell scene on the sea-shore, and on ship-board during a stormy passage which was to end in a wreck, as well as in the more conventional settings of the synagogue, the law court, and the market square.

Luke is an ancient author writing a history, and we must be aware that in the ancient world there was a strong tradition

[1] See Cadbury, *The Making of Luke-Acts*, pp. 241–2, and *The Book of Acts in History*, p. 60; Dupont, *The Sources*, p. 160.

of oratory and a widely observed convention among historians concerning the composition of speeches. In the world of the first century A.D. oratory, the carefully studied art of persuasive speech, was considered by every educated person, be he Jew, Greek, or Roman, an honourable and useful pursuit, and the art of cultivated and persuasive speech was thought to form a great part of a man's education. This means that we can at once conclude that not one of the speeches in Acts could possibly be a word-for-word reproduction of what was said, and only what was said, by the particular speaker on the particular occasion. They are all much too short, even the longest of them. They would be too short even for modern speeches.

Again, there can be no doubt that historians of about the time of Luke, whether they were Jewish, like the authors of 1 and 2 Maccabees and Josephus, or Roman or Greek, like Livy and Tacitus and Suetonius or Polybius and Plutarch and Lucian and Philostratus, allowed themselves considerable freedom in the composition of speeches. They regarded speeches as, so to speak, intervals for light music in the middle of the solid and taxing historical narrative. Speeches were meant to entertain, even to amuse, to arouse admiration and speculation. The most irresponsible of ancient historians used their speeches as an opportunity of setting out their own ideas and exhibiting their own oratorical skill, pretty well irrespective of the speaker and occasion to which they are attributed. The more responsible endeavoured to observe limits. The greatest, and one of the earliest, of them all, Thucydides, who wrote in the second half of the fifth century B.C., tells us that in the speeches he inserted into his narrative he set down what he knew to have been said on the given occasion if he himself had been present, or if he had had a reliable account of it, but that otherwise he put down what he thought was likely to have been said on the occasion. Even so, it is clear that Thucydides expressed the substance of the speeches in his own words and his own style. Lucian, writing in the second century A.D., admits that speeches provide an historian with an opportunity for displaying rhetoric, but insists that 'what is said must be above all appropriate to the character and suitable to the occasion',[1] and he censures an historian for including a hopelessly unrealistic rhetorical speech as a funeral oration over

[1] Lucian, *On Writing History*, 58 (my translation).

an unsuccessful Roman general who had committed suicide while on active service.[1] We can be confident that Luke belonged to the class of responsible ancient historians, because his speeches are short and are devoid of artificial rhetoric. Though he is not uninfluenced by the tradition of pagan historiography, he inclines more to the standards and forms of Jewish history-writing.[2] Still, we cannot assume that he is so much an exception among ancient historians that all his speeches consist of simple reporting of exactly what was said on each occasion. It is significant that though his speeches vary in style they vary in groups rather than as individual speeches. There is, for instance, stylistically speaking, a uniform group of evangelistic speeches to Jews, whether made by Peter or Paul; and the speech of Paul to Festus does not vary striking'y in style from the speech of Demetrius the silversmith to his fellow craftsmen.

To say, however, that in composing his speeches Luke followed the normal convention of ancient history-writing is not necessarily to say that Luke produced his speeches out of his own head and with no reference to any sources of historical information. It has been suggested by C. H. Dodd and others that a resemblance can be seen between the structure of the earliest speeches in Acts, and that of the gospel which Paul appears to have inherited from the primitive Church, and that of the preaching of Jesus as recorded in Mark 1[14-15]. This resemblance has been thought to point to the existence of a single pattern of primitive apostolic preaching which can be recovered from these examples. It is not nearly so easy to find a common pattern behind the other, later, speeches in Acts, partly because they were delivered to such diverse audiences and concerned such different subjects. The fact that on the whole the later speeches in Acts have very much the same style, and that this style is not easily distinguishable from the style of the narrative portions of Acts, suggests strongly that Luke's own contribution had much to do with them. The tide of scholarship, however, has in several places swung against Dodd's argument, and the consequences drawn from it, that we have reasonably reliable knowledge of the content of the Church's earliest preaching. A number of scholars believe that

[1] Ibid. 26.
[2] See B. Gärtner, *The Areopagus Speech and Natural Revelation*, pp. 26–29.

it can be shown that the contents of the 'apostolic' speeches
in the earlier chapters of Acts do not really reflect the early
kerygma (preaching), but only the preaching of the Church as
it was in Luke's day, i.e. at the end (so these scholars think) of
the first century.[1]

We have seen strong reason to believe that the author of
Acts knew very well what Christianity was like during the
period roughly A.D. 50–60. It is unlikely that such a man knew
nothing about the preaching and teaching of the primitive
Church. One early source is unmistakably evident in Acts,
and that is the proof-texts from the Old Testament, which
plentifully besprinkle the early speeches at least, as they do
the Epistles of Paul and the Synoptic Gospels. Dodd in two
works, *According to the Scriptures* and *Historical Tradition in the
Fourth Gospel*, has shown the very interesting light that these
throw on the earliest thought of the Church.[2] It would be odd
if Luke had retained the early proof-texts without retaining
any vestige or reminiscence of their early interpretation. Most
scholars admit that a Pauline colouring, a deliberate assumption or reproduction of Pauline language, can be detected at
some points in the speeches, e.g. 13[38, 39], 15[6ff.], and in several
places in the speech given in 20[18–35]. Whence are we to suppose that Luke derived this knowledge of Paul's type of
thought? We can hardly imagine that he had read Paul's
letters. And if he managed to pick up some ideas of Paul's and
some proof-texts from the earliest period of the Church, why
cannot it be conceded that he may have had some reliable
knowledge of other early material? We need not assume that
Luke is producing this material unedited, exactly as he
received it. That is not Luke's way. But neither is it necessary
to assume that his manner of treating his material leaves an
opaque, impenetrable cloud between his words and earlier
periods before he wrote those words. Such a phenomenon
would be almost unique, especially in the ancient world. We
can divide the evangelistic speeches in the first half of Acts into
two categories: speeches to Jews (all the speeches up to the end
of Acts 13), and speeches to Gentiles (Acts 14[15–17] and 17[22–31]).
The speeches in the first category are debatable, but for the

---

[1] e.g., C. F. Evans, Haenchen, U. Wilckens, O'Neill, and Conzelmann.
[2] See also the earlier work, *Testimonies*, by Rendel Harris (2 vols.), and
the recent *Early Christian Apologetic*, by B. Lindars.

speeches in the second category we have strong evidence that they reproduce accurately enough the substance of Paul's ideas in the first chapter of Romans and the first chapter of 1 Thessalonians.[1] In the case of the Areopagus speech the *expression* is quite un-Pauline, but the *contents* are well paralleled in Paul.[2] We may find a faint analogy in the writings of Philo, who has his own very individual and characteristic ideas, and can in the course of his works unblushingly place these ideas in the mouths of all sorts of characters in the Old Testament, but who at the same time betrays in a hundred different ways his knowledge of contemporary and earlier Rabbinic thought, which is quite distinct from his own.

2. *Doctrine in Acts*

Luke's *Doctrine of Christ* has marked 'subordinationist' tendencies, to use a technical term; that is to say, Luke stresses again and again the position of Christ as an instrument of God, a messenger of God, an agent of God; he has little or nothing to say about Christ as a divine being in his own right and makes no attempt to work out philosophically his relation to God. He does not, for instance, call him the *Logos* (Word) of God, as the fourth Gospel does, nor the 'image' and 'fulness' of God, as Paul does in the Epistle to the Colossians; nor can he say that Christ 'reflects the glory of God and bears the very stamp of his nature', as does the Epistle to the Hebrews in its opening verses. Many writers declare that Luke knows nothing of the 'pre-existence' of Christ, that is to say of his existing as a supernatural being before the Incarnation. But we cannot rule out the possibility, even the likelihood, that Luke's use of proof-texts from the Old Testament testifies to the belief, very widespread in the early Church and well evidenced in the New Testament in all the main parts, that Jesus was in some sense present with God's people in many of the scenes described in the Old Testament. And this is a form of pre-existence, although a Jewish rather than a Greek form.

[1] For the resemblance between the evangelistic speeches addressed to Gentiles in Acts and 1 Thess. 1[9, 10] see Wilckens, *Die Missionsreden*, pp. 72–74, and 86–88.
[2] This is what Gärtner has shown in his book *The Areopagus Speech and Natural Revelation*. For the details, see the commentary below, pp. 178–83.

Luke uses the phrase 'the Christ' of Jesus very frequently, and in this use the phrase is a title and not a name; it means 'the Messiah' (e.g., $2^{31, 36}$, $3^{18, 20}$, 4^{26}, 5^{42}, 8^5, $9^{22, 34}$, $18^{5, 28}$, 26^{23}). Luke uses it only as a name in formulae for baptizing or exorcizing or preaching (e.g. 2^{38}, 3^6, 4^{10}, $10^{36, 48}$, 11^{17}, 15^{26}, 16^{18}). Whether this is the sign of an early stage in doctrine or of a later one is disputed. Normally one would regard it as an early usage, because it means that the word has not yet become a mere name, and lost its original, Jewish, significance. On the other hand, in the writings of Paul it is well on its way to becoming a mere name. Luke constantly uses the phrase 'the Christ *of God*' and similar expressions (e.g. Acts 3^{18}, $4^{26, 27}$), indicating the peculiar relation of 'belongingness or apostolicity'[1] that Christ has towards God; and in keeping with this, Jesus is usually described (as in Acts 2^{24}) as 'being raised' by God rather than as himself rising from the dead. As 'the Christ' he is also conceived consistently as the fulfilment of Scripture, 'in whom the fulfilment of the time as the fulfilment of every Old Testament word has become actuality'.[2] With the Christ the times of refreshment have come (Acts 3^{20-26}). The title 'Lord' (*kyrios*) is certainly a very old title for Jesus, for it translates the Aramaic word *Mara*, which is found in the primitive Christian phrase *Marana tha* ('our Lord, come') in 1 Corinthians 16^{22} and Revelation 22^{20}. Luke uses it very widely indeed, usually in association with Christ or Jesus Christ; only twice does it occur by itself as a title: in Acts 2^{36}, where Peter says in a speech that 'God has made him both Lord and Christ, this Jesus whom you crucified', and in 10^{36}, where Peter in another speech speaks of the 'good news of peace' given 'by Jesus Christ (he is Lord of all)'. The retention by Luke of these two early uses of *kyrios* by itself suggests that Luke was deliberately introducing into these speeches a primitive usage, which was not that of his own day, but which he knew to be primitive. The undoubtedly primitive title, one which may go back to the lips of Jesus himself, 'Son of man', occurs once and once only in Acts (though of course it appears in Luke's Gospel), at Acts 7^{56}, in Stephen's dying words. Either this is a genuine historical reminiscence or Luke once again is using sparingly a phrase which he knows to be primitive but which is not familiar to him in contemporary

---

[1] The phrase is that of Wilckens.   [2] Wilckens, pp. 156–7.

Christian usage. But then, Paul does not use the title even once! Another title used by Luke of Christ is 'Servant' or 'Child (Gk. παῖς) of God' (Acts 3[13, 26], 4[27, 30]). The question whether this is an early title or not is disputed. Another title used by Luke of Jesus is 'the Righteous One' (Acts 3[14], 7[52],

An ancient Roman street; shop-fronts below, living quarters above.

22[14]). This has a background in the Old Testament (Isa. 42[1]; Jer. 23[5], 33[15]; Zech. 9[9]) and particularly in the line from Habakkuk 2[4] (quoted in Rom. 1[17]; Gal. 3[11]; Heb. 10[38]; and perhaps 1 Pet. 3[18]: cp. 1 John 2[1]) 'the righteous shall live by faith'. This use of Habakkuk suggests that early on the 'Righteous One' of these proof-texts was identified with Jesus, and that this title cannot be a very late one, even though it is used also in literature of the late first or early second century (1 Pet., *The Epistle of Barnabas*, and *The Epistle of Polycarp*). Jesus is also described as of the posterity (Gk. σπέρμα) of David in Acts (13[23]), and though this phrase occurs in the Pastoral

Epistles and in Ignatius it also appears in a passage in Romans
(1^3) which many scholars have regarded as coming from a
tradition taken over by Paul from some earlier source.[1] Twice
in speeches Luke describes Jesus as 'Leader' or 'Author' (Acts
3^{15} and 5^{31}). This word was certainly not in the vocabulary of
the early Church. It occurs twice in the Epistle to the Hebrews
(2^{10} and 12^2), which was written certainly no later than A.D. 95
and may be considerably earlier, though it cannot be placed
in the very earliest period. One unmistakably non-Jewish title
used by Luke is 'Saviour' (Acts 5^{31} and 13^{23}). This comes from
Hellenistic (i.e. Greek-speaking) circles in the Church; but
they must be early Hellenistic circles, for Paul uses the title
too (Phil. 3^{20} and Eph. 5^{23}). The title 'Son of God', which is
very common indeed in Paul, appears only once, at Acts 13^{33},
in a quotation of Psalm 2^7.

This brief survey of the titles used by Luke for Jesus suggests,
then, that it is inaccurate to describe Luke's Christology without qualification either as late or as early. Certainly it is
difficult to believe that the early speeches in Acts reflect as we
have them a consistently primitive, even apostolic, Christology.
On the other hand, to describe the speeches as deriving from
a 'post-Pauline' period, of about the same time as the Pastoral
Epistles, is equally unsatisfactory. There are too many
genuinely early elements in them for that. On the whole the
evidence seems to support the conclusion we have already
reached on grounds of historical evidence. Luke lived near
enough to the primitive Church to know something about it;
close enough to Paul to echo several of his phrases. But he has
to make a conscious effort to reproduce the diction of the
primitive Church. It does not come naturally to him.

The *Holy Spirit* appears prominently in Acts, so much so that
the book has been called 'the Gospel of the Holy Spirit'. The
Spirit descends in a dramatic way at Pentecost. Many people
are 'filled with the Holy Spirit', Peter (4^8), Stephen (6^5), Paul
(9^{31}, 13^9), Barnabas (11^{24}). The Spirit directs, speaks to,
instructs, inspires, and even obstructs people.[2] He appoints
bishops (20^{28}). It is impossible to deceive him ($5^{3, 9}$) or to

---

[1] Exactly the same can be said for Luke's description of Jesus as destined
to judge the quick and the dead (Acts 10^{42}, 17^{31}). The concept occurs in
the subapostolic literature, but also in Paul.

[2] $8^{29, 30}$, 10^{19}, $11^{12, 28}$, $13^{2, 4}$, 15^{28}, $16^{6, 7}$, 17^{16}, 19^{21}, $20^{22, 23}$, 21^4.

traffic in him (8^{18-21}). The Spirit normally accompanies the act of baptism (2^{38}, 9^{17-19}, 19^{1-7}). But there are exceptions. Christian converts in Samaria do not receive the Spirit at baptism, but only later, after the apostles have laid hands on them (8^{12-17}). Cornelius and his friends receive the Spirit before being baptized (10^{44-48}). The twelve apostles themselves receive the Spirit at Pentecost without even being baptized, at any point before or after. It is impossible to reduce these accounts to a tidy theological or pastoral system, though many attempts to do so have been made. Jesus himself promises that the Holy Spirit will come ($1^{5,\ 8}$), himself possesses the Holy Spirit permanently (1^2), indeed God has anointed him with the Holy Spirit (10^{38}). He gives the Spirit because he has received the Spirit from the Father (2^{33}: cp. Luke 3^{16}, 24^{49}). The Spirit, in short, is assumed to be active everywhere, as the exalted Lord is assumed to be present everywhere, so that he can be prayed to (7^{59}), and can heal (9^{34}). Luke's special way of describing the presence of Christ is to speak of 'the name' (3^{16}, 4^{12}, 8^{12}, 9^{16}, 15^{26}). This is a characteristically Jewish concept, not Hellenistic at all, and is widely used in early Jewish Christian literature. We may agree with Conzelmann when he says that Luke's account of the Spirit defines the relationship of Jesus to the Father (who anoints him with the Spirit, and gives him the special powers of the Spirit), in the world, in redemptive history, and to the Church. The period of the ministry of Jesus

appears as a redemptive epoch of a unique kind, in which the Spirit rests upon one person only. This uniqueness is underlined still more by the fact that between the Ascension and Pentecost there is an interval without the Spirit. Thus the Spirit enables us to see on the one hand the individuality of Jesus, his position in the centre of redemptive history, and on the other the continuity between him and the Church, or in other words the positive link with the present.[1]

Luke, of course, does not attempt to give any philosophical description of the relation of the Spirit to the Father or the Son.

In his *Doctrine of Salvation* Luke fails to attach special significance to the crucifixion and death of Jesus. He regards him as the fulfilment of the prophecies about the Suffering Servant

[1] *The Theology of Luke*, p. 184.

($8^{32\,f.}$), and describes God as winning the Church for himself by his own blood (20^{28}, and see the commentary on this passage below, pp. 204–5). But there is no Passion-mysticism such as is found in Paul, no appreciation of the paradox of the crucified Messiah presented as the burning centre of the Christian message. The way in which a man is saved, according to Luke, is that first he must repent (2^{38}, $3^{19,\ 26}$, 5^{31}, 11^{18}, 17^{30}, 20^{21}, 26^{20}); he is then baptized into the Name of Christ. This means transference under the power of his Name; Christ's main mission and function is as Lord and Christ to save by the power of his Name (2^{36}). The forgiveness of sins is the direct effect of baptism ($3^{19,\ 26}$, 5^{31}, 10^{43}, 13^{38}), and so (as we have seen) is, normally, the reception of the Spirit. This salvation includes membership in the redeemed people (2^{47}) and the fulfilment for them of the promises made to Israel, which are fulfilled in Jesus (2^{39}, 13^{26}). The Church has in fact taken over the role of Israel. Though baptism and repentance are closely linked in Luke, this is not true of baptism and faith; for Luke, faith sometimes appears to follow baptism ($16^{15,\ 33,\ 34}$, 19^{4}; but compare 8^{12}). Faith is sometimes associated with the forgiveness of sins (10^{43}, 13^{38}, 26^{18}). The world-wide mission of the Church plays a crucial part in Luke's thought. The Ascension of Christ is the turning-point. The fact that Acts repeats both the Resurrection Appearances and the account of the Ascension, shows that, to Luke, the Ascension is not one event with the Resurrection (as it appears to be to Matthew, to John, and to Paul), but two. It is the end of the story of the earthly work of Jesus, his triumph over death, his fulfilment of prophecy,[1] his taking his place in heaven. But it is also the beginning of the world-wide mission of the Church (Luke 24^{47}; Acts 1^{8}), which will last till the Second Coming (Acts $1^{10\,f.}$). Christ's condition in the meanwhile is described as sitting at God's right hand (Acts $2^{33\,f.}$, 5^{31}, $7^{55\,f.}$). Through his Spirit he controls the Church's work.

The *Doctrine of the Last Things* (which is usually denoted by a single useful technical term, 'eschatology') in Luke has recently attracted much attention from scholars. The eschatology to be found in the Gospels and in the New Testament generally has been the subject of intense study, and it has

---

[1] For the fulfilment of prophecy in Jesus see Acts $2^{23,\ 25}$, $3^{18,\ 24-26}$, 10^{36}, $13^{27,\ 29,\ 33-37}$.

gradually been realized that Christianity was born in an atmosphere of strong eschatological expectation. Jesus himself in some sense, and his apostles, and all the early disciples were intently expecting the end of the world, God's final intervention in history, judgement, resurrection, eternal life. Many were looking for the signs of the last day or last times. Apocalypses describing these events in figurative language were widely read. This atmosphere can be detected in the Synoptic Gospels and in the writings of Paul, and in a lesser or greater way it affects the whole New Testament. It is only recently, however, that special attention has been paid to Luke's attitude to what must have been a burning question in his day. Was the world going to end almost immediately? Would the Second Coming take place soon?

There are strong reasons for thinking that Luke was anxious to play down and relax the eschatological expectation of the early Christian period. He appears, for instance, to re-handle the words of Mark with this intention. Compare, for instance, Mark 9[1] with Luke 9[27] and Mark 13[6, 7] with Luke 21[8, 9]. For Luke the earthly life of Jesus is in the past, an historical event, so that Luke's Gospel can almost become a biography of Jesus. For him the Apostolic Age is past. The purity and innocence of the primitive Church are gone by his time. 'Fierce wolves', teachers of error, have invaded the fold (Acts 20[29]). Acts is an enlargement of Luke's Gospel designed to illustrate this view; it is almost 'an extension of the Incarnation'. The *leitmotiv* of Acts is given in 1[8]: 'But you shall receive power when the Holy Spirit has come upon you; and you will be my witnesses in Jerusalem, and in all Judea and Samaria, and to the end of the earth.' Eschatology appears to have been reduced or transformed almost into Church history. But the End has not been entirely lost sight of. There are references in Acts to the Return of Christ (1[11], 3[20, 21], 10[42], 17[31], 24[15, 25]; cp. Luke 9[27], 12[32, 34–36, 45]). It may be that Luke was anxious to deprecate, not an expectation of the Return of Christ, but a very primitive Christian idea that the Resurrection Appearances were the beginning of the Return or the End itself. Perhaps Luke was writing early enough to be able to know (in order to refute them) the very earliest Christian eschatological beliefs, earlier even than those of Paul, and perhaps he did not come on the scene too late to share the belief of Paul, and of many other Christians of Paul's day, in a Return of Christ at the End some time in the future.

The *Doctrine of the Church and the Ministry* in Acts is not a much developed one. The word Luke uses most frequently for the Church is 'the brethren'. This is his earliest designation of the Church; it occurs first in 1^{15}, and there are twenty-nine other occurrences in Acts; the word is used several times also to mean 'fellow-Jews' (1^{16}, $2^{29, 37}$, 3^{17}, 7^2, $13^{15, 26, 38}$, 22^1, $23^{1, 5, 6}$, $28^{17, 21}$) and it is likely that this word was in fact the earliest Christian word for members of the Christian Church. The next most frequent word is 'the disciples'; it occurs first in 6^1, and there are twenty-seven other occurrences of it in Acts. The word 'church' itself appears first in 5^{11} without any explanation; and thereafter frequently—to be exact, nineteen times. Once it is used, in Stephen's speech, to mean the congregation of Jews under Moses in the wilderness (7^{38}), and three times to mean the purely secular assembly of the citizens of Ephesus ($19^{32, 39, 40}$). Luke almost always uses the word to mean the local church, and quite often speaks of 'the churches'; only twice can we find the word used to mean the whole Church, considered as a single people or a single organism (9^{31} and 20^{28}). 'All who believed' is used as a description of the Church twelve times, first in 2^{44}. Very occasionally 'the saints' occurs as a description of the Church ($9^{13, 32, 41}$, 26^{10}). Christianity in Acts is sometimes called 'the way' (16^{17}, $18^{25, 26}$, $19^{9, 23}$, 22^4, 24^{14}) and once Christians are described as 'any belonging to the Way' (9^2). Luke notes the point at which members of the Church began to be called Christians (11^{26}), but only once again does he use the word (26^{28}). There is nothing in Luke of the Pauline conception of the Church as the Body of Christ, nor of the Johannine doctrine of the indwelling of believers in Christ. But of course he regards the Church as an inseparable part of Christianity. The history of the Church is the history of Christ; Saul has been persecuting the Church, but at his vision on the Damascus road the risen Lord asks him, 'Saul, Saul, why do you persecute *me*?' In this sense, Christ is in his people and experiences what they experience, even in Lukan thought. Indeed, the story of Acts is the story of the Church, no more and no less.

For Luke, the twelve apostles form a separate order. They are the witnesses of the earthly life of Jesus, and of the Resurrection (Luke 24[48]; Acts 1[22], 4[33], 10[40f.]), the leaders of the primitive Church, the initiators of the Mission to the Gentiles, the bearers of the Word of God from whom the whole missionary preaching of Christianity derives (6[2, 4]). They are not administrators, they teach (2[42], 5[25, 28], 13[12], 18[11]). Only once are they called 'the twelve' (6[2]). Their last appearance as apostles is in 16[4]; then they virtually disappear, and no mention is made of succession. Others as well as they evangelize, Barnabas, Silas, Timothy. But the apostles are unique, as Jesus was unique; they belong to the Beginning (Luke 1[2]; Acts 1[1f.]). Continuity in the Church is effected by maintaining the tradition of the works and words of Jesus, which the Spirit in the Church sustains. Elders are mentioned several times, as administering, or as being appointed to administer, the local church.[1] Once bishops (ἐπίσκοποι) are mentioned (20[28]), apparently as synonymous with elders. Deacons are never once mentioned; Luke does not call the Seven deacons. Prophets are still active.[2] In short, the picture of the early Christian ministry in Acts reflects a period when it is still very fluid, when the question of office-bearers in the Church has still scarcely arisen, and when the subject of succession in office is still in the future. By the end of the first century _I Clement_ can concern itself with the succession from the apostles of presbyters (that is, of presbyters identified with bishops, not of bishops distinct from presbyters), and recognizes two types of ministry, presbyter-bishops and deacons. The Pastoral Epistles mention presbyters, deacons, and bishops (the latter sometimes distinct from presbyters). Neither mentions Christian prophets. Judging by the picture which it gives of the ministry alone, it would be difficult to place Acts at the end of the first century. It does not breathe the same ecclesiastical atmosphere as the Pastoral Epistles.

3. _Summary_

Our review of the doctrine to be found in Acts, then, leaves us unable either to assign it decisively to the end of the first century or the beginning of the second, or to conclude that it

---

[1] Acts 11[30], 14[23], 15[2, 4, 6, 22, 23]. For this account of the ministry in Acts see Barrett, _Luke the Historian_, pp. 71–74; Conzelmann, _The Theology of Luke_, pp. 215–18; Haenchen, _Die Apostelgeschichte_, p. 91. Cp. Conzelmann, _Die Apostelgeschichte_, p. 9.   [2] Acts 11[27], 13[1], 21[10].

gives us an intact picture of the teaching and preaching of the Church at its most primitive stage. Luke knows something about the primitive Church, about its watchwords and its convictions, its Christological ideas and its names for itself, its expectations and its proof-texts. He can in a limited way think himself into its atmosphere without committing grave anachronisms. In several points, too, he uses the language which a contemporary of Paul might have used. But the primitive period is not his period, and he cannot give a consistent account of its way of thinking. There is not enough evidence to support the theory that he has access to a coherent account of what the apostles actually preached. Luke lives in a period when the apostolic age is past, and can only be evoked (as Luke intended to evoke it) as a golden memory. But when we say 'a golden memory' we do not mean a tissue of romantic inventions. Luke is a second-generation Christian. He uses more naturally language about Christ (such as 'leader' or 'Saviour') derived from Greek-speaking Christianity, not from the Christianity of the earliest period. He is concerned to discountenance early eschatological ideas, to shift the emphasis to the necessity of spreading the gospel throughout the world. But he is not utterly out of touch with the primitive period, so far out of touch that his information about its thought is worthless. He can produce a good imitation of apostolic preaching, a version of it which, while it is the composition of Luke and not of Peter or Paul, is not valueless. He does not reflect the ideas, the interests, or the conditions of the late first century, its concern with ecclesiastical organization and with Christian behaviour. On the whole we can say with some confidence that an examination of the doctrine of Acts agrees with the examination of its historical references. It reflects the outlook of a man writing in the seventies or eighties of the century who has known Christianity in the fifties and sixties.

III. *The Composition of Acts*

1. *The Sources of Acts*

In the past quite extensive theories have been advanced attempting to identify continuous and written sources behind Luke's narrative in Acts. One theory was that at any rate the early speeches in Acts could be demonstrated to derive from a written source, because they could be shown in various passages to be translations from an Aramaic original. But it has not proved possible to maintain this theory. Dibelius showed effectively how many difficulties lie in the way of theories such as this. In Acts 15^{14}, for instance, James is represented as calling Peter *Symeon* (a form nearer the Aramaic), rather than Simon (which could be a normal Greek name). But in the same speech he quotes a text from the Greek Old Testament where it differs significantly from the Hebrew.[1] This is a mistake which no Aramaic speaker or writer of Aramaic is ever likely to have made. Again, Peter would use Aramaic to address the Jerusalem crowd (Ch. 3), whereas Paul would have spoken Greek to the synagogue congregation at Pisidian Antioch (Ch. 13); but the style of the two speeches is exactly the same. In Acts 22^2 we are expressly told that Paul is about to speak in Aramaic, but in the speech that follows there are no signs of translation from the Aramaic whatever. In Acts 26^{14} the account says that the Voice from heaven spoke in Aramaic; but the Voice quotes a well-known proverb from Greek literature, 'It hurts you to kick against the goads.'[2] Fifty years ago many scholars would have agreed with the theory advanced by Harnack that behind the early chapters of Acts can be discerned two different written sources, describing in different words much the same events; their presence is revealed by occurrences of two accounts of the same incident— two escapes of the apostles from prison, for instance, and two descriptions of how the early Christians shared their possessions.[3] One of these sources was supposed to emanate from Antioch and the other from Jerusalem. But today scholarship is not as ready to identify documentary sources as were scholars of an earlier day, and most scholars would see mainly oral sources (though possibly still two different accounts of the same incidents) behind the first six chapters of Acts. We can, however, with some confidence identify a few documentary sources in later chapters of Acts. There is very widespread

---

[1] Acts 15^{17} reproducing in a citation of Amos 9^{12} the error of the Greek version in mistaking Edom for Adam.

[2] These examples are taken from Dibelius, *Studies in the Acts of the Apostles*, pp. 178–9.

[3] Compare Acts 2$^{44-46}$ with 4$^{32-35}$, and 4$^{1-3}$ with 4$^{17-21}$.

agreement that Stephen's speech, which constitutes the seventh chapter of Acts, betrays one of these.[1] As we have seen, the 'Apostolic Decree' in Acts 15 probably reached Luke in written form.[2]

Haenchen points out that at the earliest period nobody had any particular interest in the sayings of the apostles, especially if most people were preoccupied by an expectation of the end of the world. It is therefore unlikely that there were in existence for Luke's use collections of apostolic sayings or accounts of apostolic deeds.[3] He makes an attempt to analyse the material in Acts into Form-Critical categories, but it is not a successful one.[4] We can learn little or nothing from it about the history or significance of the material analysed. He is more successful, however, in estimating Luke's own contribution to the narrative. This consists of the speeches which Luke uses to direct the intention and supply the theology of the narrative; the summaries that occur from time to time (e.g. 2^{43-47}, 16^5, 19^{17-20}), serving to knit together the otherwise loose and disparate material for his narrative; and finally Luke's own 'literary reconstructions' of such scenes as the conversion of Cornelius and the 'Apostolic Council'.[5]

But when all is said and done, it is very difficult indeed to reconstruct, or even tentatively to identify, Luke's sources for the book of Acts. We have nothing corresponding to the Gospel of Mark, with which we can compare Luke's Gospel. It is primarily this difficulty of identifying Luke's sources, combined with the remarkable signs of historical accuracy visible in the second half of the book, which constitutes the strongest argument that Luke was the author of the 'we' passages and a companion of Paul during some part of his journeys.

2. *The Design of Acts*

A good case could be made for dividing Acts into only two parts, the part devoted to the mission to the Jews, and that devoted to the mission to the Gentiles. In that case, the division might well come, following O'Neill's suggestion,[6] at

---

[1] See the commentary on this chapter below, pp. 93–94.
[2] See above, p. 18. [3] Haenchen, *Die Apostelgeschichte*, pp. 86–87.
[4] Ibid., pp. 95–96. [5] Ibid., pp. 96–102.
[6] O'Neill, *The Theology of Acts*, pp. 62–63, 70.

19²¹. We are provided with a summary at 19¹⁰⁻²⁰. All Asia had heard the gospel. Verse 21 runs: 'Now after these events, Paul resolved in the Spirit to pass through Macedonia and Achaia and go to Jerusalem; saying, "After I have been there, I must also see Rome." ' And there are many indications from this point onward of a divine compulsion on Paul to go up to Jerusalem and beyond it to Rome.¹ This present commentary, however, has contented itself with dividing the material in Acts into four sections, the exact endings and beginnings of which are not always capable of being decided, entitled 'The Primitive Jewish-Christian Church' (1–5), 'First Encounters between the Church and the Gentiles' (6¹–14²⁸), 'The Church Spreads to the Gentiles' (15¹–21¹⁶), and 'Paul's Road to Rome' (21¹⁷–28³¹).

Lucian, writing in the second century A.D., maintains that the two primary necessities for an historian are 'an understanding of society' and 'the capacity to interpret'.² The historian, he says, should take trouble to discover by research what really happened, 'best of all if he has been present and witnessed it, but if not, by listening to those who describe it in the most impartial way'. And then, 'he must have a power of imagination and be able to put together the most credible story'. When he has collected all the facts he must work them together into a series of notes; and this in turn has to be moulded into a presentable narrative.³ Luke comes out of these tests very well. He professes, in the words of the Preface to his Gospel and by his occasional lapses into the first person plural, to have been present at some at least of the events narrated, and to have derived his material otherwise from 'eyewitnesses and ministers of the word' (Luke 1²). Could 'eyewitnesses' refer to the material for the Gospel and 'ministers of the word' to the material for Acts? His remarkable accuracy in referring to social and political details and to the historical events in the second half of Acts bears out his 'understanding of society'. His 'literary reconstructions', his carefully devised, unrhetorical speeches, and his summaries serve as interpretation, articulation, and construction of the narrative. The evidence

---

¹ Ibid., pp. 62–63; for these indications, see Acts 20²²ᶠ·, ²⁵, 21⁴, ¹⁰⁻¹⁴, 23¹¹, 27²⁴.
² Lucian, *On Writing History*, 34 (my translation).
³ Ibid., 47, 48 (my translation).

that Luke was a painter is worthless. But that he was an artist, a very skilful literary artist, is visible on every page of Acts. This does not mean that he was a novelist *manqué*, constructing an imaginary plot by the use of some genuine historical materials. He was indeed an historian, the first Church historian and in many ways the finest of all. But in order to compose a history out of the disparate, disconnected, and sometimes scanty materials available to him he employed skilfully and with restraint all the resources of interpretation, of imagination, of arrangement, of style, of language at his disposal. So successful was he that the Church rewarded him by giving his Church History a unique place in the canon of its New Testament.

3. *The Language of Acts*

Luke comes nearer to writing Attic Greek (which was the literary, ideal, language for Greek writers of his period) than any other writer in the New Testament. But this deliberately literary style is not maintained consistently nor for long passages; and it is clear that the ordinary Greek of his period, the Greek of commercial correspondence and of the spoken language of the middle and lower classes, the *lingua franca* of the eastern half of the Roman Empire (called the *koinē*), came more naturally to him, as it did to almost all the other writers of the New Testament. Further, Luke at times wrote a deliberately 'biblical' language, when he imported into his style expressions and idioms derived from or in imitation of the Greek Old Testament. Even in an English version the first point in his two-volume work at which he adopts this style is obvious; read the first four verses of his Gospel, and then the next two chapters: the contrast in style is unmistakable. In Acts he usually attributes to the apostolic speakers in the first half of the book this 'biblical' style; it is a kind of 'sacred language'. This is only one example of his tendency to alter his language in order to suit the speaker and the occasion. We have seen how James, the Aramaic-speaker, in Acts 15 refers to Peter as *Symeon*.[1] The Voice which addresses Paul, in Aramaic, calls him by his Semitic name, Saul, not his Roman name, Paul (Acts 9[4], 22[7], 26[14]). When Paul in Acts 26 is

---

[1] See above, p. 49.

speaking before the Jewish king Agrippa and the Roman procurator Festus he exhibits an interesting and appropriate mixture of Semitisms (i.e. expressions ultimately deriving from Hebrew or Aramaic) for the Jew, and Hellenistic speech suitable for the educated Roman. Wherever his usual *koinē*-Greek takes on a more than usually literary garb there are reasons for it: 17^{16-34}—the Areopagus speech; 19^{21-40}—the scene in the theatre at Ephesus; 24^{1-23}—Tertullus' speech and all the proceedings before Felix. In varying his style in this manner Luke is conforming to the convention of ancient historians. Lucian recommends historians to do this very thing, and says that the style should become grand (but not too grand) in relating grand events. He mentions a sea battle as one of the 'grand' subjects, for which the style should be borne along the tops of the waves, so to speak, spreading its sail.[1]

4. *The Text of Acts*

The most valuable manuscripts for determining the text of Acts are those which are regarded as most valuable for determining the text of the New Testament generally, often called the 'great uncials', because they are written in a script (like our capital letters) of a greater antiquity than the running, or cursive, script (like our written hand), and are in fact the oldest codices (i.e. manuscripts in book-form) of the New Testament known. These are:

B. *Codex Vaticanus*, of the fourth century, written in Egypt, now in the Vatican Library at Rome.

ℵ. *Codex Sinaiticus*, late fourth or early fifth century, probably written in Egypt. Tischendorf found it in the remote monastery of St. Catherine at Mt. Sinai in 1844. It is now in the British Museum.

A. *Codex Alexandrinus*, fifth or early sixth century, origin uncertain. It was given to King Charles I of England in 1628 by Cyril Lucar, then Patriarch of Alexandria, and is now in the British Museum.

D. *Codex Bezae*, probably of the fifth century, a bilingual (Greek and Latin) manuscript. It is in the Library of the University of Cambridge, having been presented to that

---

[1] Lucian, *On Writing History*, 45.

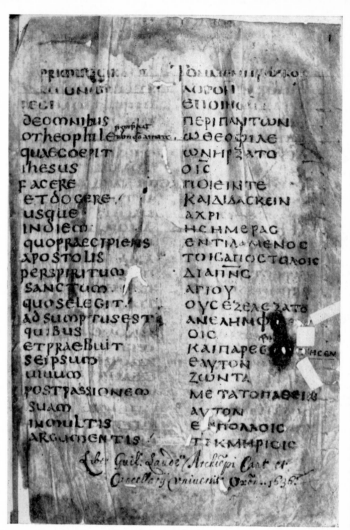

The opening verses of Acts (1¹⁻³ᵃ) in Codex Laudianus in Greek and Latin, with the signature of Archbishop Laud below

University by Theodore Beza, the Reformation scholar, in 1581.

C. *Codex Ephraemi* or *Rescriptus*, probably of the fifth century, origin unknown. It is now in the Bibliothèque Nationale in Paris.

E. *Codex Laudianus*, probably of the late sixth or early seventh century, bilingual. It came into the possession of Archbishop Laud, who presented it to the Bodleian Library, Oxford, where it is now to be seen. It contains Acts only.

To these we should add, for Acts, a cursive manuscript, 81, written in 1044, containing fragments of Acts, now in the British Museum; another part of the same manuscript is preserved in the Patriarchal Library in Cairo.

As well as these uncials and cursives there are several papyrus manuscripts that were preserved in the sands of Egypt, and discovered by archaeologists in recent years. Of these the most remarkable is $\mathfrak{P}^{45}$, of the third century, which contains Chapters 4 to 17 of Acts. Part of it is now in Dublin, and part in Vienna. But there are several other very early papyri containing fragments of Acts. The other sources from which scholars today reconstruct the text of Acts (as of any book of the New Testament) are early translations (known as Versions), such as the Latin translations, the Syriac ones, and the translations into two different dialects of the Egyptian language, Sahidic and Bohairic; and quotations of the New Testament from the early Christian Fathers.

Undoubtedly the most remarkable feature of the text of Acts is its unusually large contribution to the type of readings known as the 'Western Text'. The chief witnesses for reconstructing this type of text are *Codex Bezae*, D (which is not, however, by any means a pure representative of the 'Western' text); some readings given between asterisks in the margin of the Syriac Version known as the Harklean Syriac (Sy[h]); and the Old Latin Versions of the New Testament (represented by such manuscripts as gig, h, p, and the Latin column of D known as d). This type of text exhibits so many startling and interesting variant readings in Acts that some scholars have argued that it represents the original text and that the text witnessed to by the majority of manuscripts is a later rewriting. This view, however, has not obtained widespread support. The most that can be said on a subject which is still full of uncertainty is that 'Western' readings represent a type of text which goes back to a very early period, even as far as the middle of the second century. It is not unreasonable to conclude that among these curious 'Western' readings we can detect the hand of at least one early consistent interpolator into the text of Acts; his activity will occasionally be noted in the Commentary. This text is called 'Western' because most of the manuscripts witnessing to it happen to be of Western *provenance*, but there is no reason at all to think that this proves that the revision itself was made in the Western Church. One of the earliest witnesses to it, Irenaeus, probably got his text of the New Testament from Asia Minor. We shall be noting several remarkable 'Western' readings in the course of the Commentary. But the 'Western' type is not simply an interesting curiosity. It represents a period when the text of Acts was fluid and had not become stereotyped into different textual traditions, which are represented for us today for the most part by the 'great uncials', and therefore the 'Western' text may still throw valuable light on our search for the original text of Acts.

THE ACTS

1 IN the first book, O Theophilus, I have dealt with all that
2 Jesus began to do and teach, until the day when he was taken
up, after he had given commandment through the Holy
3 Spirit to the apostles whom he had chosen. To them he presented himself alive after his passion by many proofs,
appearing to them during forty days, and speaking of the
4 kingdom of God. And while staying*a* with them he charged

a Or eating

I. THE PRIMITIVE JEWISH-CHRISTIAN CHURCH
CHAPTERS 1—5

1: 1–11. *Jesus initiates the Church's Mission*

1   Theophilus is completely unknown. The name may be one invented
to disguise the real name of the person to whom the Gospel and Acts
are addressed, but it is wholly unlikely that Theophilus is a fictitious
person. The epithet 'most excellent' given to him in Luke 1³ may
imply that he held an official position, but it need not do so.

2   *taken up* probably means no more than 'removed, taken away' (cp.
Luke 9⁵¹), without the added sense 'upwards, into heaven', as in an
Ascension. But it is quite possible that the word 'taken up' is an early
interpolation, and that the verse originally read 'until the day when
he gave commandment through the Holy Spirit to the apostles and
chose them'.

3   *forty days* is a conventional period of time and must not be taken
exactly—the period that Moses spent on the top of Sinai and Elijah
in his journey to Horeb and Jesus in the wilderness. 13³¹ describes the
same period more generally as 'many days'. Notice how gradually
the transition from preface to narrative takes place, in marked contrast to the violent change of style after the preface in the Gospel (cp.
Luke 1⁴ with 1⁵ᶠᶠ.). Perhaps Luke had learnt something from criticism of his style (? by Theophilus) since he had written his first work.
Lucian (*On Writing History*, 55) says that the transition from preface
to narrative must be gradual and smooth.

4   *staying with them* (Gk. συναλιζόμενος) could mean either 'forgathering

them not to depart from Jerusalem, but to wait for the pro-
5 mise of the Father, which, he said, 'you heard from me, for
John baptized with water, but before many days you shall be
baptized with the Holy Spirit.'

6   So when they had come together, they asked him, 'Lord,
7 will you at this time restore the kingdom to Israel?' He said
to them, 'It is not for you to know times or seasons which the
8 Father has fixed by his own authority. But you shall receive
power when the Holy Spirit has come upon you; and you
shall be my witnesses in Jerusalem and in all Judea and
9 Samaria and to the end of the earth.' And when he had said
this, as they were looking on, he was lifted up, and a cloud
10 took him out of their sight. And while they were gazing into

---

or 'eating salt with'. The contrast implied here between baptism
with water and baptism with Spirit (and presumably not with water)
is not one that Luke attempts to emphasize during the course of his
narrative. It may therefore represent an early tradition here.

6–8   There is evident here a deliberate intention on Luke's part to discourage an expectation of the immediate Return of Jesus. Paul had
issued similar discouragements (1 Thess. 5^{1-11}; 2 Thess. 2^{1-12}), but
always in a situation where the Event was only postponed for a little
longer. But here the postponement seems much more indefinite.

8   This verse sets the keynote of Acts and provides it with its subject.

9–11   Luke has already described this event, in Luke 24^{50-53}, where
Christ is represented as the Priest of God in glory, blessing his people
before passing away (based on Ecclesiasticus 50). Here the same event
is presented differently. Christ ascends, becomes invisible, is removed
on or in a cloud. The imagery of a cloud meant for both Jews and
Greeks a 'supernatural abduction'[1] (cp. Rev. 11^{12}). The emphasis is
upon the removal of the visible presence of Jesus. The Lord will
return some time, but meanwhile mere gaping after wonders is futile
(v. 11). The apostles must return to Jerusalem and bend their energies
to the task of proclaiming the gospel; the immediate necessities of the
Church must occupy them. Cp. Matt. 28^{16-20} and John 20^{19-29} to see
how two other writers in the New Testament manage this event.

[1] The words are those of P. A. van Steempvoort, to whose article 'The
Interpretation of the Ascension in Luke and Acts' (*New Testament Studies*,
v (1938), pp. 30–42) the comment here is much indebted.

heaven as he went, behold, two men stood by them in white
11 robes, and said, 'Men of Galilee, why do you stand looking
into heaven? This Jesus, who was taken up from you into
heaven, will come in the same way as you saw him go into
heaven.'

12 Then they returned to Jerusalem from the mount called
Olivet, which is near Jerusalem, a sabbath day's journey
13 away; and when they had entered, they went up to the upper
room, where they were staying, Peter and John and James
and Andrew, Philip and Thomas, Bartholomew and Matthew,
James the son of Alphaeus and Simon the Zealot and Judas
14 the son of James. All these with one accord devoted themselves to prayer, together with the women and Mary the
mother of Jesus, and with his brothers.

15 In those days Peter stood up among the brethren (the
company of persons was in all about a hundred and twenty),
16 and said, 'Brethren, the scripture had to be fulfilled which the

---

1: 12–26. *The Church faces its immediate tasks*

12   *a sabbath day's journey* was a little over half a mile.
13   The list of the apostles is identical with that of Luke 6[13–16], with
the order a little changed and Judas Iscariot omitted; cp. Matt.
10[2–4]; Mark 3[13–19].
        upper room: it was a well-known custom in Jerusalem to let off the
upper room in a house to poverty-stricken people, and it was very
usual for rabbis to hire such rooms to study in.
14   This is the only mention of any of the relations of Jesus in the Book
of Acts, except for James, the Lord's brother.
15   *In those days* is an extremely vague indication, suggesting that Luke
really had little idea of the length of the interval between the last
event described and this one.
ff.   We here for the first time encounter a quotation from the Book of
Psalms, used in a manner characteristic of primitive and early
Christian biblical interpretation; examples of this abound in Acts.
The assumption was made that every one of the Psalms was written

Holy Spirit spoke beforehand by the mouth of David, concerning Judas who was guide to those who arrested Jesus.
17 For he was numbered among us, and was allotted his share
18 in this ministry. (Now this man bought a field with the
reward of his wickedness and falling headlong^a he burst
19 open in the middle and all his bowels gushed out. And it
became known to all the inhabitants of Jerusalem, so that the
field was called in their language Akeldama, that is, Field of
20 Blood.) For it is written in the book of Psalms,

> "Let his habitation become desolate,
> and let there be no one to live in it";

and

> "His office let another take."

a Or swelling up

---

by David, under the direct inspiration of the Holy Spirit; that he
had been inspired to utter direct predictions of what was to happen
in the distant future; and that this inspiration included the actual
words God spoke to, or concerning, his Messiah and his Chosen
People. This assumption was common to both Judaism and Christianity. It can be found both in the works of early Jewish Rabbis and
in the literature of the Dead Sea Sect. The Christians applied the
words of the Psalms to their own Messiah, Jesus Christ, but they were
using a technique or a convention which would have been perfectly
understandable to Jews; it occurs in almost every book of the New
Testament.

Brethren, the very first term used to describe the Christian Church,
earlier even than the use of the word 'church' (ἐκκλησία) itself.

18, 19   Matt. 27³⁻¹⁰ gives a completely different account of the end of
Judas Iscariot; the only point the two accounts have in common is
that both incidents are connected with the place called Akeldama
(though they are differently connected). They cannot both be true.
It has been suggested that Akeldama is a corruption of another
Aramaic term meaning 'Field of Sleep', i.e., cemetery, and that
Christian popular sentiment altered the term and connected it with
the death of Judas. But there are no satisfactory parallels for calling
a cemetery a Field of Sleep and the Aramaic term is not a very
natural one.

21 'So one of the men who have accompanied us during all the
22 time that the Lord Jesus went in and out among us, beginning
    from the baptism of John until the day when he was taken
    up from us—one of these men must become with us a witness
23 to his resurrection.' And they put forward two, Joseph called
24 Barsabbas, who was surnamed Justus, and Matthias. And
    they prayed and said, 'Lord, who knowest the hearts of all
25 men, show which one of these two thou hast chosen to take
    the place in this ministry and apostleship from which Judas
26 turned aside, to go to his own place.' And they cast lots for
    them, and the lot fell on Matthias; and he was enrolled with
    the eleven apostles.

---

f.   Notice the qualifications for an apostle—companionship with Jesus
from what Luke always regards as the beginning of Jesus' ministry,
his baptism by John (Acts 1^{22}, 10^{37}, $13^{24, 25}$), and testimony to a
vision of the Risen Lord. It was perhaps because on neither of these
points was his record comparable to that of the Twelve that Paul
found difficulty in establishing his claim to apostleship. We hear
nothing more about either of the men between whom the choice lay,
but their very insignificance argues in favour of our accepting their
names as genuine.

25   *ministry and apostleship*. The apostles are not officers whose places
must be filled on the present holders' vacating office, for this is the
only example of an apostle's place being filled. When James the
brother of John, son of Zebedee, was executed by Herod Agrippa
(Acts $12^{1, 2}$) no attempt was made to fill his place. Judas' defection
was altogether exceptional (John 17^{12}); Matthias' function was
primarily that of witness, and the sooner a witness is chosen after
the event to which he witnesses the better. In their primary function,
that of founding the Church by witnessing to what they have seen
and know (*apostleship*), the apostles have no successors. But in the
much wider and less definite field of ministry, of course they have
successors and assistants, as Acts will show abundantly.

26   This casting of lots was not intended as a deliberate throwing of
the choice into the lap of chance, like our spinning of a coin, but as
a way of putting the choice entirely in the hands of God, who was
assumed to direct the fall of the lot. The concept of the lot as the sign
of God's activity is particularly prominent in the literature of the
Dead Sea Sect. Notice that Peter, as leader of the apostles, takes the

2 WHEN the day of Pentecost had come, they were all together

initiative; the whole people gathered there choose the candidates;[1]
God decides the election; and then (presumably) the apostles arrange
the official enrolment. Matthias is not ordained; none of the Twelve
was, any more than they were baptized, for Jesus himself had
chosen them (the prayer in v. 24 may be addressed to Jesus).

2: 1–13. *The Coming of the Holy Spirit*

The association of the first appearance of the Holy Spirit in
the Church with the Jewish Feast of Pentecost is by no means
self-explanatory. Pentecost was originally an agricultural festival; this is its Greek name, meaning the fiftieth day, roughly
seven weeks after the Feast of the Passover; the Hebrew and
Aramaic name is 'Feast of Weeks' (Lev. 23[15–21]; Deut. 16[9]).
By the first century A.D. this festival was observed by the Jews
primarily as a commemoration of the giving of the Law on
Mount Sinai. Later it was associated especially with the
thought of the Covenant made between God and Israel. But
neither of these associations is particularly appropriate to the
coming of the Spirit, and Luke makes no attempt to exploit
them. The rabbis did know of a story telling how the Law at
Sinai was promulgated in seventy languages, but they did not
associate this story with Pentecost. The best Old Testament
parallel to the story of Pentecost is perhaps Isa. 66[15ff.] (LXX),
which has nothing to do with the Law or with Pentecost.
There was a popular notion that at the End-time there would
be only one language; see Isa. 66[18] (presumably reversing
the division of the primal language of mankind into different
languages, Gen. 11[1–9]); it is found in post-biblical apocalyptic
literature too (*The Testament of Judah* 25[3]). Again, fire suggests
judgment, and so do storm and wind (2 Thess. 1[8]; 4 Esdras
13[10]; Philo, *De Decalogo* 46). It looks as if the association of the
Coming of the Holy Spirit with Pentecost is not to be found in
some theological or exegetical connexion of the Holy Spirit
with the Festival, but because the event happened during the
Festival of Pentecost, the next occasion after the Passover
Festival when there would be large numbers of Jews in

---

[1] The 'Western' text has a singular verb in v. 23, 'he put forward',
making Peter responsible for the choice of the two. This is not the only
point at which this interpolator appears to desire to enhance Peter's status.

2 in one place. And suddenly a sound came from heaven like
   the rush of a mighty wind, and it filled all the house where
3 they were sitting. And there appeared to them tongues as
4 of fire, distributed and resting on each one of them. And

Jerusalem. But early on, at a stage before the account of it
reached Luke, the event was interpreted as a sign of the
arrival of the End-time (i.e., eschatologically), the Spirit
being thought of as both Precursor and Bringer of salvation
and judgement. Luke re-handled this early account according
to his own ideas.

1 *When the day of Pentecost had come* is not necessarily the best translation here. If we are guided by the meaning of exactly the same phrase
   ($\epsilon\nu$ $\tau\hat{\omega}$ $\sigma\nu\mu\pi\lambda\eta\rho\sigma\hat{\nu}\sigma\theta\alpha\iota$) in Luke 9^{51}, we shall render it as 'when it was
   going on for the day of Pentecost'. The idea of fulfilment, which still
   survives in the word 'fully', which appears in several English translations, is not really there in the Greek. Further, the Feast of Pentecost
   was not a single day, but several days. This is a vague phrase, not
   untypical of Luke, suggesting that he does not know the exact time
   of the coming of the Spirit.

2 For the Spirit as wind see Ezek. 37^{9-14} and John 3^8.

3 *distributed* is the correct translation; there is no authority in the
   text for the idea that the tongues of fire were divided.

4 It is usually assumed that we have to do here with a phenomenon
   called 'glossolalia', people speaking in unintelligible language under
   the stress of religious emotion. It has from the beginning been a recurring feature at periods of religious excitement in the history of
   Christianity. That it was a well-known phenomenon in the primitive
   Church is clear from Paul's letters (1 Cor. $12^{10, 28, 30}$, $14^{2-27, 39}$);
   Paul does not discourage the practice directly; indeed, he says that
   he does it himself (1 Cor. 14^{18}). But he is anxious to depreciate its
   importance in comparison with other gifts. There evidently were
   people in the Christian community who professed to interpret these
   unintelligible 'tongues', but even so there is no doubt that to most
   people they remained (as they do when the phenomenon occurs
   today) unintelligible. Luke obviously knows of the existence of this
   phenomenon, but tends to identify it with prophecy, as Paul does
   not (Acts 10^{46} and 19^6). This may represent a further stage, slightly
   beyond Paul's, in the domestication and regulation of this turbulent
   phenomenon. It seems that Luke is representing what was an out-
   burst of glossolalia, under the stress of great religious excitement, as
   a miraculous endowment of the primitive Christian community with

they were all filled with the Holy Spirit and began to speak
in other tongues, as the Spirit gave them utterance.

5   Now there were dwelling in Jerusalem Jews, devout men
6 from every nation under heaven. And at this sound the
multitude came together, and they were bewildered, because
7 each one heard them speaking in his own language. And they
were amazed and wondered, saying, 'Are not all these who
8 are speaking Galileans? And how is it that we hear, each of
9 us in his own native language? Parthians and Medes and
Elamites and residents of Mesopotamia, Judea and Cappa-
10 docia, Pontus and Asia, Phrygia and Pamphylia, Egypt and
the parts of Libya belonging to Cyrene, and visitors from
11 Rome, both Jews and proselytes, Cretans and Arabians, we
hear them telling in our own tongues the mighty works of
12 God.' And all were amazed and perplexed, saying to one

---

temporary skill in languages; and this as a sign of the universality of
the Christian religion. It should be noted that the gift is given to all
Christians present, not just to the Twelve, and that all present,
Christians or non-Christians, are nevertheless of the Jewish race or
attached to the Jewish religion.

9–11   The list of nationalities who witnessed the results of the outpouring
of the Spirit has been identified as almost exactly the same as an
astrological list, known from other writers, in which each land corresponded to a sign of the Zodiac (only *Judea* is out of place; it was
not, after all, a foreign land; Luke may have made it replace another
name). The list gives evidence of deriving from a period before the
Roman Empire, during the time of the Successor-States to Alexander's
empire, and can be compared with similar lists in earlier, pagan
writers. Luke may not have been the first to use the list in this
context.

10   *visitors from Rome* is not a correct translation. The phrase means
'visitors who were Roman citizens'; they formed in Luke's mind
a class distinct from provincials, who were included in the last nine
nationalities mentioned. For this use of 'Romans' (*'Ρωμαῖοι*) cp. Acts
16[21, 37, 39], 22[25], 23[27–28].

11   *Cretans and Arabians* may mean 'Westerners and Easterners' or
'island-dwellers and continent-dwellers'.

3 another, 'What does this mean?' But others mocking said,
'They are filled with new wine.'

4   But Peter, standing with the eleven, lifted up his voice and

---

2: 14–47. *The first preaching of the gospel and its results*

The first speech of Peter in Acts (vv. 14–36) sets the keynote
for all the subsequent speeches by apostles. Two preliminary
points should be noted in it. First, the writer probably relied
on the Septuagint translation of the O.T. not only for his
quotations but for his argument. Peter emphasizes the word
Lord (v. 36) as it occurs in the quotation from Joel (2^{32}); in
the LXX version the word for Lord is *Kyrios*, which could
apply, and which here evidently did apply in the mind of the
writer to the Lord Jesus, whereas in the Hebrew original the
word in question is the Incommunicable Name for God.
Again in the quotation at 2^{26} of Ps. 16^9 the words *in hope* rely
on the rendering of the LXX, not of the Hebrew, where the
phrase means 'in safety'. It is therefore unlikely that the writer
read his Old Testament in Hebrew, as any very primitive
Christian, Peter or any other apostle, would do. This suggests
that the speech was composed by a Greek-speaking Christian.

Secondly, not only does the speech contain a curious
typically Rabbinic argument about David's witness to the
Christ (vv. 29–35), but it assumes that the Resurrection is
identical with the Ascension (vv. 32, 33), an assumption which
Luke elsewhere emphatically does not make. The speech's
style, however, has exactly the same characteristics as all the
early speeches in Luke. These facts seem to point to the conclusion that Luke has worked over some earlier traditions in
the interests of his aims in the book, and that the speech
represents a compromise between his materials and his
convictions.

This conclusion is borne out if we look at the structure of
this speech, which is very similar to the structure of all the
early speeches in Acts. It can be summarized thus:

(1) The age of Fulfilment has dawned, a Messianic Age
(2^{16}; cp. $3^{18, 24}$).

(2) This Fulfilment has happened through Jesus, through
his Davidic descent ($2^{30–31}$), his ministry (2^{22}; cp. 3^{22}), death

addressed them, 'Men of Judea and all who dwell in Jerusa-
15 lem, let this be known to you, and give ear to my words. For
these men are not drunk, as you suppose, since it is only the
16 third hour of the day; but this is what was spoken by the
prophet Joel:

17   "And in the last days it shall be, God declares,
           that I will pour out my Spirit upon all flesh,
           and your sons and your daughters shall prophesy,
           and your young men shall see visions,

(2^{23}; cp. 3^{13-14}), and Resurrection (2^{24}; cp. 3^{15}, 4^{10}), with proof of this from the Scriptures.

(3) By the Resurrection, Jesus has been proclaimed as the glorified Messiah, sitting at the right hand of God, Head of the New Israel (2^{33-36}; cp. 3^{13}, 4^{11}).

(4) The Holy Spirit now lives in the Church (2^{33}).

(5) An appeal for repentance, with the offer of forgiveness, the Spirit and salvation (2^{38-39}; cp. $3^{19, \ 25-26}$, 4^{12}, 5^{31}).[1] The evidence viewed as a whole suggests that though Luke has given to these early speeches in Acts a certain uniformity and has admitted into their vocabulary some of the phrases and ideas of his own day, though he has in fact retouched them as he retouched so much else, he was working on existing materials and had some reliable information about the type of preaching that Christians had used when in the early days they began their missionary enterprise by entering the local synagogue and speaking to Jews.

15   *the third hour* was 9.00 a.m. by our time. Luke, like the other evangelists, reckons by the Roman method, in which the day began at 6.00 a.m. By Jewish reckoning the new day began at sunset.

17   *in the last days* is a substitution by Luke for the words 'and afterwards' which appear in both Hebrew and LXX. 'In the last days' was a very loose general term: cp. 1 Tim. 4^1; 2 Tim. 3^1. F. F. Bruce suggests the influence on Luke of such an Old Testament passage as Isa. 2^2. The Scriptural proof-texts are the material most likely of all to be inherited by Luke.

[1] For an account of the structure of the early speeches in Acts see C. H. Dodd, *The Apostolic Preaching and Its Developments,* from which this summary is largely taken.

and your old men shall dream dreams;

18 yea, and on my menservants and my maidservants in
those days

I will pour out my Spirit; and they shall prophesy.

19 And I will show wonders in the heaven above

and signs on the earth beneath,

blood, and fire, and vapor of smoke;

20 the sun shall be turned into darkness

and the moon into blood,

before the day of the Lord comes,

the great and manifest day.

21 And it shall be that whoever calls on the name of the Lord
shall be saved."

22 'Men of Israel, hear these words: Jesus of Nazareth, a
man attested to you by God with mighty works and wonders

---

19 *blood and fire and vapor of smoke*, omitted by the 'Western' text, but
retained, no doubt, by Luke, who shows thereby that he does not
necessarily take all Old Testament imagery in a literal sense; cp. v. 20.

20 *manifest*, because the LXX at this point mistranslated a Hebrew
word (whose real meaning is 'terrible') and Luke (or his source)
followed it.

21 *calls on the name of the Lord*, a technical term in Paul's letters, see Rom.
10$^{13, 14}$; 1 Cor. 1^2: it occurs again in Acts 9$^{14, 21}$, 22^{16}. It means 'to
invoke God and thereby to acknowledge allegiance to him'; for
Christians, this invocation was to give allegiance to God *as revealed
in Christ*.

22 *Jesus of Nazareth*, Ναζωραῖος in Greek, the regular adjective in the
Synoptic Gospels for describing Jesus. The Christians are called
'*Nazoraioi*' at Acts 24^5. There is some reason for thinking that the
followers of John the Baptist may have been called *Nazoraioi* (=
'keepers') originally, and that the followers of Jesus were confused
with them. The word has no etymological connexion with Nazareth,
but the early Christians, or their opponents, may have thought that
it had. It may also have been connected in the minds of the early
Christians with a word *neṣer* meaning 'the Branch' (i.e. the Messiah;
cp. Isa. 11^1), and even with *nazir*, a Nazirite, one who observed
a special ascetical discipline and lived under a vow of religion.

and signs which God did through him in your midst, as you
23 yourselves know—this Jesus, delivered up according to the
definite plan and foreknowledge of God, you crucified and
24 killed by the hands of lawless men. But God raised him up,
having loosed the pangs of death, because it was not possible
for him to be held by it.

25   For David says concerning him,
        "I saw the Lord always before me,
        for he is at my right hand that I may not be shaken;
26   therefore my heart was glad, and my tongue rejoiced;
        moreover my flesh will dwell in hope.
27   For thou wilt not abandon my soul to Hades,
        nor let thy Holy One see corruption.

---

23   *lawless men*, not licentious men, but Gentiles, who do not observe
     the Jewish Law, precisely as the Jews themselves would describe the
     Romans; this is a Jewish touch, whether devised or inherited by Luke.
24   *pangs of death*, literally, birth-pangs of death, a very odd phrase,
     which some have thought to indicate the mis-translation of an original
     Aramaic word behind this passage which could mean either 'bonds'
     or 'pangs'. But 'birth-pangs of death' was, however odd, quite a well-
     known expression in the LXX (2 Sam. 22[6]; Job 21[17], 39[3]; Ps. 18[5], 116[3];
     Hos. 13[13]; Isa. 13[8], 26[17]; Jer. 13[21]), and it is much more likely that
     Luke used it here to impart a suitably Scriptural colour to the diction
     of the apostle's speech. M. Wilcox (*The Semitisms of Acts*, pp. 23–24,
     47–48) suggests that it indicates the use by Luke's source of a Targum,
     i.e. an early translation-mingled-with-commentary, in Aramaic,
     rather than a direct use of the LXX.
25–31 The quotation of Ps. 16[8–11] is introduced on the assumption that
     the passage represents David reporting the words of the Messiah,
     who declares that he always kept the thought of God before him and
     the steadfast belief that God would prevent his body corrupting, i.e.
     would raise it. Vv. 29–31 explain that the passage could not refer
     to David.
25   *the Lord* means God the Father, of whom the Messiah is supposed
     here to be speaking. The MSS. which read 'my Lord' here make it
     refer to Christ, and spoil the sense.
27   *Hades* here simply stands for death. There is no doctrine of the
     Descent into Hell in Luke's writings.

28 Thou hast made known to me the ways of life;
    thou wilt make me full of gladness with thy presence."

29 'Brethren, I may say to you confidently of the patriarch
David that he both died and was buried, and his tomb is
30 with us to this day. Being therefore a prophet, and knowing
that God had sworn with an oath to him that he would set
31 one of his descendants upon his throne, he foresaw and
spoke of the resurrection of the Christ, that he was not
32 abandoned to Hades, nor did his flesh see corruption. This
33 Jesus God raised up, and of that we all are witnesses. Being
therefore exalted at the right hand of God, and having
received from the Father the promise of the Holy Spirit, he
34 has poured out this which you see and hear. For David did
not ascend into the heavens; but he himself says,

    "The Lord said to my Lord, Sit at my right hand,
35   till I make thy enemies a stool for thy feet."
36 Let all the house of Israel therefore know assuredly that God
has made him both Lord and Christ, this Jesus whom you
crucified.'

37   Now when they heard this they were cut to the heart, and
said to Peter and the rest of the apostles, 'Brethren, what
38 shall we do?' And Peter said to them, 'Repent, and be

---

35 The citation of Ps. 110 as a proof-text of the Resurrection–Ascension
and of Christ's Lordship is a very old usage in primitive Christianity,
and occurs again and again in the N.T. Cp. Mark 12³⁵ᶠ·, 14⁶²;
1 Cor. 15²⁵; Heb. 1¹³; and it occurs frequently in early Christian
literature.

36 The heart of Luke's Christology in a single sentence. It is not by
any means incompatible with that of Paul. There is no need to see
here the idea that God only made Jesus the Christ at his baptism or
his Resurrection; no such idea occurs elsewhere in Luke.

38 The reception of the Spirit is here associated with baptism, as it
normally is in Acts. Where it is not, we may suspect a source. *In the
name of Jesus Christ* is an old baptismal formula.

baptized every one of you in the name of Jesus Christ for the
forgiveness of your sins; and you shall receive the gift of the
39 Holy Spirit. For the promise is to you and to your children
and to all that are far off, every one whom the Lord our God
40 calls to him.' And he testified with many other words and
exhorted them, saying, 'Save yourselves from this crooked
41 generation.' So those who received his word were baptized,
and there were added that day about three thousand souls.
42 And they devoted themselves to the apostles' teaching and
fellowship, to the breaking of bread and the prayers.
43   And fear came upon every soul; and many wonders and
44 signs were done through the apostles. And all who believed

---

42   Luke sets out the characteristic features of the life of the primitive
Church in an unforgettable phrase. Fellowship (κοινωνία) is a word
full of meaning. L. S. Thornton (in *The Common Life in the Body of
Christ*, pp. 5 ff., and *passim*) calls it the focus of a new relationship
between God and man in Christ. It includes having goods in common (κοινά), Acts 2⁴⁴, 4³²; collecting funds to support the poverty-
stricken Christians in Jerusalem (in the course of which James,
Cephas, and John give the right hand of fellowship (κοινωνίας) to
Paul, Gal. 2⁹, ¹⁰), and later the breaking down of the barrier between Jew and Gentile; for in one sense nothing is now κοινόν
(common in the sense of 'inferior', Acts 10²⁸) and in another everything is κοινόν ('shared').
      breaking of bread: the exact phrase occurs again only in Luke 24³⁵,
but very similar expressions occur in several places in the N.T., and
in 1 Cor. 10¹⁶ and 11²⁴ are used of the Eucharist. It would therefore
be unwise to follow the use of the phrase in Rabbinic literature and
take it as referring only to the beginning of a meal, or the first part of
the Eucharist, or to confine it to the Love-feast or Agape which in
Paul's time, and probably in Luke's also, accompanied the Eucharist
(cp. 1 Cor. 10¹⁴⁻³¹, 11¹⁷⁻³⁴). No doubt it refers to the Eucharist
primarily; but in those early days the Eucharist was also an ordinary
meal eaten in common with fellow Christians, or was held in the
middle of one.
43–47 One of the many Lukan 'summaries', designed both to direct and
control the narrative, to bind it together and to fill up gaps caused by
scantiness of material.

were together and had all things in common; and they sold
their possessions and goods and distributed them to all, as

The monogram Chi Rho=CHR(istos), from a wall of Lullingstone Roman
villa, Kent, with Alpha and Omega on each side. Date *c.* 350.

any had need. And day by day, attending the temple together
and breaking bread in their homes, they partook of food with
glad and generous hearts, praising God and having favor

with all the people. And the Lord added to their number day
by day those who were being saved.

3 Now Peter and John were going up to the temple at the
2 hour of prayer, the ninth hour. And a man lame from birth
was being carried, whom they laid daily at that gate of the
temple which is called Beautiful to ask alms of those who
3 entered the temple. Seeing Peter and John about to go into
4 the temple, he asked for alms. And Peter directed his gaze
5 at him, with John, and said, 'Look at us.' And he fixed his
attention upon them, expecting to receive something from
6 them. But Peter said, 'I have no silver and gold, but I give
you what I have; in the name of Jesus Christ of Nazareth,

---

47   *to their number* translates too smoothly a phrase which in most other
contexts in Acts means 'together' (e.g. 1^{15}, 2^{44}), but which cannot
mean that here.[1] The suggestion that it represents the mistranslation
of an Aramaic original has not found general favour. The best suggestion to explain this minor but very thorny problem is that of H. J.
Cadbury, that it has the meaning which it often bears in papyri, 'in
total', 'in all', and that Luke forgot to add the number after it.

3: 1–10. *The Apostles' first miracle*

1   The *ninth hour*, three o'clock in the afternoon, was the time of the
evening sacrifice ('evening oblation'), when all pious Jews would
make a point of praying, whether they were within reach of the
Temple or not. Cp. Dan. 9^{21}; Judith 9^1.

2   No other sources mention this *Beautiful* gate. Josephus mentions
a 'Corinthian' or a 'Brazen' gate, and this is to be identified with what
the Mishna (the great source of Rabbinic material, containing
traditions going back in many cases as far as the first century A.D.)
calls the 'Nicanor' gate. The account here suggests a gate giving access
to the men's court, or Court of the Israelites, which bounded on three
sides the Court of the priests that in its turn enclosed the altar of burnt
offering and the Holy of Holies. Luke seems to imagine, erroneously,
that Solomon's porch was reached after traversing an access-court,
whereas it was in fact attached to the outside perimeter of the
building.

[1] Some of the early versions found it puzzling. The Latin (rendering *in
idipsum*) was content to leave it meaningless.

7 walk.' And he took him by the right hand and raised him up;
8 and immediately his feet and ankles were made strong. And
leaping up he stood and walked and entered the temple with
9 them, walking and leaping and praising God. And all the
10 people saw him walking and praising God, and recognized
him as the one who sat for alms at the Beautiful Gate of the
temple; and they were filled with wonder and amazement at
what had happened to him.

11 While he clung to Peter and John, all the people ran
together to them in the portico called Solomon's, astounded.
12 And when Peter saw it he addressed the people, 'Men of
Israel, why do you wonder at this, or why do you stare at
us, as though by our own power or piety we had made him
13 walk? The God of Abraham and of Isaac and of Jacob, the
God of our fathers, glorified his servant*a* Jesus, whom you

a Or child

3: 11–26. *Peter's speech after the healing*

11 The 'Western' text attempts to rescue Luke from giving the
impression that Solomon's porch was attached to an inner court; it
reads: 'and as Peter and John went out, he went with them, holding
them; but they [the people] stood in the Porch which is called
Solomon's, in amazement.'

16 Peter's second speech exhibits many characteristically Lukan
touches, such as the firm attribution of the blame for the death of
Jesus to the Jews and not to the Romans (vv. 13, 14), the conception
of ignorance as a temporary excuse (v. 17), and the expression *Author
of life* (v. 15), which is certainly not a primitive title for Jesus. But the
speech is not without earlier elements too.

13 *servant*, or child. This title, it is true, does not contain for Luke the
thought of sin-bearing or atonement; and it does occur in later
Christian authors writing between A.D. 90 and 150 (*1 Clement, Didache,
The Epistle of Barnabas*, and *The Martyrdom of Polycarp*). But Luke confines its use to these early speeches (3²⁶, 4²⁵, ²⁷, ³⁰ as well as here),
which suggests that he thought it was an early title. It occurs elsewhere usually in liturgical expressions, and liturgical formulae are
notoriously conservative; and it appears in proof-texts used by the
early Church to delineate the Righteous Sufferer (servant or slave)

delivered up and denied in the presence of Pilate, when he
14 had decided to release him. But you denied the Holy and
Righteous One, and asked for a murderer to be granted to
15 you, and killed the Author of life, whom God raised from
16 the dead. To this we are witnesses. And his name, by faith
in his name, has made this man strong whom you see and
know; and the faith which is through Jesus[a] has given the
man this perfect health in the presence of you all.

17   'And now, brethren, I know that you acted in ignorance, as

a *Greek* him

---

mentioned in the Psalms and in Isaiah. The word occurs here in
what seems to us an odd juxtaposition of Exod. 3^6 with Isa. 52^{13};
this is a type of conflated proof-text which is to be found everywhere
throughout the N.T., in Mark and Paul as much as in other writers,
and there is no reason why we should imagine that Luke invented
rather than inherited it (for the first quotation see Acts 7^{32} also).

15   God raises Jesus from the dead; Jesus is passive rather than active
in the Resurrection. This is typically Lukan doctrine; cp. 5^{30}, 10^{40},
$13^{30, 37}$.

16   The translation does in fact make sense of this verse, but only at
the cost of not translating the Greek, for the Greek as it stands cannot be construed into any intelligible meaning. Literally translated,
it would run: 'And at the faith of his name this man, whom you see
and know, his name has made strong, and the faith which is through
him has given him this wholeness in the presence of you all.' This is
one of those passages where the suggestion that an Aramaic phrase
has been misunderstood finds most support, though the theory is by
no means certain. Another suggestion is that the second mention of
'his name' is a later gloss, for if it were removed, God, who is the
subject of the sentence before the difficult one, would be the subject
of the verb 'strengthened', and thus construed the verse would make
good sense. C. F. D. Moule has suggested that we have here three
alternative forms which Luke had put down for this sentence without
finally deciding upon any of them, and that this has naturally produced confusion. For another possibility of unfinished syntax see the
note on 2^{47}. The question of the exact reference of the expression
'the faith which is through him' is a difficult one also. The RSV
decides the matter by translating 'through Jesus', but it could equally
well refer to the faith of the healed man.

did also your rulers. But what God foretold by the mouth of all the prophets, that his Christ should suffer, he thus fulfilled. Repent therefore, and turn again, that your sins may be blotted out, that times of refreshing may come from the presence of the Lord, and that he may send the Christ appointed for you, Jesus, whom heaven must receive until the time for establishing all that God spoke by the mouth of his holy prophets from of old. Moses said, "The Lord God will raise up for you a prophet from your brethren as he raised me up. You shall listen to him in whatever he tells you. And it shall be that every soul that does not listen to that prophet shall be destroyed from the people." And all the prophets who have spoken, from Samuel and those who came afterwards, also proclaimed these days. You are the sons of

---

8   Luke is deeply convinced that Christ's sufferings were determined beforehand as part of God's plan (Acts 17³, 26²³; Luke 24²⁶, ⁴⁴ᶠ·). This is perhaps the nearest he approaches to a theory of the Atonement. But this conviction can be traced throughout the New Testament.

9   *times of refreshing* does not mean occasional visits by a usually absentee Holy Spirit, nor intervals for recuperation during the eschatological afflictions, but the final time of salvation.

I   a reference to the Parousia or Second Coming, a feature which is not absent from Luke's Gospel, though it does not feature very prominently there.

4   It is very difficult to envisage this passage as simply reproducing the relatively late ideas and vocabulary of Luke's own day. It has a primitive colour and ring. The conflated proof-text, Deut. 18¹⁵, ¹⁹ (cp. Acts 7³⁷) and Lev. 23²⁹, is a very early Christian one, and indeed goes back to pre-Christian use in the literature of the Dead Sea Sect.

4   A first-century Christian, like a first-century Jew, was perfectly capable of classing *Samuel* among the prophets.

5   Another conflated proof-text, Gen. 12³ with 22¹⁸; *posterity* is the translation of a word which literally means a seed, and it is clear from the next verse that Luke meant the seed or posterity to be singular—'in your descendant'. This meaning is explicitly drawn out by Paul in Gal. 3¹⁶, where Gen. 12⁷ is referred to. It is likely that both Paul and Luke were reproducing an argument which they had

the prophets and of the covenant which God gave to your fathers, saying to Abraham, "And in your posterity shall all
26 the families of the earth be blessed." God, having raised up his servant,[a] sent him to you first, to bless you in turning every one of you from your wickedness.'

4 AND as they were speaking to the people, the priests and the captain of the temple and the Sadducees came upon them,
2 annoyed because they were teaching the people and pro-
3 claiming in Jesus the resurrection from the dead. And they arrested them and put them in custody until the morrow, for
4 it was already evening. But many of those who heard the word believed; and the number of the men came to about five thousand.

[a] Or child

---

inherited; the alternative is to admit a flagrant 'Paulinism' in Luke. Paul quotes the text used by Luke (Gen. 12³) at Gal. 3⁸, where he correctly reproduces the LXX. But Luke here alters the 'nations' of the original to 'families'. It is not clear why he should do so, unless he wants to reserve reference to the possibility of blessing brought to the Gentiles (which is another rendering of the Greek word for nations, ἔθνη) till later in his story.

4: 1–22. *Peter and John arraigned before the Sanhedrin*

1   *the captain of the temple* was the chief of the Temple police, who ranked next after the high priest. In Luke 22⁴, ⁵² Luke places him in the plural, which suggests that he was not very exactly informed about the administration of the Temple.

4   Objection has been made that the number of 5,000 is impossibly large as an estimate of the total strength of the Church at this time, on the ground that Jeremias has conjectured the population of Jerusalem at this date to be 25,000–30,000. But this must surely be a gross underestimate. Hecataeus of Abdera said that the population of Jerusalem about 300 B.C. was 120,000 (Diodorus Siculus, XL. iii. 8; Josephus, *Against Apion*, i. 194, 197). Even allowing for the tendency of ancient historians to exaggerate numbers, this suggests a very large population, and V. Tcherikover (*Hellenistic Civilisation and the Jews*, ET, p. 119) accepts it as approximately correct. Josephus (*Jewish War*, vi. 422–5) says that during his procuratorship Cestius (*c.* A.D. 65)

On the morrow their rulers and elders and scribes were
gathered together in Jerusalem, with Annas the high priest
and Caiaphas and John and Alexander, and all who were of
the high-priestly family. And when they had set them in the
midst, they inquired, 'By what power or by what name did
you do this?' Then Peter, filled with the Holy Spirit, said
to them, 'Rulers of the people and elders, if we are being
examined today concerning a good deed done to a cripple,
by what means this man has been healed, be it known to you
all, and to all the people of Israel, that by the name of Jesus
Christ of Nazareth, whom you crucified, whom God raised

---

wanted to ascertain the population of the city and asked the chief
priests to conduct a census; they did this during the Feast of the
Passover, and reached the figure of 2,700,000. Even supposing this
figure to be ten times too large, we reach a population of Jerusalem
vastly in excess of Jeremias's calculation. It is in any case difficult
to believe that Jerusalem about the year 30 was no bigger than
Durham or Wells, and even more difficult to imagine that the Church,
whose extraordinary growth in numbers is one of the remarkable
phenomena of the first and second centuries, had not at a very early
stage indeed reached the modest total of 5,000. Luke's figure is, of
course, only an approximate estimate, but we need not doubt its
substantial accuracy.

Annas was certainly not high priest at this time, though he was
from A.D. 6 to 14. Luke elsewhere is uncertain as to Annas, for in
Luke 3^2 he has the extraordinary expression 'in the high-priesthood
of Annas and Caiaphas', although there is no evidence that two
people ever were high priests at the same time. Caiaphas (who
according to John 18^{13} was Annas' son-in-law) was high priest from
about 26 to 36. He was then deposed and one of Annas' sons,
Jonathan (who may be the *John* mentioned in this verse) was High
Priest for a year. Nothing is known of Alexander. The *high-priestly
family* could refer to the family of Annas, for no less than five of his
sons were high priests at one time or another, as he himself had been.
But it could mean, more generally, all who belonged to the small
group of families from whom the high priests were chosen.

This construction with relative clauses (*whom you crucified, whom
God raised from the dead*) is characteristic of Luke's style in the early
speeches in Acts ($2^{24, 32, 36}$, $3^{13, 15}$, 4^{27}, 5^{30}, $10^{38, 39}$, $13^{31, 37}$), when

from the dead, by him this man is standing before you well.

11 This is the stone which was rejected by you builders, but
12 which has become the head of the corner. And there is salvation in no one else, for there is no other name under heaven given among men by which we must be saved.'

13   Now when they saw the boldness of Peter and John, and perceived that they were uneducated, common men, they wondered; and they recognized that they had been with
14 Jesus. But seeing the man that had been healed standing
15 beside them, they had nothing to say in opposition. But when they had commanded them to go aside out of the council,
16 they conferred with one another, saying, 'What shall we do with these men? For that a notable sign has been performed through them is manifest to all the inhabitants of Jerusalem,

---

reference is made to the activity of God through Jesus. It is possible that Luke is in these expressions reproducing early doctrinal formulae. This 'relative-style' is not particularly characteristic of the Septuagint, whose style Luke sometimes consciously or unconsciously imitates.

11   This quotation of Ps. 118^{22} represents a very early proof-text found elsewhere in the N.T. (Mark 12^{10}; Luke 20^{17}; Matt. 21^{42}; 1 Pet. 2^{7}), and the idea of Christ as a stone of stumbling, the expression of which is associated with other citations from the O.T., is found in Rom. 9$^{32, 33}$; 1 Pet. 2$^{6, 8}$. But in this verse the translation appears to be taken direct from the Hebrew and not reproduced from the LXX. Further, the sentence is very clumsily formed, because '*this*' in v. 11 refers to Christ, though *this man* in v. 10 (exactly the same word, οὗτος, in the Greek, which does not express 'man') referred to the man who was healed. These features may well point to the existence of a source for Luke here.

12   A very Jewish way of expressing what is in fact an unlimited claim for the significance of Christ (cp. Isa. 45$^{21-22}$). There is some evidence that in early Jewish-Christian apocalyptic literature 'the Name' was used as a title for Christ.

13   *uneducated* (ἀγράμματοι) does not mean that they were illiterate, but that they had not received the formal education of an upper-class gentleman in the Graeco-Roman world; they were ignorant of philosophy and literature and rhetoric.

and we cannot deny it. But in order that it may spread no
further among the people, let us warn them to speak no more
to any one in this name.' So they called them and charged
them not to speak or teach at all in the name of Jesus. But
Peter and John answered them, 'Whether it is right in the
sight of God to listen to you rather than to God, you must
judge; for we cannot but speak of what we have seen and
heard.' And when they had further threatened them, they
let them go, finding no way to punish them, because of the
people; for all men praised God for what had happened. For
the man on whom this sign of healing was performed was
more than forty years old.

When they were released they went to their friends and
reported what the chief priests and the elders had said to
them. And when they heard it, they lifted their voices

---

in this name includes the meaning 'by this authority'.

4: 23–5: 16. *General description of Church life*

Until he comes to relate the appointment of the Seven and
of Stephen, Luke has only isolated, and rather vague, pieces
of information to retail. He skilfully weaves them together by
including such material as a prayer (4^{24-30}), some further
details of early Christian communism (4^{32-37}), and summaries
$(5^{12-16, 40-42})$.

chief priests does not imply that there was more than one high priest
in office at the time. The word is frequently used in the plural by
Josephus to indicate the group of people who had at one time been
high priests but who had been deposed by the Romans, as often
happened. They still retained considerable authority and respect.
One may compare the not inconsiderable group of ex-Premiers of
France before the Fifth Republic. The word 'chief priests' occurs in
the same sense elsewhere in the N.T.[1]

[1] Matt. 2^4, 16^{21}, 20^{18}, $21^{15, 23, 45}$, $26^{3, 14, 47}$, $27^{1, 3, 6, 12, 20, 41, 62}$, 28^{11};
Mark 8^{31}, 10^{33}, $11^{18, 27}$, $14^{1, 10, 43, 53, 55}$, $15^{1, 3, 10, 11, 31}$; Luke 9^{22}, $20^{1, 19}$,
$22^{2, 4, 66}$, $23^{4, 10, 13}$, 24^{20}; John $7^{32, 45}$, 11^{57}, 12^{10}, $18^{3, 35}$, $19^{6, 15, 21}$; and
elsewhere in Acts 5^{24}, $9^{14, 21}$, 22^{30}, 23^{14}, $25^{2, 15}$, $26^{10, 12}$.

together to God and said, 'Sovereign Lord, who didst make
the heaven and the earth and the sea and everything in
25 them, who by the mouth of our father David, thy servant,[a]
didst say by the Holy Spirit,

"Why did the Gentiles rage,
and the peoples imagine vain things?

26   The kings of the earth set themselves in array,
and the rulers were gathered together,
against the Lord and against his Anointed"—[b]

27 for truly in this city there were gathered together against thy
holy servant[a] Jesus, whom thou didst anoint, both Herod and
Pontius Pilate, with the Gentiles and the peoples of Israel,
28 to do whatever thy hand and thy plan had predestined to take
29 place. And now, Lord, look upon their threats, and grant to

> _a Or_ child   _b Or_ Christ

---

25   The verse as it stands is wholly ungrammatical, and must be either
corrupt or unfinished. The possibility of an Aramaic source has been
canvassed. C. F. D. Moule has suggested that here too we have an
example of several alternative clauses left undeleted by Luke and all
copied in by a later copyist. It may be that he is reproducing awk-
wardly part of an early fixed formula of prayer. _Sovereign Lord_ (literally
'Despot') Conzelmann describes as 'a Hellenistic form of address in
prayer', and Moule (_The Birth of the New Testament_, p. 21) calls the
whole passage 'undoubtedly liturgical', and sees it as falling into
a typically Jewish form of prayer.

25, 26   This text (Ps. 2[1ff.]) is found cited as a Messianic proof-text in _The
Psalms of Solomon_ (a Pharisaic work of 70–40 B.C.), is probably implied
in Mark 1[11], 9[7], and Matt. 3[17], and is referred to in Heb. 1[5].

27   Herod and Pilate are here associated with the Jews in the guilt of
putting Jesus to death. But Luke's usual tendency is to shift the guilt
from other authorities to the Jews. This increases the impression that
Luke is indebted to an earlier source in this passage. When the _Servant_
was _anointed_ (a reference to Isa. 61[1]) is not stated. Earlier Christologies,
which might have been present in Luke's source, may well have
placed the occasion at the baptism of Jesus (cp. Mark 1[11]) or the
Resurrection (cp. Rom. 1[4], which is thought by some to derive from
a period earlier than Paul). Luke himself, as his Birth Narrative shows,
regarded Jesus as Messiah from birth.

o thy servants[a] to speak thy word with all boldness, while thou
   stretchest out thy hand to heal, and signs and wonders are
1 performed through the name of thy holy servant[b] Jesus.' And
   when they had prayed, the place in which they were gathered
   together was shaken; and they were all filled with the Holy
   Spirit and spoke the word of God with boldness.

2   Now the company of those who believed were of one heart
   and soul, and no one said that any of the things which he
   possessed was his own, but they had everything in common.
3 And with great power the apostles gave their testimony to
   the resurrection of the Lord Jesus, and great grace was upon
4 them all. There was not a needy person among them, for as
   many as were possessors of lands or houses sold them, and
5 brought the proceeds of what was sold and laid it at the
   apostles' feet; and distribution was made to each as any had
6 need. Thus Joseph who was surnamed by the apostles
   Barnabas (which means, Son of encouragement), a Levite,
7 a native of Cyprus, sold a field which belonged to him, and
   brought the money and laid it at the apostles' feet.

      a Or slaves   *b Or* child

---

3   The *testimony to the resurrection of the Lord Jesus* did not so much lie
in their producing historical proofs of the event as in the impression
made by the apostles' behaviour and character (*power*), which convinced their hearers that their testimony to the Resurrection was
true. It is quite possible that the true reading here is: 'The apostles
of the Lord Jesus gave their testimony to the Resurrection.'

5   *Barnabas* does not mean *Son of encouragement*, but 'son of Nebo' or
'son of a prophet', and it is unlikely that anybody who knew Aramaic
could have made this mistake. But Menaen (Menahem) mentioned
in a list, which includes Barnabas, at Acts 13[1], could be interpreted
to mean 'son of encouragement'. It is quite likely that in the list of
names used by Luke at 13[1] 'son of encouragement' was written against
Menaen's name, and Luke mistook this as applying to Barnabas, and
reproduced it here. *A native of Cyprus* means that he was born there,
not that he was a Cypriot by race.

5 BUT a man named Ananias with his wife Sapphira sold
2 a piece of property, and with his wife's knowledge he kept
back some of the proceeds, and brought only a part and laid
3 it at the apostles' feet. But Peter said, 'Ananias, why has
Satan filled your heart to lie to the Holy Spirit and to keep
4 back part of the proceeds of the land? While it remained unsold, did it not remain your own? And after it was sold, was
it not at your disposal? How is it that you have contrived this
deed in your heart? You have not lied to men but to God.'
5 When Ananias heard these words, he fell down and died.
6 And great fear came upon all who heard of it. The young men
rose and wrapped him up and carried him out and buried him.
7   After an interval of about three hours his wife came in,
8 not knowing what had happened. And Peter said to her. 'Tell
me whether you sold the land for so much.' And she said,
9 'Yes, for so much.' But Peter said to her, 'How is it that you
have agreed together to tempt the Spirit of the Lord? Hark, the
feet of those that have buried your husband are at the

5:1-11   The point of the fate of Ananias and Sapphira was that they had
lied to God and not man, i.e, that publicly, in the presence of the
Christian Church, they had promised to give the whole of the proceeds
of the sale of their piece of land to the apostles, as trustees for the
Church, and that they had cheated in the transaction. Public profession in the Church was thought of as direct profession to God. The
people of the early Church lived a great deal of their lives communally.
They discussed each other's incomes and means of support publicly,
arranged that the needy and sick should be subsidized, and confessed
their sins to each other publicly. Peter does not punish Ananias and
Sapphira; he merely draws the moral and drives home the point. The
writer's intention clearly is to describe God as punishing.

4   The intention of this sentence is obscure. The meaning would be
more satisfactory if we could translate 'Was it not yours while it
remained unsold? And once it was sold, did it remain under your
control?' (expecting the answer, No). Though such a rendering is
a little strained, it is not impossible.

6   *wrapped him up* could be alternatively translated 'removed'.

10 door, and they will carry you out.' Immediately she fell
   down at his feet and died. When the young men came in they
   found her dead, and they carried her out and buried her
11 beside her husband. And great fear came upon the whole
   church, and upon all who heard of these things.

12   Now many signs and wonders were done among the
   people by the hands of the apostles. And they were all
13 together in Solomon's Portico. None of the rest dared join
14 them, but the people held them in high honor. And more

---

11   The first mention of the normal Greek word for *church*, ἐκκλησία.
From now on, Luke uses it frequently. It says something for his sense
of history that he has not used it hitherto, for it is clear that this was
not the earliest word used by the Christians to describe themselves
(see Introduction, pp. 46–47). It is unlikely that the two passages in the
Gospels which describe Jesus using the word (or an Aramaic equivalent) represent his *ipsissima verba* (Matt. 16[18] and 18[17]), as these are the
only places in the Gospels where the word is attributed to Jesus, and
Matthew's source at this point looks like a secondary one. The word
has two uses behind it. First, it is used in the LXX as one of the words
to describe the congregation of the people of Israel, especially in their
experiences in the wilderness under Moses (cp. Acts 7[38]). Secondly,
it was used quite often by Josephus to describe a kind of unofficial
mass meeting called by some authority to sound public opinion on
a certain point and to gain, if possible, a unanimous vote of approval.
Herod the Great, for instance, accused his sons at such a meeting
before putting them to death. Salome, his sister, called such a meeting
after Herod's death to ensure the succession of his son Archelaus.
Members of the high-priestly clique could summon such a meeting
in order to influence public opinion (Josephus, *Jewish War*, i. 550,
666; iv. 159). This use contributed quite as much to the Christian
use of the word *ecclesia* as the other.

14   There seems to be a complete contradiction between these two
verses. If *none of the rest* refers, as in its present context it must, to the
people, then it is impossible both that *none of the rest should dare to join
them* and also *multitudes both of men and women* should have joined the
Church. It is best to fall back on the theory of an unassimilated
source; perhaps vv. 12*b* to 14 are from a separate hand, and *the rest*
refers to some group already mentioned in this source. Or vv. 12*b* to
14 may be a very early interpolation. Certainly v. 15, *so that they even
carried out . . .* follows very easily upon v. 12*a*, which describes *signs and
wonders done by the apostles*.

than ever believers were added to the Lord, multitudes both
15 of men and women, so that they even carried out the sick
into the streets, and laid them on beds and pallets, that as
Peter came by at least his shadow might fall on some of
16 them. The people also gathered from the towns around
Jerusalem, bringing the sick and those afflicted with unclean
spirits, and they were all healed.

17 But the high priest rose up and all who were with him, that

---

15   Cp. 19[11, 12] and Mark 6[56].

5: 17–42. *The Apostles again arrested and again released*

This section repeats in a surprising way the pattern of
incidents which has already appeared in 4[1-31]—arrest, threat,
defence, release, rejoicing. Various theories have been produced to explain this recurrence. Harnack thought that the
two narratives went back to two different written sources,
coming from different places but in substance describing the
same events. But there is not enough evidence to support the
theory of a continuous written source behind these stories, or
indeed behind any part of the early chapters of Acts. More
recently Jeremias has put forward the theory that the two
arraignments of the apostles represent two different stages of
a judicial procedure which can be reconstructed from Rabbinic
literature; the first a process of warning or, as it were, putting
on probation, the second a trial after the warning had gone
unheeded or the probation had been broken, followed by the
execution of a sentence of flogging. But the whole narrative
is too vague to be fitted into as precise a form as this. It is
more likely that Luke learnt that rabbi Gamaliel had on one
occasion been known to defend the Christians to the Temple
authorities and that at some time or other the leaders of the
primitive Church had endured flogging from the Jews, a
punishment which Paul was later to experience (2 Cor. 11[24]).
He wove these isolated pieces of information with his usual
skill into a narrative.

17   There is some MS. support for the suggestion that originally this
verse began 'But Annas the high priest' instead of *But the high priest*

8 is, the party of the Sadducees, and filled with jealousy they
   arrested the apostles and put them in the common prison.
19 But at night an angel of the Lord opened the prison doors and
20 brought them out and said, 'Go and stand in the temple and
21 speak to the people all the words of this Life.' And when they
   heard this, they entered the temple at daybreak and taught.

   Now the high priest came and those who were with him
   and called together the council and all the senate of Israel,
22 and sent to the prison to have them brought. But when the
   officers came, they did not find them in the prison, and they
23 returned and reported, 'We found the prison securely locked
   and the sentries standing at the doors, but when we opened
24 it we found no one inside.' Now when the captain of the
   temple and the chief priests heard these words, they were
   much perplexed about them, wondering what this would
25 come to. And some one came and told them, 'The men whom
   you put in prison are standing in the temple and teaching the
26 people.' Then the captain with the officers went and brought
   them, but without violence, for they were afraid of being
   stoned by the people.

---

rose up (Gk. Ἄννας=Annas for ἀναστάς=*anastas* ('rising up')). But
it is easier to understand how Annas could have been substituted later
than to explain how an original reading of 'Annas' could have been
corrupted into the other expression.
19   An extremely vague and casual angelic deliverance, which we can
hardly take as serious history.
21   It looks at first sight as if Luke thought that there was some distinction between the *council* and the *senate* of Israel, whereas in fact
there was only one council or senate, viz., the Sanhedrin. But Conzelmann adduces passages in 1 and 2 Maccabees and in Josephus to
show that the word for *senate* (γερουσία) can mean the Sanhedrin, and
an inscription has been found containing the phrase 'to the most
reverend Sanhedrin of Senate' (συνεδρίῳ γερουσίας), so that if Luke
errs here he errs in good company. In fact when the apostles stand
before the Sanhedrin (v. 27) the senate has disappeared.

27 And when they had brought them, they set them before
28 the council. And the high priest questioned them, saying,
'We strictly charged you not to teach in this name, yet here
you have filled Jerusalem with your teaching and you intend
29 to bring this man's blood upon us.' But Peter and the apostles
30 answered, 'We must obey God rather than men. The God
of our fathers raised Jesus whom you killed by hanging him
31 on a tree. God exalted him at his right hand as Leader and
Savior, to give repentance to Israel and forgiveness of sins.
32 And we are witnesses to these things, and so is the Holy
Spirit whom God has given to those who obey him.'

33 When they heard this they were enraged and wanted to
34 kill them. But a Pharisee in the council named Gamaliel,

---

28   The phrase *We strictly charged you* suggests an official intimation by
a court, analogous to the serving of a summons.

29   According to Plato (*Apology*, 29 d), Socrates at his trial said 'I will
obey the god rather than you.'

29–32   Peter's little speech here, though clearly a composition by Luke, is
not devoid of primitive features. *Hanging him on a tree*, with its reference
to the significance of this condition for observers of the Law (Deut.
21[23]), recalls Gal. 3[13] and could be designed only for a Jewish audience.
Leader and Saviour are not early Christological titles, but the phrase
repentance to Israel and forgiveness of sins is one wholly within the world
of Jewish thought. One gains the impression that Luke is not here
using a source, but that he knows the vocabulary and to some extent
the thought of an earlier period than his and is at times deliberately
reproducing it.

34–39   Gamaliel's speech must certainly be wholly a composition by Luke.
In the first place, Gamaliel could not have referred to the rebellion
of Theudas, which took place in the procuratorship of Cuspius Fadus,
i.e., not earlier than 44, whereas this speech could not have been
delivered after 35 at the latest, and was probably earlier. In the
second place, it is hard to imagine how Luke could have secured an
accurate record of a speech by a rabbi at a private session of the
Sanhedrin. The theory was advanced that Luke's mistake arose from
a misreading by him of a passage in Josephus' *Antiquities*, xx. 97, in
which the historian first describes the rebellion of Theudas and a little
later on mentions Judas, who started the rebellion at the census,

A praying figure from the wall of Lullingstone Roman villa.

a teacher of the law, held in honor by all the people, stood up
35 and ordered the men to be put outside for a while. And he
said to them, 'Men of Israel, take care what you do with
36 these men. For before these days Theudas arose, giving himself out to be somebody, and a number of men, about four
hundred, joined him; but he was slain and all who followed
37 him were dispersed and came to nothing. After him Judas
the Galilean arose in the days of the census and drew away
some of the people after him; he also perished, and all who
38 followed him were scattered. So in the present case I tell
you, keep away from these men and let them alone; for if
39 this plan or this undertaking is of men, it will fail; but if it is
of God, you will not be able to overthrow them. You might
even be found opposing God!'
40   So they took his advice, and when they had called in the
apostles, they beat them and charged them not to speak in
41 the name of Jesus, and let them go. Then they left the
presence of the council, rejoicing that they were counted
42 worthy to suffer dishonor for the name. And every day in the

---

because Judas' sons were involved in a similar rebellion later. But
this theory is now widely discredited. At the same time, it is unnecessary to go so far as to dismiss as altogether fictitious the statement that Gamaliel on one occasion defended the Christians, or at
least urged caution in dealing with them, on the ground that Paul's
writings and Paul's behaviour before his conversion reveal that there
always had been irreconcilable enmity between Christians and
Pharisees. This Gamaliel must be the rabbi known as Gamaliel I to
students of Rabbinic literature. Very little is known about him,
beyond the fact that he was a teacher of St. Paul (Acts 22³), whereas
his grandson Gamaliel II left quite a mark on Rabbinic traditions.

37   Luke mentions the *census* in his Gospel also (Luke 2²). It took place
in A.D. 6 and sparked off a nationalist uprising under Judas in protest
against this first step towards the imposition of direct Roman rule
(including Roman taxation) over Judaea.

42   Here ends Luke's account of the Church in its earliest, wholly

temple and at home they did not cease teaching and preaching
Jesus as the Christ.

Now in these days when the disciples were increasing in
number, the Hellenists murmured against the Hebrews
because their widows were neglected in the daily distribution.
And the twelve summoned the body of the disciples and said,

Jewish, phase. It is significant that it ends with the apostles still
teaching in the Temple.

II. FIRST ENCOUNTERS BETWEEN THE CHURCH AND THE GENTILES (CHAPTERS 6: 1–14: 28)

6: 1–14. *Stephen appears upon the scene*

The introductory formula tells us that Luke does not know the
exact date of the next events to be recorded, or their exact relationship to what has gone before. He has to link his unconnected information with his narrative. The contrast between *Hellenists* and *Hebrews*
suddenly appears without further explanation. These *Hellenists* must
be Jews whose native language was Greek, in contrast to the *Hebrews*,
whose native language was Aramaic. The word *Hellenists* does not
denote the race of those to whom it applies, nor their theological or
political views. They were not necessarily Hellenizers, though as
Greek-speakers they would be more likely to be conversant with the
non-Jewish world and readier to view it as a possible field for the
Church's mission. It is no coincidence that the non-Christian Jews
show more violent opposition to the *Hellenists* than to the Palestinian
Christians, nor that it was Christian Jews from Cyprus and Cyrene
(who would certainly be Greek-speaking) who first began deliberately to evangelize Gentiles (11[20]). In 9[29] *Hellenists* is used to refer
to Greek-speaking non-Christian Jews. *The disciples* here first appears
as a title for the Christians. Conzelmann thinks that this indicates
a source which gave the Palestinian Christians' name for themselves.
The reader must assume that a considerable time has elapsed,
because not only has the gospel, preached first by Aramaic-speakers
to Aramaic-speakers, now spread to Greek-speaking communities,
but a recognizable class or group of *widows* has appeared. In a later
period these *widows* formed a special order or group within the
Church, with their own discipline and customs (1 Tim. 5[3–11], [16]).
This is the only place in the whole of Acts where the apostles are

'It is not right that we should give up preaching the word of
3 God to serve tables. Therefore, brethren, pick out from
among you seven men of good repute, full of the Spirit and
4 of wisdom, whom we may appoint to this duty. But we will
devote ourselves to prayer and to the ministry of the word.'

---

called *the Twelve* (though of course the expression occurs in Luke's
Gospel); it is a name which Paul uses for them once (1 Cor. 15⁵).

2–5   There are plenty of parallels in Rabbinic literature for the appointment of a board of seven men as delegates or representatives of others.
And there is no reason whatever to disbelieve Luke's statement that
seven men were at an early stage in the history of the Church
appointed in order to relieve the apostles of some of the burden of
administering the funds and resources of the Church. It was universally assumed in the Church of the third and later centuries that
we have here a description of the origin of the office or order of deacon.
Certainly deacons from the third century onwards, and probably
earlier, were regarded as people specially charged with the administration of the funds and the other property of the Church.
Further, the verb connected with the word *deacon*, 'to deacon'
(διακονεῖν), meaning 'to serve', occurs in v. 2, with 'tables'; to
'deacon tables' is a typically concrete Jewish way of saying to superin-
tend the administration of relief. On the other hand, the apostles
declare (v. 4) that they are going to 'deacon the word', so that διακονεῖν can hardly be a technical term to indicate deacons in this context, and Luke never calls them deacons; in fact 'deacon' as a noun
is a word Luke never uses. Paul once mentions deacons (Phil. 1¹),
and applies the term once (though hardly in a technical sense, Rom.
16¹) to Phoebe, a woman. Otherwise his quite frequent use of the
word simply means 'minister' in the widest possible sense. It is only
in 1 Tim. (3⁸, ¹², 4⁶) that the word again appears to suggest an office
rather than a function. But a much stronger argument against seeing
here the origin of the order of deacons is the fact that the only two of
the 'Seven' about whose later career we know anything do not behave
at all according to the pattern laid down for them in vv. 2 and 3.
Stephen preaches polemically and Philip evangelizes (8⁵⁻⁴⁰, 21⁸).
Some scholars have been anxious to see in this passage the origin of
presbyters. But, quite apart from the fact that presbyters were a well-
known Jewish institution already, Luke knows of the office of presbyter and mentions it frequently, and would surely indicate if he
meant us to understand that it originated in the appointment of the
Seven.

And what they said pleased the whole multitude, and they chose Stephen, a man full of faith and of the Holy Spirit, and Philip, and Prochorus, and Nicanor, and Timon, and Parmenas, and Nicolaus, a proselyte of Antioch. These they set before the apostles, and they prayed and laid their hands upon them.

It is worth noting that the names of all the Seven are Greek names, though this does not, of course, preclude their having had Jewish names as well. The fact that one of them, Nicolaus, is described as a proselyte makes it certain that the others were Jews.

Who *laid their hands upon* the Seven? The apostles? or the people? In favour of the latter is that at this point Codex Bezae (no doubt here representing the 'Western' text), alters the wording from 'these they set before the apostles, and they prayed' to 'these were set before the apostles, who prayed', thereby explicitly assigning the laying-on of hands to the apostles. This suggests that originally the apostles initiated the decision to choose the Seven, the people chose them, and then the people laid their hands on them. This view is upheld by Daube (*The New Testament and Rabbinic Judaism*, pp. 237 ff.), who believes that by this act the people made the Seven their representatives, just as the children of Israel in the wilderness of old had made the Levites their representatives by laying hands on them (Num. 27[18] and Deut. 34[9]). If this view is the true one, then the suggestion that Luke is here reading into an earlier situation the ritual practice of his own day must be disallowed, for ordination by the people is likely to be an earlier practice than ordination by official ministers. But it is on the whole more likely that Luke here means us to understand that the apostles laid their hands on the Seven. *Whom we may appoint* of v. 3 suggests that the actual making of them into ministers is to be done by the apostles, and if they do not appoint the Seven by laying on hands, how are we to suppose that they appoint them? Again, if we allow that the apostles ordain here, we can see that the whole process of instituting the Seven follows the same process as the appointing of Matthias (1[15–26]). The apostles initiate the process; the people choose the men; the apostles then enrol or ordain. But it is not necessary to assume that because Luke thinks that the apostles laid hands on the Seven we must therefore regard this as nothing but an anachronism on Luke's part. Daube insists (op. cit., pp. 229–33) that the rabbis used laying-on of hands for two purposes, and two only: in the Temple ritual of sacrifice, and in ordaining a rabbi (whom he equates with an elder); and Daube has therefore to

7   And the word of God increased; and the number of the
disciples multiplied greatly in Jerusalem, and a great many
of the priests were obedient to the faith.

8   And Stephen, full of grace and power, did great wonders
9 and signs among the people. Then some of those who belonged to the synagogue of the Freedmen (as it was called),
and of the Cyrenians, and of the Alexandrians, and of those
10 from Cilicia and Asia, arose and disputed with Stephen. But
they could not withstand the wisdom and the Spirit with
11 which he spoke. Then they secretly instigated men, who said,

---

assume that the men of the early Church adapted this ordination
to the Rabbinate to a number of quite different purposes. It is simpler
to assume that the ceremony of laying-on of hands was in much wider
use in the first century than existing Rabbinic literature (which is
not an exhaustive source) would lead us to think. It was a widely used
ceremony entirely outside Jewish circles too. The examples of it in
the N.T. cannot all be fitted into the relatively narrow category of
ordination to the Rabbinate. The example in Acts 8[17] is not easy to
explain on these grounds. 1 Tim. 5[22], for instance, suggests that the
gesture implied forgiveness of sins; and the occurrence in Heb. 6[2]
can be fitted readily into no known use of the ceremony. We know too
little about the subject to refuse veracity to Luke's account here.

9   *the synagogue of the Freedmen* includes the synagogue of the Cyrenians
and Alexandrians, and the men of Cilicia and Asia (i.e. the com-
paratively small Roman province of Asia), a synagogue of wor-
shippers of mixed origin. It is Jews of similar origin who are the most
violent opponents of Paul in 9[29]. The *Freedmen* probably means the
freedmen descendants of those Jews who were brought by Pompey to
Rome in 63 B.C. (Philo, *Leg. Gai* 155).

11   It is impossible to decide whether Stephen's trial was an official
one according to due legal form or a lynching. It is on the whole
unlikely that the Sanhedrin should have been given formal power to
put people to death for serious offences against the Law, though it is
certain that the Romans permitted the Temple authorities to kill
non-Jews who ventured beyond the Court of the Gentiles. But an
execution might be carried out in the absence from Jerusalem of the
procurator, or if there was an interregnum between the departure of
one and the arrival of his successor. Conzelmann notes that the
Jewish people of Jerusalem generally are here represented as hostile

'We have heard him speak blasphemous words against Moses and God.' And they stirred up the people and the elders and the scribes, and they came upon him and seized him and brought him before the council, and set up false witnesses who said, 'This man never ceases to speak words against this holy place and the law; for we have heard him say that this Jesus of Nazareth will destroy this place, and will change the customs which Moses delivered to us.' And gazing at him, all who sat in the council saw that his face was like the face of an angel.

---

to Stephen, and takes this as a sign that Luke is using a source, for in his generalizing summaries he represents the people as favouring the Christians (2^{47}, $5^{13, 26}$).

the *holy place* is a Rabbinic expression for the Temple; cp. 21^{28}.

The claim that Jesus would destroy the Temple is found in Matt. 26^{61}, 27^{40}; Mark 14^{58}, 15^{29}; and John 2^{19}, but, surprisingly, Luke does not include this saying in his Gospel. *The customs* probably refers to the *Halakah* or elaborate interpretation of the Law which the Pharisees had devised in order to make the legislation of the Pentateuch applicable to communities of Jews living under the very different conditions of society in Palestine in Hellenistic times. This was to become a burning issue later. Whether the accusation was true that Stephen attacked the *Halakah* Luke does not provide us with enough evidence to determine. It is not impossible.

6:15–8:3. *Stephen's speech and his martyrdom*

Almost all scholars agree that in Stephen's speech we can trace a separate source used by Luke. Though from the point of view of style it does not differ markedly from the rest of the book and we must recognize that Luke has worked over his source, there are too many novel features about it, unparalleled in Acts, to allow it to be regarded as one of Luke's free compositions—its subject, its length, its method of expounding the O.T. The question of what exactly is its subject has puzzled many scholars. As a speech for the defence against specific charges it appears at first sight to be gravely defective, if not totally irrelevant. The long historical introduction (7^{1-34}) and the sudden ending, apparently breaking off in mid argument, give an impression of incoherence and obscurity. Scholars have been greatly divided as to whether Stephen is in favour of the Jewish Law or whether he is attacking it. Is he reproaching the Jews because they did not keep the Law or because they did keep it? Certainly he appears to be attacking rather than defending. But what is he attacking?

In fact, the whole speech will always seem out of proportion and ill suited to its context until its central theme is understood; but when this is grasped, then the speech can be seen not only as a coherent whole but as a direct and specific answer to the charge against Stephen that he taught that *Jesus of Nazareth will destroy this place, and will change the customs which Moses delivered to us* (6¹⁴). This theme is that God from the beginning of his dealings with his people intended that they should recognize his Christ, look forward to his Advent, acknowledge his representatives, and accept no place of worship as permanent before the coming of him who was to be the true Temple, the true place where God should be worshipped. It is at once an answer to the accusation against him and a counter-charge against his accusers, who are to Stephen the contemporary representatives of those Jews who had failed to see God's intention through the ages. This theme, which must necessarily be occupied largely with biblical exposition, is carried out mainly by means of a typological interpretation of the text of the O.T. This type of exegesis is paralleled generally throughout the N.T., but specifically in two works, the Epistle to the Hebrews, and in a product of the subapostolic period, *The Epistle of Barnabas*. (For details see the Commentary below. See also R. P. C. Hanson, *Allegory and Event*, pp. 91, 94–98.) We are justified in concluding from these facts that Stephen's speech comes from a source, worked over by Luke, bearing strong affinities to the Epistle to the Hebrews and *The Epistle of Barnabas*, both of which are usually associated with Alexandrian, or Hellenistic-Jewish thought. This does not necessarily mean that we must attribute the speech to an Alexandrian provenance, but it does assign it to an Hellenistic origin, to a type of thought which cannot be regarded as coming from the most primitive period of the Church. There is a certain appropriateness in Luke's assigning it to Stephen, the *Hellenist*, the man who may at the earliest period have

AND the high priest said, 'Is this so?' And Stephen said:
'Brethren and fathers, hear me. The God of glory appeared

---

been most forward in demanding that Christianity should look
to wider horizons than Palestinian Judaism; but it is most
improbable that the speech really derives from Stephen. Yet
properly understood, it is not open to the charge of irrelevance
and incoherence, and in fact it fits remarkably well into its
context and into Luke's general plan of preparing for the
extension of the gospel to the Gentiles. His usual skill did not
desert him when he inserted the speech at this point.

Several little discrepancies between the statements of both Hebrew
and Greek texts of the O.T. and Stephen's account here can be
observed. (a) The traditional text locates the place where *the God of
glory appeared to our father Abraham* in Palestine, not Haran (Gen. 12⁷).
(b) The command *Depart from your land* is recorded as reaching Abraham when he was in Haran (Gen. 12¹) and not (as Stephen says) in
Ur. (c) If the traditional text is followed it must be concluded that
Abraham's father Terah was alive when Abraham left Haran, for
Gen. 11²⁶ says that Terah was 70 years old when Abraham was born,
Gen. 11³² says that Terah lived to be 205 years old, and Gen. 12⁴ says
that Abraham was 75 years old when he left Haran. Therefore at that
point Terah must have been 145 years old and have had 60 years of
life still before him. But (a) *The Genesis Apocryphon* (among the literature of the Dead Sea Sect) also assumes that God 'appeared' to
Abraham in Ur; this idea may derive from a contemporary Tar-
gum, i.e., translation of the sacred text from Hebrew to Aramaic,
with interpretation and comment, designed for synagogue reading.
(b) Gen. 15⁷ itself, Neh. 9⁷, and Philo (*De Abraham* 62 ff.) all assume
that the command *Depart from your land* came to Abraham when he
was in Ur, not in Haran. (c) In view of Gen. 11³² anyone could be
pardoned for making the mistake about the death of Terah made in
this speech; both the Samaritan Pentateuch and Philo (*De Mig.
Abraham*, 177) give the figure 145 as Terah's age at Gen. 11³². The
emphasis upon the fact that God promised Abraham a *land* but did
not give it to him as a possession, so that he and his family lived as
temporary squatters, in tents (7¹⁻⁶), is probably intended to suggest
that God was indicating to Abraham that the true land (or as
Hebrews puts it 'the homeland . . . the better country, the heavenly
one', Heb. 11¹³⁻¹⁶) was yet to come, that is, the final home and
destination and inheritance given to God's chosen people in Christ.
Heb. 11¹³ quotes Gen. 15¹³ as Stephen does (Acts 7⁶). Similarly *The

to our father Abraham, when he was in Mesopotamia, before
3 he lived in Haran, and said to him, "Depart from your land
and from your kindred and go into the land which I will show
4 you." Then he departed from the land of the Chaldeans, and
lived in Haran. And after his father died, God removed him
5 from there into this land in which you are now living; yet
he gave him no inheritance in it, not even a foot's length, but
promised to give it to him in possession and to his posterity
6 after him, though he had no child. And God spoke to this
effect, that his posterity would be aliens in a land belonging
to others, who would enslave them and ill-treat them four
7 hundred years. "But I will judge the nation which they serve,"
said God, "and after that they shall come out and worship
8 me in this place." And he gave him the covenant of circumcision. And so Abraham became the father of Isaac, and
circumcised him on the eighth day; and Isaac became the
father of Jacob, and Jacob of the twelve patriarchs.

9   'And the patriarchs, jealous of Joseph, sold him into
10 Egypt; but God was with him, and rescued him out of all
his afflictions, and gave him favor and wisdom before
Pharaoh, king of Egypt, who made him governor over Egypt

Epistle of Barnabas interprets the 'good land' of Exod. 33[1, 3] as meaning the incarnate Christ (*Ep. Barn.* vi. 8 f.; cp. xi. 9). It is quite
possible too that the reference in Stephen's speech to *inheritance,
posterity*, and to God's promising (7[5, 6]), refers covertly to the coming
Christ; cp. Gal. 3[16, 18], 4[28]; Rom. 4[13], 8[17], where the same themes
are used to describe fulfilment in Christ.

9–16   It is likely that the author of the original speech intends us to see
a parallel between the fate of Joseph and the fate of Jesus Christ. It
is even possible that Jacob's going down to Egypt and being put
in a tomb which was bought by somebody else may be likened to
Christ's going to Jerusalem, 'that great city, which is allegorically
called Sodom and Egypt, where their Lord was crucified' (Rev. 11[8]),
and there dying and being put into a tomb bought by somebody else.

and over all his household. Now there came a famine throughout all Egypt and Canaan, and great affliction, and our fathers could find no food. But when Jacob heard that there was grain in Egypt, he sent forth our fathers the first time. And at the second visit Joseph made himself known to his brothers, and Joseph's family became known to Pharaoh. And Joseph sent and called to him Jacob his father and all his kindred, seventy-five souls; and Jacob went down into Egypt. And he died, himself and our fathers, and they were carried back to Shechem and laid in the tomb that Abraham had bought for a sum of silver from the sons of Hamor in Shechem.

'But as the time of the promise drew near, which God had granted to Abraham, the people grew and multiplied in Egypt till there arose over Egypt another king who had not known Joseph. He dealt craftily with our race and forced our fathers to expose their infants, that they might not be kept alive. At this time Moses was born, and was beautiful before

---

These verses develop the parallel between Moses and Christ. He was sent as a *ruler and deliverer* (vv. 25, 35) by God to his people, to perform wonders and signs (v. 36), to lead the people out of Egypt into the Promised Land. But he was *thrust aside* (vv. 27, 39) and *our fathers refused to obey him* (v. 39). But Moses at the same time is presented not only as a type of Christ, but as one who was in direct contact with Christ. He sees God's *angel* (v. 30), who is immediately referred to as *the Lord* (vv. 31–33). It is likely that Stephen thought of this figure as Christ himself, who appeared in a pre-incarnate state to some chosen individuals under the old dispensation (the *angel* appears again in vv. 35 and 38): cp. 1 Cor. 10[1-4]; 2 Cor. 3[15-18]; John 12[41]. Moses knows that the great prophet, the Christ, will appear later (v. 37, referring to Deut. 18[15, 18]). It is probable that *the angel who spoke to him at Mount Sinai* (v. 38) is also identified with Christ. Paul (Gal. 3[19f.]) interprets the angels who gave the Law (a later, Rabbinic conception) as a sign of its inferiority to Christ, but this speech comes from a different tradition of exegesis (cp. 7[53]).

God. And he was brought up for three months in his father's
21 house; and when he was exposed, Pharaoh's daughter
22 adopted him and brought him up as her own son. And Moses
was instructed in all the wisdom of the Egyptians, and he
was mighty in his words and deeds.

23 'When he was forty years old, it came into his heart to
24 visit his brethren, the sons of Israel. And seeing one of them
being wronged, he defended the oppressed man and avenged
25 him by striking the Egyptian. He supposed that his brethren
understood that God was giving them deliverance by his
26 hand, but they did not understand. And on the following day
he appeared to them as they were quarreling and would have
reconciled them, saying, "Men, you are brethren, why do you
27 wrong each other?" But the man who was wronging his
neighbor thrust him aside, saying, "Who made you a ruler
28 and a judge over us? Do you want to kill me as you killed the
29 Egyptian yesterday?" At this retort Moses fled, and became
an exile in the land of Midian, where he became the father of
two sons.

30 'Now when forty years had passed, an angel appeared to
him in the wilderness of Mount Sinai, in a flame of fire in
31 a bush. When Moses saw it he wondered at the sight; and
32 as he drew near to look, the voice of the Lord came, "I am
the God of your fathers, the God of Abraham and of Isaac
and of Jacob." And Moses trembled and did not dare to
33 look. And the Lord said to him, "Take off the shoes from
your feet, for the place where you are standing is holy
34 ground. I have surely seen the ill-treatment of my people
that are in Egypt and heard their groaning, and I have come

---

32   The quotation of Exod. 3⁶ here is not an accurate reproduction of
the LXX, but has affinities with the Samaritan Pentateuch.

down to deliver them. And now come, I will send you to Egypt."

5 'This Moses whom they refused, saying, "Who made you a ruler and a judge?" God sent as both ruler and deliverer by the hand of the angel that appeared to him in the bush.
6 He led them out, having performed wonders and signs in Egypt and at the Red Sea, and in the wilderness for forty
7 years. This is the Moses who said to the Israelites, "God will raise up for you a prophet from your brethren as he raised
8 me up." This is he who was in the congregation in the wilderness with the angel who spoke to him at Mount Sinai, and with our fathers; and he received living oracles to give
9 to us. Our fathers refused to obey him, but thrust him aside,
10 and in their hearts they turned to Egypt, saying to Aaron, "Make for us gods to go before us; as for this Moses who led us out from the land of Egypt, we do not know what has
11 become of him." And they made a calf in those days, and

---

8   *living oracles* certainly does not suggest that Stephen is depreciating the Law; cp. 7⁵³. But it is likely that the original author of this speech regarded the Law as primarily valuable in its function of predicting Christ (a function which almost all writers in the N.T. recognize, not least Paul), and not in its function as providing regulations for the conduct of daily life and worship. If behind this speech was an intention of disparaging the ceremonial part of the Pentateuch, not only would it make relevant one of the charges against Stephen (6¹⁴) but it would be consistent with much later Christian thought.[1]

10   The subject changes to the Jews' methods of worship. Implied in this rather obscure passage is the argument that the Jews should have recognized that all forms and places of worship were temporary and provisional until the arrival of the Messiah, who would in his person fulfil the office of providing a satisfactory place for worshipping and a method of worshipping the true God. The tent (v. 44) emphasized the provisional nature of the Jews' worship. David, who pleased God, did not provide a permanent place of worship; Solomon, who did not please God, wrongly attempted to provide a permanent Temple (vv. 46, 47). But God never wanted anything of the sort (vv. 49, 50).

[1] See Marcel Simon, *Verus Israel* and *St. Stephen and the Hellenists*.

offered a sacrifice to the idol and rejoiced in the works of
42 their hands. But God turned and gave them over to worship
the host of heaven, as it is written in the book of the prophets:

"Did you offer to me slain beasts and sacrifices,
forty years in the wilderness, O house of Israel?
43 And you took up the tent of Moloch,
and the star of the god Rephan,
the figures which you made to worship;
and I will remove you beyond Babylon."

44 'Our fathers had the tent of witness in the wilderness, even

---

42   *God turned* could mean, transitively, not reflexively, that God
turned the people back.

42, 43   The exact reference of the quotation from Amos 5^{25-27} is uncertain.
It could mean (*a*) 'Did you sacrifice to me in the desert (as you
should have)? No, you sacrificed to pagan gods.' Or (*b*) 'Did you
offer sacrifice in the desert, I would like to know ($\mu o\iota$ as an ethic
dative)? No, and you were quite right; your sacrificial cult now is
nothing but a sacrifice to pagan gods.' We must ask, which interpretation did Amos mean us to take, and which did Stephen follow? It is
likely that Amos intended meaning (*b*): The Golden Age in the
wilderness was one when all this sacrificial cult was unnecessary;
your present excessive indulgence in sacrifice in order to salve your
bad consciences is equivalent to sacrificing to the gods of the surrounding nations and gains you no favour with God. Stephen probably took the meaning (*a*): Instead of worshipping God, who had
through Christ or Christ-like figures provided living oracles for the
people to live by, they rejected God's representative and worshipped
pagan idols, an action characteristic of their moral blindness. Stephen
(or some earlier hand) has substituted *Babylon* for 'Damascus' in the
original quotation (exercising hindsight); otherwise the quotation
keeps to the LXX. But the LXX itself is a rather muddled translation. It has taken the name of the god Siccuth as equivalent to
succoth, meaning 'booths', and the name of the other god, Raiphan or
Rompha, has become badly corrupted in the textual tradition.

44   The idea that the historical, empirical tent or Temple corresponded
as a provisional copy to the real tent or Temple, or place where God
dwells, is found also in Heb. 8^5, 9^{24} and *The Epistle of Barnabas*, xvi. 1;
cp. Wisd. 9^8.

as he who spoke to Moses directed him to make it, according
to the pattern that he had seen. Our fathers in turn brought
it in with Joshua when they dispossessed the nations which
God thrust out before our fathers. So it was until the days of
David, who found favor in the sight of God and asked
leave to find a habitation for the God of Jacob. But it was
Solomon who built a house for him. Yet the Most High does
not dwell in houses made with hands; as the prophet says,

> "Heaven is my throne,
> and earth my footstool.
> What house will you build for me, says the Lord,
> or what is the place of my rest?
> Did not my hand make all these things?"

Joshua and Jesus as written in Greek are precisely identical names.
From *The Epistle of Barnabas* (xii. 8); cp. Heb. 4⁸) onwards many early
Christian writers regard Joshua as a prefiguration of Jesus. *When they
dispossessed the nations* could be translated 'when he gained possession
of the Gentiles'. It may be that the original author of the speech
intended us to draw this double meaning here.

a habitation for the God of Jacob: the reading 'house of Jacob' has
better MSS. support. But the reading in the text makes better sense
in view of v. 47.

Stephen has chosen one of the few texts in the O.T. which denounce
the Temple cult root-and-branch (Isa. 66¹⁻²). Philo and some of his
predecessors in the tradition of Hellenistic Judaism (e.g. the author of
The Epistle of Aristeas) had regarded the cult as something to be carried
out literally, but only for the sake of its allegorical (i.e., philosophical
or psychological) meaning. The followers of the Dead Sea Sect had
criticized the cult as carried on in the Temple of their day without
intending to deprecate animal and other sacrifices in principle. There
were some pagan circles where the offering of animal sacrifices was
denounced (notably in neo-Pythagoreanism). Apollonius of Tyana
in the first century was an exponent of this doctrine. Several of the
Apologists of the early Church exploited this body of opinion by
presenting Christianity as a religion without material sacrifices,
without images and without Temple. This speech seems to be an
early example of this line of thought, springing particularly from the
conviction (found elsewhere in the N.T., e.g. John 2¹⁹, ²¹; 2 Cor.

51   'You stiff-necked people, uncircumcised in heart and ears,
        you always resist the Holy Spirit. As your fathers did, so do
52 you. Which of the prophets did not your fathers persecute?
        And they killed those who announced beforehand the coming
        of the Righteous One, whom you have now betrayed and
53 murdered, you who received the law as delivered by angels
        and did not keep it.'

54   Now when they heard these things they were enraged, and
55 they ground their teeth against him. But he, full of the Holy
        Spirit, gazed into heaven and saw the glory of God, and Jesus
56 standing at the right hand of God; and he said, 'Behold,
        I see the heavens opened, and the Son of man standing at

---

6$^{15, 16}$; Eph. 2$^{19-22}$; 1 Pet. 2^5) that Christ is the New Temple where
alone men can offer pure worship, or that Christians are the true
Temple where God dwells, because they are in Christ. We are not
justified in concluding that this polemic against the Temple shows
that this speech was written after the Fall of Jerusalem and Destruction of the Temple in A.D. 70. On the contrary, the very ferocity of
the onslaught suggests that the writer is attacking an existing abuse,
and not denouncing a system of worship which is known to everybody
no longer to exist.

50–52   Though these verses employ the rhetorical device of breaking off
short, in fact they make a most effective ending for the speech. God
has continually supplied the Jews with signs and oracles and intima-
tions that the Christ was to come, but they have regularly disregarded
his messages and ill-treated his messengers. The culmination of this
was their rejection and killing of the Christ himself when he came.
The speech does not so much prepare us for the movement of the
Church's mission towards the Gentiles as for its movement away from
the Jews.

51   *uncircumcised in heart and ears*, a conflation of biblical texts, Lev. 26^{41};
Deut. 10^{16}; Jer. 6^{10}; and Ezek. 44^7.

52   The idea that all the prophets had been martyred grew up in late
Judaism and is reflected elsewhere in the N.T. (cp. Matt. 23$^{29-37}$;
Luke 13^{34}; 1 Thess. 2^{15}; Heb. 11^{36}).

56   This is the only occurrence in the whole of Acts of the title *Son* of
man. Whether Jesus actually applied it to himself or not, there is no
doubt that it was a very primitive Christological title indeed. It may

the right hand of God.' But they cried out with a loud voice and stopped their ears and rushed together upon him. Then they cast him out of the city and stoned him; and the witnesses laid down their garments at the feet of a young man named Saul. And as they were stoning Stephen, he prayed, 'Lord Jesus, receive my spirit.' And he knelt down and cried with a loud voice, 'Lord, do not hold this sin against them.' And when he had said this, he fell asleep.

AND Saul was consenting to his death.

And on that day a great persecution arose against the

---

well here represent a reminiscence of the actual dying words of Stephen himself. The exact significance of *standing* is uncertain. It may indicate that Christ is rising to receive the martyr, achieving the final stage of his heavenly work, preparing to come again, or acting as a witness in judgement.

Stoning was indeed the punishment for blasphemy under the Law (Lev. 24[10 ff.]), and also the way in which some of the prophets had been killed (2 Chron. 24[21]). But this verse illustrates the uncertainty about whether Stephen was unofficially lynched or officially executed. Official stoning as described in Rabbinical literature consists in the victim's being thrown over a precipice and having stones rolled on top of him from above; and though no mention is made of the perpetrators' removing their own clothes it is laid down that the victim's clothes are to be taken off. If, however, this was a lynching, presumably it would be an affair of the lynchers' taking off their outer garments to make stone-throwing easier. This is presumably the sort of action the fourth evangelist envisaged when he represented the Jews as threatening Jesus with stoning (John 10[31ff.], 11[8]), and this is what Paul had to endure more than once (Acts 14[19]; 2 Cor. 11[25]). It is much more likely that Stephen was lynched by stoning after denunciation by the Temple authorities than that the Sanhedrin thought itself strong enough to carry out the cumbrous process of an official stoning or precipitation. It may be that Luke wanted to represent an unofficial lynching as an official trial.

It is likely that the Passion of Stephen has been assimilated to the Passion of Jesus; cp. Luke 23[34, 46].

This *persecution* cannot, of course, have been an official one conducted by the Roman government, but must have been violent pressure brought on Christians in Jerusalem on the initiative of the

church in Jerusalem; and they were all scattered throughout
2 the region of Judea and Samaria, except the apostles. Devout
men buried Stephen, and made great lamentation over him.
3 But Saul laid waste the church, and entering house after
house, he dragged off men and women and committed them
to prison.

4   Now those who were scattered went about preaching the
5 word. Philip went down to a city of Samaria, and proclaimed
6 to them the Christ. And the multitudes with one accord gave
heed to what was said by Philip, when they heard him and
7 saw the signs which he did. For unclean spirits came out of
many who were possessed, crying with a loud voice; and
8 many who were paralyzed or lame were healed. So there was
much joy in that city.

---

authorities of the Temple. The government of the Roman Empire
was the most efficient that the world had up to then seen, and
immensely impressed many even of those who benefited little from
it, such as Josephus. But its police forces, in as far as it had any, were
very inadequate, extremely inefficient by modern standards, and
much more likely to punish a few individuals in a haphazard way
after violence had been done than to take measures beforehand to
prevent the violence. It is therefore quite easy to imagine an able
man like Paul, armed with the fury of religious bigotry, conducting
a minor and covert campaign of terrorism without attracting the
serious attention of the authorities, especially if the Sanhedrin could
represent him as simply enforcing local law upon local inhabitants
who were not Roman citizens.

   except the apostles is very difficult to explain, except as an editorial
addition by Luke, who for the sake of his narrative wishes to retain
them in Jerusalem. The 'Western' text labours to make even clearer
the point that they did not leave the city.

8: 4–25. *The incident of Simon Magus and Philip's evangelizing in
Samaria*

7   Several commentators have noted Luke's special interest in healings
of the paralysed and the lame.

But there was a man named Simon who had previously practiced magic in the city and amazed the nation of Samaria, saying that he himself was somebody great. They all gave heed to him, from the least to the greatest, saying, 'This man is that power of God which is called Great.' And they gave heed to him, because for a long time he had amazed them with his magic. But when they believed Philip as he preached good news about the kingdom of God and the name of Jesus

---

In later tradition this Simon became a considerable figure, as an arch-magician and the enemy of the apostolic Church. Justin Martyr, writing in the middle of the second century, confuses him with a local Latin god in Rome called Semo Sancus, but he also tells us (*Apology*, I. xxvi. 3) that Simon called himself 'the Great Power'. By Irenaeus (writing between A.D. 170 and 180) he is represented as claiming to be the epiphany of the highest god (*Adv. Haer.* I. xxiii. 1). Both writers represent him as the founder of a Gnostic sect, but this is very doubtful. Gnostics of the middle and end of the second century were fond of claiming bogus contact-men with the apostles as the originators of their secret tradition. It may be that one sect of them hit upon Simon as a useful eponymous founder to support their claim. Luke certainly knows nothing of Gnosticism. In the Pseudo-Clementine literature, a body of writings composed in the third century in the interest of extreme Jewish-Christian anti-Pauline heterodoxy, but including a good deal of material dating from the second century or earlier, Simon Magus appears in the part of the villain, opposing the apostles wherever he can. In Acts he is no more than a mercenary-minded sorcerer, and he gives no sign of being likely later to offer opposition to the Church. The ending of the episode is lame: 'Simon hoped that he might be forgiven. *Finis*.' On the other hand, if Luke and his hearers knew the beginnings of the later story-material about Simon, then the episode here related has much more point: 'This man who claimed later so much occult power in rivalry to the Church was converted and baptized by Philip and rebuked by Peter and humbly accepted the rebuke.'

Luke has a particular detestation of *magic*; cp. Acts 13[6ff.], 19[18, 19].

The name of Jesus Christ does not necessarily imply that the baptism was into this name alone (in contrast to the triple Name, as in Matt. 28[19]), though this is highly likely. On the other hand, it is quite fanciful to see in baptism into the single Name a defect which had to be remedied by the intervention of the apostles from Jerusalem.

13 Christ, they were baptized, both men and women. Even
Simon himself believed, and after being baptized he continued with Philip. And seeing signs and great miracles performed, he was amazed.

14   Now when the apostles at Jerusalem heard that Samaria

14–18   This laying-on of hands by the apostles on people already baptized
has caused great bewilderment to the commentators, and justly. We
may dismiss immediately the suggestion that the account is simply
a reconstruction by Luke designed to bring out the fact that the
Church in Samaria was recognized legally by authority from Jerusalem. In what sense was the baptism of the Ethiopian eunuch, described
immediately after this one, authorized from Jerusalem? Why did
Luke not produce a reconstruction to provide this? Again, it should
be obvious to everybody that for Luke the association of the Spirit
with baptism is normal practice. When we find abnormalities, such
as baptism without the Spirit, as here and in 19[6], or the Spirit given
without, or before baptism, as in the case of Cornelius (10[44]), we are
justified in assuming that Luke is *not* reconstructing, because these
instances are clearly not the practice of the Church contemporary
with Luke. Are the apostles, then, instituting a rite of 'confirmation',
a necessary ingredient of Christian initiation, without which the
Spirit cannot normally be received? A case for this point of view was
made some time ago by Mason, and more recently by Dix and L. S.
Thornton. But this attitude encounters overwhelming difficulties.
Who 'confirmed' the Ethiopian eunuch? or did he return to Ethiopia
without the Holy Spirit? The silence of the rest of the New Testament
upon the subject of 'confirmation' as a necessary accompaniment to
baptism (with the exception of Acts 19[6] and—very doubtful—Heb. 6[2])
is a significant one, particularly as Paul in 1 Cor. 1[14–17] appears to
disavow any particular right to baptize as belonging to an apostle.
G. W. H. Lampe, in *The Seal of the Spirit*, has made a powerful case
against the view that any rite other than water-baptism was regarded
as a necessary part of initiation in the early Church. Still less is the
view justified that the apostles are here conducting a 'confirmation'
in the sense of the term in the Anglican *Book of Common Prayer* (allowing
that the view of Mason, Dix, and Thornton, is, roughly, that of the
Orthodox Church), i.e., a rite granting to those who have been baptized a strengthening addition to their existing endowment with the
Holy Spirit. Not only is this idea unknown in the N.T., it is also
almost wholly foreign to the ancient Church.[1]

[1] For an excellent summary of this subject see Appendix 3 in C. S. C.
Williams's Commentary.

The baptistery from the Christian Church at Dura-Europos on the Euphrates, *c.* 230. The candidate for baptism stood in the trough below the arch and water was poured over him.

had received the word of God, they sent to them Peter and
15 John, who came down and prayed for them that they might
16 receive the Holy Spirit; for it had not yet fallen on any of
them, but they had only been baptized in the name of the
17 Lord Jesus. Then they laid their hands on them and they
18 received the Holy Spirit. Now when Simon saw that the
Spirit was given through the laying on of the apostles' hands,
19 he offered them money, saying 'Give me also this power, that
any one on whom I lay my hands may receive the Holy
20 Spirit.' But Peter said to him, 'Your silver perish with you,
because you thought you could obtain the gift of God with
21 money! You have neither part nor lot in this matter, for your
22 heart is not right before God. Repent therefore of this
wickedness of yours, and pray to the Lord that, if possible,
23 the intent of your heart may be forgiven you. For I see that
you are in the gall of bitterness and in the bond of iniquity.'
24 And Simon answered, 'Pray for me to the Lord, that nothing
of what you have said may come upon me.'

It is likely that this story reflects a period when the apostles were
gradually losing direct control over the Church. With the expansion
of the Christian message that resulted from Stephen's death, and the
exodus of Christians from Jerusalem after it, went a varied and un-
controlled evangelizing activity over which the Jerusalem Church
could keep no strict supervision. The visit to Samaria of two of them
(perhaps as representatives of the Church of Jerusalem) suggests an
effort to keep up with the pace of events, a pace which was bound in
the end to outstrip the efforts of the mother Church to keep control
over her people. This will not be the last of such efforts in Acts.

14   John, as usual, has only a walking-on part. The suggestion that
this is John Mark, and not John son of Zebedee, brother of James,
has little to commend it.

20   In later legend it is always Peter who is the chief antagonist to
Simon.

23   A curious and obscure mixture of Deut. 29^{18} and Isa. 58^6.

24   The 'Western' text has at this point the strange addition 'and he
continued for a long time lamenting greatly'. As a closing sentence

Now when they had testified and spoken the word of the Lord, they returned to Jerusalem, preaching the gospel to many villages of the Samaritans.

But an angel of the Lord said to Philip, 'Rise and go toward the south[a] to the road that goes down from Jerusalem to Gaza.' This is a desert road. And he rose and went. And behold, an Ethiopian, a eunuch, a minister of Candace the

[a] Or at noon

---

to the story it is quite ineffective. But if it was written in the knowledge that tradition had assigned to Simon a later career which marked him clearly as on the road to ruin, it would have some point, for it would present Simon as believing in Peter's power of prediction. As most of the incidents later connected with Simon are located in Rome, it is possible that we have here a faint indication (which has a little more evidence elsewhere in Acts to support it, see below, pp. 126-7, 254) that the interpolator worked in Rome. This in its turn slightly strengthens the hypothesis that Acts was written in Rome and for the Church of Rome.

8: 26–40. *The baptism of the Ethiopian eunuch*

An air of vagueness and fragmentariness hangs over this incident, enhanced by the introduction of an angel at 8[26]. The *Philip* last mentioned in Acts is Philip who was one of the Seven (8[4 ff.]), so presumably this *Philip* is he, and not Philip the Apostle (1[13]). The activities of the Seven, of whom Philip was one, and of the Twelve seem to have little to do with each other. The suggestion has been made that this story has been either invented to fit in with some prophetic passages in the O.T. (which is most unlikely) or modified from its original form so as to appear to fulfil these passages. Zeph. 2[4, 11f.], 3[4, 10] mentions in the LXX version 'Gaza' and 'Azotus at noonday' (or 'of the south'), prophets borne by the spirit, and the welcoming of men from Ethiopia. The word Gaza can also mean 'treasury' (γάζα in Greek).

Candace was not a proper name but a title, borne by successive queens. Ethiopia was for the men of the Graeco-Roman world a somewhat legendary place, representing the ultimate limit of the known world to the south, called by them also *Natapa-Meroe*. Today we call it the Sudan. This territory was indeed ruled by queens, not

queen of the Ethiopians, in charge of all her treasure, had
28 come to Jerusalem to worship and was returning; seated in
29 his chariot, he was reading the prophet Isaiah. And the
30 Spirit said to Philip, 'Go up and join this chariot.' So Philip
ran to him, and heard him reading Isaiah the prophet, and
31 asked, 'Do you understand what you are reading?' And he
said, 'How can I, unless some one guides me?' And he
32 invited Philip to come up and sit with him. Now the passage
of the scripture which he was reading was this:

> 'As a sheep led to the slaughter
> or a lamb before its shearer is dumb,
> so he opens not his mouth.
> 33   In his humiliation justice was denied him.
> Who can describe his generation?
> For his life is taken up from the earth.'

34 And the eunuch said to Philip, 'About whom, pray, does the
prophet say this, about himself or about some one else?'
35 Then Philip opened his mouth, and beginning with this
36 scripture he told him the good news of Jesus. And as they

---

kings, who were thought to be semi-divine consorts of the Sun.
Minister, literally 'Dynast' ($\delta\upsilon\nu\acute{\alpha}\sigma\tau\eta\varsigma$), the word used in the LXX of
Jer. 34[19] to translate the Aramaic title for an official, *saris*, who was
not necessarily a eunuch.

28   All reading in the ancient world, even by solitary persons, was
reading aloud, and one suspects that this was true of most of the
praying too, even praying by solitary persons. Exceptions to this,
such as Ambrose, the great fourth-century Bishop of Milan, as noted
by Augustine, were regarded as surprising.

31 f.   Here is unmistakable evidence that the main Suffering Servant
passage in Deutero-Isaiah (Isa. 53[7, 8]) attracted the interest of
Christian students at an early stage; exactly how early that stage was,
this narrative does not enable us to determine with accuracy. Luke
does not read an atonement theory into the passage, beyond using it
to show that it was predetermined and predicted that Jesus should
suffer, die, and rise again. But this does not preclude the possibility
of others' having done so.

went along the road they came to some water, and the eunuch said, 'See, here is water! What is to prevent my being baptized?'[a] And he commanded the chariot to stop, and they both went down into the water, Philip and the eunuch, and he baptized him. And when they came up out of the water,

[a] *Other ancient authorities add all or most of verse 37,* And Philip said, 'If you believe with all your heart, you may.' And he replied, 'I believe that Jesus Christ is the Son of God.'

O. Cullmann has conjectured that the words *What is to prevent my being baptized?* reflect a very old formula used in the baptism of Christians in the early Church. He points to the recurrence of the formula *Who is to prevent* (τίς κωλύει) in Acts 10[47] and 11[17] in baptismal contexts and suggests that it is also reflected in the use of the same word *prevent* in Mark 9[39], 10[14] and parallels. His case is, of course, strengthened by v. 37, even though it is not original. We must, however, face the fact that there is no satisfactory evidence that this formula was used in the early Church during the administration of baptism, apart from these occurrences of it in the N.T., and that evidence is lacking that there was during the first, or even during the second, century any fixed form of words for administering baptism, apart from the interrogatory creed itself, put in the form of questions and answers.

This verse is supplied wholly by the 'Western' text, and so is not printed in the text of the RSV. Not only is the textual evidence not sufficient to support this verse as the original reading, but the formula of belief in 11[17] ('we believed in the Lord Jesus Christ') is different from this one, and in 16[31] the formula is 'Believe in the Lord Jesus' (but cp. 9[20]). This verse, however, is valuable for giving us a very early doctrinal formula which is independent of the N.T. It probably represents the earliest known form of a baptismal creed. Clearly the interpolator thought that the eunuch could not have been baptized without repeating some sort of creed.

It is usually held that baptism at this stage involved going right under the water (total immersion). But the earliest known baptistery, in the Christian church at Dura-Europos on the Euphrates, dating from some point not very long before 246, did not allow for immersion but for water poured on top of the candidate as he stood in a kind of trough (see Illustration, p. 107). It may be that the practice of pouring water on the candidate was the custom which prevailed from the earliest times, at least as an alternative method of baptism.

At this point some MSS. and some Fathers read 'and when they came up out of the water, the Spirit fell on the eunuch, but the angel

the Spirit of the Lord caught up Philip; and the eunuch saw
40 him no more, and went on his way rejoicing. But Philip was
found at Azotus, and passing on he preached the gospel to
all the towns till he came to Caesarea.

9 BUT Saul, still breathing threats and murder against the
2 disciples of the Lord, went to the high priest and asked him

---

of the Lord caught up Philip', etc. This cannot be the original reading. Perhaps it shows that some early readers felt that since the
coming of the Spirit upon the Christians in Samaria had been
specifically mentioned in the narration of the last incident, it might
be thought that the Spirit had not come on the eunuch unless
explicit mention were made of the fact.

40   We do not hear of Philip again until 21⁸, when we find him
apparently settled at Caesarea (his final point of call here) with four
daughters.

9: 1–31. *First account of Paul's conversion*

1, 2   How was Paul able to continue his campaign of intimidation
against the Christians beyond the bounds of Jerusalem? 1 Macc.
15¹⁶⁻²¹ has been adduced as a proof that the Sanhedrin could arrest
people beyond their own country. It is the account of an order given
by the government of the Roman republic early in the second half
of the second century B.C. to afford the Jews (i.e. the High Priest,
along with the Temple authorities) facilities for extraditing criminals
or people obnoxious to them from Egypt to Judaea; the order is
addressed to the current Ptolemy, Hellenistic King of Egypt. But we
cannot assume that so wide-ranging an authority, given to a Jewish
native government at the very beginning of its period of power,
survived intact during all the vicissitudes of the next 150 and more
years, during which all forms of self-government had been taken away
from the Jews. It is much more likely that Paul was armed with
official authorization from the Sanhedrin to injure and even kidnap
leading Christians, *if he could with impunity.* As we have already noted
(see above, pp. 103, 104), the police systems of the ancient world were
very defective and an enterprising and determined bigot could probably
achieve a good deal in the way of violence without attracting un-
welcome notice. Paul himself admits that he persecuted the Church
and persecuted it with peculiar violence (Gal. 1¹³, ²³, Phil. 3⁶), and
in the ancient world persecution did not end with smear campaigns
and hostile propaganda. Paul tells us (2 Cor. 11³²) that an official

for letters to the synagogues at Damascus, so that if he found
any belonging to the Way, men or women, he might bring
them bound to Jerusalem. Now as he journeyed he

---

of King Aretas did his best to arrest him when he was in Damascus;
it is quite possible that this *ethnarch* did not have jurisdiction at all,
but was simply ordered by his king to kidnap Paul if he could. After
all, successful, though illegal, kidnapping is not unknown even in
well-policed twentieth-century society.

Paul himself, in the single passage in his letters where he refers to
his conversion (Gal. 1¹⁵, ¹⁶), characteristically tells us nothing about
it from the point of view of his religious experience or spiritual
feelings, but his account agrees in its main outlines with that of Luke,
and all the more impressively because it does so incidentally or
casually. He reveals that this experience took place away from
Jerusalem ('nor did I go up to Jerusalem', Gal. 1¹⁷), and he implies
that it took place at Damascus—'again I *returned* to Damascus', a city
he has not previously mentioned (Gal. 1¹⁷). Luke is careful not to say
that Paul saw any form during this vision; he suggests that Paul saw
a blinding light which caused him instantly to shut his eyes, and not
open them until the vision was past, though he does not hesitate in
a later description to call it a vision (Acts 26¹⁹). Paul consistently
claims in his letters that the appearance of the Lord to him on this
occasion was on a level with the other Resurrection appearances and
constituted him thereby an apostle (Gal. 1¹⁷; 1 Cor. 9¹⁻⁵, 15⁸). But
this difference is greater in appearance than reality. Paul never puts
himself in all respects on a level with the Twelve (and he knows this
term, see 1 Cor. 15⁵); he never, so to speak, calls himself the Thirteenth. It is difficult to avoid the conclusion that for him the term
'apostle' meant a group larger than the Twelve-plus-Paul. Luke does
indeed twice call Paul an apostle (Acts 14⁴, ¹⁴), but he preferred
to see him as the chosen instrument (9¹⁵), the great evangelizer of the
Gentiles. If this was, in the light of a certain historical perspective,
the role which he chose to give to Paul, rather than presenting him
precisely as Paul presented himself in his letters, we are not bound to
conclude that Luke could not have known Paul and must have been
moving in circles and living at a period too distant from Paul to
enable him to give us a tolerably accurate picture of him.

We may indeed agree that his account of the exact movements
of Paul after his conversion must be corrected in view of Paul's statements in Gal. 1. Luke represents him as visited by Ananias almost
immediately after the vision, as spending a long but indefinite period
in Damascus, and as then leaving the city, owing to the plots against
him, and going to Jerusalem. Paul says that immediately after the

approached Damascus, and suddenly a light from heaven
4 flashed about him. And he fell to the ground and heard
a voice saying to him, 'Saul, Saul, why do you persecute me?'
5 And he said, 'Who are you, Lord?' And he said, 'I am Jesus,
6 whom you are persecuting; but rise and enter the city, and
7 you will be told what you are to do.' The men who were
traveling with him stood speechless, hearing the voice but
8 seeing no one. Saul arose from the ground; and when his
eyes were opened, he could see nothing; so they led him by
9 the hand and brought him into Damascus. And for three
days he was without sight, and neither ate nor drank.

---

vision, he 'did not confer with flesh and blood' (Gal. 1^16, NEB
'without consulting any human being'). He went to Arabia, later
returned to Damascus, and then three years after (presumably after
his conversion) went to Jerusalem (Gal. 1^17, 18). It is easy to imagine
that the incident of Ananias' visit did not come under the rubric of
consulting a human being. How are we to imagine that Paul's baptism (Rom. 6^3 certainly compels us to conclude that he *was* baptized)
took place, if we take his words with strict undeviating literalness?
Paul can say both that he received the gospel through a revelation
of Jesus Christ and not through man (Gal. 1^12) and that he has
received traditions of the most important sort about Jesus from those
who were in Christianity before him (1 Cor. 11^23, 15^2ff.—where he
describes what he received as 'the gospel'). Similarly he can say
'I conferred not with flesh and blood', without denying the fact that
he was received and baptized by Christians in Damascus immediately
after his conversion; here we can use Luke to supplement, if not
correct, Paul. But no doubt Luke has telescoped the events which took
place after that. He has not realized that Paul went away to Arabia,
returned to Damascus, and only then was forced by threats to leave
the city. (For a discussion of the three different accounts of Paul's
conversion see below, p. 216.)

5   It has often been pointed out that Luke assumes that Jesus himself
was being persecuted in the persons of his disciples, and that this
implies a far-reaching doctrine of the Church: cp. Matt. 25^34-45;
Rom. 12^4, 5; 1 Cor. 12^12-27; Eph. 5^30.

9   This abstinence from food is more likely to be intended to indicate
the effects of shock after his experience on the road to Damascus than
to constitute a period of fasting and repentance before baptism.

Now there was a disciple at Damascus named Ananias. The Lord said to him in a vision, 'Ananias.' And he said, 'Here I am, Lord.' And the Lord said to him, 'Rise, and go to the street called Straight, and inquire in the house of Judas for a man of Tarsus named Saul; for behold, he is praying, and he has seen a man named Ananias come in and lay his hands on him so that he might regain his sight.' But Ananias answered 'Lord, I have heard from many about this man, how much evil he has done to thy saints at Jerusalem; and here he has authority from the chief priests to bind all who call upon thy name.' But the Lord said to him, 'Go, for he is a chosen instrument of mine to carry my name before the Gentiles and kings and the sons of Israel; for I will show him how much he must suffer for the sake of my name.' So Ananias departed and entered the house. And laying his hands on him he said, 'Brother Saul, the Lord Jesus who appeared to you on the road by which you came, has sent me that you may regain your sight and be filled with the Holy Spirit.' And immediately something like scales fell from his eyes and he regained his sight. Then he rose and was baptized, and took food and was strengthened.

For several days he was with the disciples at Damascus. And in the synagogues immediately he proclaimed Jesus, saying, 'He is the Son of God.' And all who heard him were

---

11 What can Luke's point be in including the name of *Straight* Street or *Judas*, the owner of the house where Paul was? Fanciful invention? Allegorizing based on images from the O.T.? Or is it not more likely to be reliable information from his source?

15 *chosen instrument*, literally 'vessel'; the background is Jer. 50²⁵.

18 Notice how implicitly Luke identifies baptism with the gift of the Holy Spirit. This was his regular assumption. When we find divergences from this view, it is time to look for sources.

22 *He is the Son of God* and *Jesus was the Christ* were certainly two of the

amazed, and said, 'Is not this the man who made havoc in
Jerusalem of those who called on this name? And he has
come here for this purpose, to bring them bound before the
22 chief priests.' But Saul increased all the more in strength,
and confounded the Jews who lived in Damascus by proving
that Jesus was the Christ.

23   When many days had passed, the Jews plotted to kill him,
24 but their plot became known to Saul. They were watching
25 the gates day and night, to kill him; but his disciples took

---

basic convictions about Jesus held by Paul, as he himself declares in
the brief doctrinal formula with which he opens his letter to the
Romans (1$^{1-4}$).

23   Luke attributes the plots to the Jews; Paul, more accurately,
ascribes them to 'the ethnarch of Aretas the King' (2 Cor. 11^{32}).
Aretas is a figure well attested from inscriptions. His kingdom was
in Nabataea and its capital was Petra; he was a semi-independent
princeling on the edge of the Roman Empire. Herod Antipas had
married his daughter, but had divorced her in order to marry
Herodias—the act which caused him to incur the denunciation of
John the Baptist. There is no evidence that Damascus was included
in his kingdom at this time. In the reign of Tiberius Damascus had
been under Roman rule, and in the reign of Nero we know that it was
also. The likelihood that Aretas' ethnarch was ruling the city for
him (which the RSV translation at 2 Cor. 11^{32}, 'governor under King
Aretas', implies) is not very strong. The two other alternatives are
that the ethnarch was supervising the Arab community in Damascus
on behalf of Aretas, who regarded himself as their protector (there
are parallels for this position), or that Paul means that the ethnarch
of Aretas watched the *outside* of the city. (See H. J. Cadbury, *The
Book of Acts in History*, pp. 19, 20.) Either of these alternatives would
make it likely that the commissioner of Aretas (so NEB in loc.) was
exercising unofficial but tolerated coercion against Paul. Conzelmann
makes the attractive suggestion that as Paul had just come from
Aretas' territory (Arabia) he had made himself obnoxious to Aretas
by causing disturbances among the Jews there. Aretas died about
A.D. 39, and his death provides us with an approximate date for
Paul's conversion, 35 or 36.

25   The reliability of Luke's source of information at this point is confirmed by the striking coincidence that Paul also mentions his being
lowered from the wall in a basket (2 Cor. 11^{33}). *His disciples* is odd,

him by night and let him down over the wall, lowering him in a basket.

And when he had come to Jerusalem he attempted to join the disciples; and they were all afraid of him, for they did not believe that he was a disciple. But Barnabas took him, and brought him to the apostles, and declared to them how on the road he had seen the Lord, who spoke to him, and how at Damascus he had preached boldly in the name of Jesus. So he went in and out among them at Jerusalem, preaching boldly in the name of the Lord. And he spoke and disputed against the Hellenists; but they were seeking to kill him. And when the brethren knew it, they brought him down to Caesarea, and sent him off to Tarsus.

So the church throughout all Judea and Galilee and Samaria had peace and was built up; and walking in the fear of the Lord and in the comfort of the Holy Spirit it was multiplied.

Now as Peter went here and there among them all, he

---

for Paul could hardly have acquired disciples by now. Perhaps it would be better to read 'the disciples took him by night' (as the AV does), even though the manuscript support for this is not entirely convincing.

This presumably corresponds to the 'fifteen days' which Paul says that he spent on his first visit to Jerusalem after his conversion (Gal. 1¹⁸⁻²²). This period hardly allows time for Paul to go *in and out among them at Jerusalem*, to *preach boldly in the name of the Lord*, and *dispute against the Hellenists*. But Paul's being sent off to Tarsus via Caesarea corresponds fairly enough to Paul's statement that he 'went into the regions of Syria and Cilicia' (Gal. 1²¹).

the church here means, not the local church, but the church throughout a much wider area, in fact the whole Church, as manifested in the regions of Judaea, Galilee, and Samaria; cp. 20²⁸.

9: 32–43. *Healings by Peter*

Peter is represented as going on a tour of inspection. Luke makes

33 came down also to the saints that lived at Lydda. There he found a man named Aeneas, who had been bedridden for
34 eight years and was paralyzed. And Peter said to him, 'Aeneas, Jesus Christ heals you; rise and make your bed.'
35 And immediately he rose. And all the residents of Lydda and Sharon saw him, and they turned to the Lord.

36 Now there was at Joppa a disciple named Tabitha, which means Dorcas or Gazelle. She was full of good works and
37 acts of charity. In those days she fell sick and died; and when
38 they had washed her, they laid her in an upper room. Since Lydda was near Joppa, the disciples, hearing that Peter was there, sent two men to him entreating him, 'Please come to us
39 without delay.' So Peter rose and went with them. And when he had come, they took him to the upper room. All the widows stood beside him weeping, and showing coats and
40 garments which Dorcas made while she was with them. But Peter put them all outside and knelt down and prayed; then turning to the body he said, 'Tabitha, rise.' And she opened

---

no attempt to correlate his activity here with that of Philip in much the same area, no doubt betraying thereby the fragmentary nature of his sources. Lydda is on the road between Azotus and Caesarea; its Greek name was Diospolis.

34 The words translated *make your bed* could mean 'lay yourself a meal'.
35 *Sharon* is not a town but the coastal plain extending from Lydda northwards to Mount Carmel.
36 *Joppa* is the modern Jaffa, a few miles north of Lydda. The etymology of Tabitha as 'Gazelle' is correct. *Gazelle* is here supplied by the RSV as a translation of the Greek *Dorcas* but is not in Luke's text.
39 *the widows stood weeping* because they were poor folk who had been deprived by Tabitha's death of her charity. They do not yet form a special group or order within the Church.
40 *Tabitha, rise* (Gk. Ταβιθά, ἀνάστηθι) may be a deliberate echo of the words of Jesus recorded at the healing of Jairus' daughter in Mark 5⁴¹, 'Little girl, I say to you, arise.' But Luke omits these words in his account of the incident (Luke 8⁵⁴), which weakens the case for this suggestion.

her eyes, and when she saw Peter she sat up. And he gave her his hand and lifted her up. Then calling the saints and widows he presented her alive. And it became known throughout all Joppa, and many believed in the Lord. And he stayed in Joppa for many days with one Simon, a tanner.

AT Caesarea there was a man named Cornelius, a centurion

Luke likes to mention details about the hosts who entertained the heroes of his story; cp. 9[11], 16[14, 15], 18[3], 21[8, 9, 16].

10: 1–11: 18. *The story of Cornelius*

Conzelmann, following Dibelius, is anxious to distinguish, in the original tradition behind this story, between the question of clean and unclean food and the question of Gentiles' being permitted to enter the Church. An analysis following this line of argument would detect two quite different sources and strands here, one a very primitive story about a Gentile centurion who came to join the Church as a result of a remarkable divine prompting, and another a vision introduced by Luke to emphasize that for Christians there can ultimately be no binding regulations about adopting one sort of food and refusing another, based ultimately perhaps on the teaching of Jesus himself (Mark 7[17–23]). In favour of this is the fact that the vision of Peter seems to be about clean and unclean food, whereas the discussion in 11[1–18] is about circumcised or uncircumcised persons (which was certainly the question at issue in the meeting described in Gal. 2[1–10]). This confusion seems to permeate the whole subject as developed in Ch. 15, for in it, if we are to judge by the 'decree', the subject at issue is food and other ceremonial regulations, not circumcision (which appears to be true also of the controversy recorded in Gal. 2[11–16]). It is clear that however the materials underlying this story may be analysed Luke himself has contributed a great deal to it.

But the simplicity introduced by distinguishing these two themes, which at first sight is attractive, on closer inspection becomes deceptive. As long as the Christian Church was confined to Jews there is no reason at all to think that controversy would have arisen about food regulations; everybody would have observed the traditional rules, and no vision about clean or unclean food would have been called for. It is only when the question of the entry of Gentiles into the Church is raised that the issue of food regulations becomes a burning one. Gentiles, to strict Jews, were unclean: they ate unclean food, they touched unclean objects, they associated with women when they were unclean (menstruous). The fact that they were uncircumcised also made them unfit to be associated with (and we can see this clearly implied in Gal. 2¹¹ ff.). The subject of table-fellowship was involved with the subject of food regulations, and both with the subject of circumcision. When therefore Luke introduces into his story of the acceptance into the Church of an uncircumcised Gentile a sub-plot describing a vision about clean and unclean food, it may well be that he is combining two different traditions, two different pieces of material, but they are not incompatible. Ultimately they are both concerned with the same subject; and Luke knows this. These themes cross each other several times up to the end of the fifteenth chapter, and though it is virtually impossible now to determine in what order they arose, and the exact course of the controversies about them, and though we cannot avoid the conclusion that Luke has admitted, or has failed to dispel, confusion in his materials relating to the subject, we can allow that he is right in treating both subjects within the context of the problem of admitting Gentiles into the Church.

1   *Cornelius* is described with a gentile *nomen* alone, exactly as would be expected of older officers in the Roman army at this period (Sherwin-White, *Roman Society and Roman Law*, pp. 160, 161, and see above, Introduction, p. 11). He was a centurion of the auxiliary forces, not of the legions, for no legionary forces were allowed in Judaea; his *Italian Cohort* is known from inscriptions, and cohorts styled 'Italica' are evidenced in Syria from the first century B.C. to the second A.D. No troops, auxiliary or legionary, were stationed in Caesarea between A.D. 41 and 44, while Herod Agrippa was king of Judaea.[1] But there is no difficulty in imagining that the incident of Cornelius took place before 41. Casearea, which formerly had been

---

[1] But, as Sherwin-White reminds us (*Roman Society and Roman Law*, pp. 11, 12), neither client kingdoms nor territories administered by the Emperor's own officials (such as Egypt) were 'outside' the Roman Empire. We are perhaps too much influenced by the quite modern conception of national sovereignty if we make this rule absolute and without exceptions.

of what was known as the Italian Cohort, a devout man who feared God with all his household, gave alms liberally to the people, and prayed constantly to God. About the ninth hour of the day he saw clearly in a vision an angel of God coming in and saying to him, 'Cornelius.' And he stared at him in terror, and said, 'What is it, Lord?' And he said to him, 'Your prayers and your alms have ascended as a memorial before God. And now send men to Joppa, and bring one Simon who is called Peter; he is lodging with Simon, a tanner, whose house is by the seaside.' When the angel who spoke to him had departed, he called two of his servants and a devout soldier from among those that waited on him, and having related everything to them, he sent them to Joppa.

The next day, as they were on their journey and coming near the city, Peter went up on the housetop to pray, about the sixth hour. And he became hungry and desired something to eat; but while they were preparing it, he fell into a trance and saw the heaven opened, and something descending, like a great sheet, let down by four corners upon the earth. In it were all kinds of animals and reptiles and birds of the air. And there came a voice to him, 'Rise, Peter;

---

a Greek city called Strato's Tower, was refounded by Herod the Great *c.* 12 B.C. and given an artificial harbour, some fragments of which still remain. There was a large Greek as well as a Jewish population in it, and the two were frequently at odds with each other.

Cornelius was not a proselyte (and therefore not circumcised), but a pagan attracted to Judaism, who followed its requirements (e.g. about the hours of prayer, 10[3]) as far as an uncircumcised pagan could. Such people are mentioned again in Acts 13[50], 16[14].

Caesarea is about 32 miles from Joppa.

The roof-top would be quiet and also would probably be shaded from the heat by an awning. It was a suitable place for a *siesta*, into which Peter's period for prayer seems to have turned.

14 kill and eat.' But Peter said, 'No, Lord; for I have never eaten
15 anything that is common or unclean.' And the voice came to
him again a second time, 'What God has cleansed, you must
16 not call common.' This happened three times, and the thing
was taken up at once to heaven.

17   Now while Peter was inwardly perplexed as to what the
vision which he had seen might mean, behold, the men that
were sent by Cornelius, having made inquiry for Simon's
18 house, stood before the gate and called out to ask whether
19 Simon who was called Peter was lodging there. And while
Peter was pondering the vision, the Spirit said to him, 'Be-
20 hold, three men are looking for you. Rise and go down, and
accompany them without hesitation; for I have sent them.'
21 And Peter went down to the men and said, 'I am the one
you are looking for; what is the reason for your coming?'
22 And they said, 'Cornelius, a centurion, an upright and God-
fearing man, who is well spoken of by the whole Jewish
nation, was directed by a holy angel to send for you to come
23 to his house, and to hear what you have to say.' So he called
them in to be his guests.

    The next day he rose and went off with them, and some of
24 the brethren from Joppa accompanied him. And on the

---

13   The Greek word for *kill* can mean 'sacrifice' (θῦσον). But there is
no reason for thinking that it should have this meaning here.
15   The voice in the dream does not lay down a law, that now the
distinction between clean and unclean food is abolished, but simply
declares that the coming of Christianity involves inevitably and
logically the abolition of this distinction; cp. Rom. 14[14-17], where the
same word *common* (κοινόν) is used.
24   Cornelius appears to be living with his kinsmen in Caesarea. He
was probably a provincial and not a Roman citizen; auxiliaries
gained the right to become Roman citizens only after twenty-five
years' service.

following day they entered Caesarea. Cornelius was expecting them and had called together his kinsmen and close friends. When Peter entered, Cornelius met him and fell down at his feet and worshiped him. But Peter lifted him up, saying, 'Stand up; I too am a man.' And as he talked with him, he went in and found many persons gathered; and he said to them, 'You yourselves know how unlawful it is for a Jew to associate with or to visit any one of another nation; but God has shown me that I should not call any man common or unclean. So when I was sent for, I came without objection. I ask then why you sent for me.'

And Cornelius said, 'Four days ago, about this hour, I was keeping the ninth hour of prayer in my house; and behold, a man stood before me in bright apparel, saying, "Cornelius, your prayer has been heard and your alms have been remembered before God. Send therefore to Joppa and ask for Simon who is called Peter; he is lodging in the house of Simon, a tanner, by the seaside." So I sent to you at once,

---

The 'Western' text has at this point an elaborate addition: 'As Peter was approaching Caesarea, one of the slaves ran on ahead and announced his arrival. And Cornelius leapt up and met him and fell at his feet. . . .' It is apparently motivated by the desire to explain how Peter discovered where Cornelius lived. It is worth noting that the interpolator assumes that Peter will keep slaves, a most unlikely assumption; perhaps it reflects faintly the position of the interpolator himself.

Other instances of the disavowal of worship by people to whom it is offered can be found in the N.T.: Acts 14[14, 15]; Rev. 19[10], 22[9].

The Greek of Cornelius' explanation here is confused; taken in its literal sense it should mean that Cornelius had been praying continuously for four days, but in fact it must mean that four days before he had been praying at 3 p.m., and that now it was 3 o'clock on the fourth day. Peter and his company had taken two days on the road (v. 24). The 'Western' text, characteristically, tries to tidy up the sentence.

and you have been kind enough to come. Now therefore
we are all here present in the sight of God, to hear all that
you have been commanded by the Lord.'

34 And Peter opened his mouth and said: 'Truly I perceive
35 that God shows no partiality, but in every nation any one
who fears him and does what is right is acceptable to him.
36 You know the word which he sent to Israel, preaching good
37 news of peace by Jesus Christ (he is Lord of all), the word
which was proclaimed throughout all Judea, beginning from

34–43   Peter's speech certainly contains no reminiscences of what was said
on the actual occasion for which it has been devised. Wilckens points
out that the expression *you know the word which he sent to Israel* does not
fit the situation, because the Gentiles addressed by Luke could not
have any previous knowledge of Christianity. It is in fact a traditional
Christian formula for introducing the Jesus-Kerygma (the preaching
about Jesus).[1] We may indeed recognize it as a speech for Jews
adapted by the prefixing of the first sentence to suit Gentiles; its
pattern is exactly that of the speeches to Jews we have already
encountered, and quite unlike the two speeches to Gentiles which we
shall encounter (14^{15-18}, 17^{21-31}). For this very reason it becomes very
difficult to regard it as an entirely free composition of Luke, designed
simply to fit the occasion. It is one of the most ungrammatical pieces
of Greek that Luke ever wrote. One cannot avoid the impression that
though, as usual, Luke has fixed its final form, older elements are
included in it.

34   Peter does not mean that Gentiles can be saved without hearing
the gospel, but he is stressing the entire readiness of the Gentiles for
the gospel.

36, 37   The grammatical looseness reaches its apogee in this verse, which
has been smoothed out in the RSV translation. Literally it runs: 'The
word (in the accusative) which he sent to the sons of Israel giving good
news of peace through Jesus Christ; he is Lord of all.' There is no
main verb to govern *the word*. *Lord of all* is an Hellenistic cosmological
religious expression (i.e. expressing Lordship over the whole cosmos
or universe); but it had been adopted by Judaism (Wisd. 6^7, 8^3).
Here it has no particular cosmological force but merely expresses the
universality of salvation for all people; it simply states in a different
way what has already been said in 4^{12}. *Beginning* ($ἀρξάμενος$) is wholly

[1] Wilckens, *Die Missionsreden*, p. 65.

Galilee after the baptism which John preached: how God anointed Jesus of Nazareth with the Holy Spirit and with power; how he went about doing good and healing all that were oppressed by the devil, for God was with him. And we are witnesses to all that he did both in the country of the Jews and in Jerusalem. They put him to death by hanging him on a tree; but God raised him on the third day and made him manifest; not to all the people but to us who were chosen by God as witnesses, who ate and drank with him after he rose from the dead. And he commanded us to preach to the people, and to testify that he is the one ordained by God to be judge of the living and the dead. To him all the prophets bear witness that every one who believes in him receives forgiveness of sins through his name.'

While Peter was still saying this, the Holy Spirit fell on all

---

ungrammatical; it is a participle in the nominative masculine singular, and can apply to no noun in the sentence, but must assume Jesus as its subject. There is a precisely parallel construction (or lack of construction) at Luke 24⁴⁷, where the words 'beginning at Jerusalem' (ἀρξάμενοι, m. pl. nom.) are just as ungrammatical as is the construction with 'beginning' here.

For Jesus' being *anointed with the Holy Spirit and power* cp. Luke 4¹⁶ff.; Acts 4²⁷. This is one of the few references in the N.T., outside the Gospels, to the activity of Jesus in healing and teaching.

The fact that Jesus ate and drank after the Resurrection showed that he was really risen, and no ghost; cp. Luke 24⁴¹⁻⁴³.

the people here can only mean the Jews.

The Spirit given before baptism or baptism given apart from the Spirit was irregular and abnormal for Luke. This incident therefore requires explanation. It is not satisfactory to say that this is a 'Pentecost for the Gentiles', because the analogy with the coming of the Holy Spirit at Pentecost will not hold. The apostles and disciples upon whom the Spirit came at Pentecost were not baptized, whereas this group of Gentiles are baptized as soon as it is clear that they have the Spirit. There is no reason why Luke should not have recounted quite as impressive a story if it had ended with the Gentiles' asking for baptism and receiving it, and then receiving the Spirit, or receiving

45 who heard the word. And the believers from among the
circumcised who came with Peter were amazed, because the
gift of the Holy Spirit had been poured out even on the Gen-
46 tiles. For they heard them speaking in tongues and extolling
47 God. Then Peter declared, 'Can any one forbid water for
baptizing these people who have received the Holy Spirit
48 just as we have?' And he commanded them to be baptized in
the name of Jesus Christ. Then they asked him to remain for
some days.

11 NOW the apostles and the brethren who were in Judea
heard that the Gentiles also had received the word of God.
2 So when Peter went up to Jerusalem, the circumcision party

---

the Spirit after Peter had laid hands upon them. This detail must be
an original part of the story inherited by Luke.

48   Peter himself does not baptize; cp. 1 Cor. 1¹⁴⁻¹⁷.

11: 1–18   Luke takes the opportunity in describing Peter's return to Jerusalem and reporting the entry of Cornelius and his group into the
Church to prepare for the controversy over circumcision. But in fact
it is very difficult to imagine that the conversion of Cornelius was
marked as signally and publicly as this, for it happened in some way
involving no deliberate evangelizing activity among the Gentiles.
The great controversy came several years later (if we assume that
Cornelius' adherence took place in A.D. 40 or earlier), when a regular
policy of evangelizing Gentiles had been embarked upon by more
than one group in the Church. Luke has for his own purposes given
special publicity to this rather obscure incident.

2   *the circumcision party*, literally 'those from the circumcision', or
Luke's own showing a wholly anachronistic expression, because
apart from Cornelius and his small group, and possibly one eunuch
in far-away Ethiopia, the entire Church was at this moment composed of *the circumcision party*, of Jews and only Jews. The 'Western'
interpolator at vv. 1 and 2 exhibits a complete rewriting of the text
representing Peter as exhorting Cornelius and his people for some
time, and travelling through neighbouring places and teaching there
before reaching Jerusalem. This alteration may have been motivated
by a desire to represent Peter as more in charge of affairs than Luke

criticized him, saying, 'Why did you go to uncircumcised men and eat with them?' But Peter began and explained to them in order: 'I was in the city of Joppa praying; and in a trance I saw a vision, something descending, like a great sheet, let down from heaven by four corners; and it came down to me. Looking at it closely I observed animals and beasts of prey and reptiles and birds of the air. And I heard a voice saying to me, "Rise, Peter; kill and eat." But I said, "No, Lord; for nothing common or unclean has ever entered my mouth." But the voice answered a second time from heaven, "What God has cleansed you must not call common." This happened three times, and all was drawn up again into heaven. At that very moment three men arrived at the house in which we were, sent to me from Caesarea. And the Spirit told me to go with them, making no distinction. These six brethren also accompanied me, and we entered the man's house. And he told us how he had seen the angel standing in his house and saying, "Send to Joppa and bring Simon called Peter; he will declare to you a message by which you will be saved, you and all your household." As I began to speak, the Holy Spirit fell on them just as on us at the beginning. And I remembered the word of the Lord,

---

had represented him (and could therefore be interpreted as the beginnings of a proprietorial interest shown in Peter by Christians at Rome). Or it could be thought of as designed to assimilate the movements described in Ch. 11 to those described in Ch. 15, and therefore as an attempt to solve or mitigate what is the central difficulty of Acts.

all your household reminds us that in the ancient world when people joined a new religion they usually did so, not as individuals, but as families. It also suggests the possibility that children were baptized when they formed members of a household which had turned Christian: cp. 16$^{15, 31f.}$, 18^8; 1 Cor. 1^{16}.

No doubt this verse is a reminder of 1^5. But this contrast between John's baptism as one of water and the Messiah's baptism as one of

how he said, "John baptized with water, but you shall be
17 baptized with the Holy Spirit." If then God gave the same
gift to them as he gave to us when we believed in the Lord
18 Jesus Christ, who was I that I could withstand God?' When
they heard this they were silenced. And they glorified God,
saying, 'Then to the Gentiles also God has granted repentance
unto life.'

19   Now those who were scattered because of the persecution

---

fire or of Spirit was not invented by Luke. It occurs in Mark 1[8] and
parallels, and lies behind John 3[3-8]. Luke is aware that though reception of the Spirit and water-baptism are regularly linked together in
his time, in an earlier period this was not always necessarily so.

17   The 'Western' text adds at the end of this verse 'so that I should
not give them the Holy Spirit when they believed in him', aptly
illustrating the point of the last comment. The interpolator cannot
envisage a time when the Holy Spirit was not linked with baptism.
But Luke knows enough of the earlier period to be able to do so.

18   John's baptism was for repentance, that of Jesus for *repentance
unto life.*

11: 19–30. *The Church in Antioch*

That there lie behind this section traditions coming from the
church in Antioch almost everyone agrees. But it is no longer
usual among scholars to attribute this information to a written
or continuous source traceable elsewhere in the early narratives of Acts, as commentators were inclined to do early in
this century. The most important fact to be gleaned from this
section is that regular and organized evangelizing of non-Jews
was first undertaken at Antioch, that the mission to the Gentiles originated in fact from Antioch, whatever isolated
incidents foreshadowing or anticipating this important new
development may have taken place earlier and elsewhere. We
also learn that Paul was associated with this development.
Luke relates that this new move had the blessing of the Church
in Jerusalem and that at some time (the indication is indefinite)
the Church of Antioch gave material help to the Church in
Jerusalem. He does not indicate here any tension at all about
the admission of Gentiles to the Church, though earlier (11[2])
he has done so, and later (15[1-5]) he will do so again.

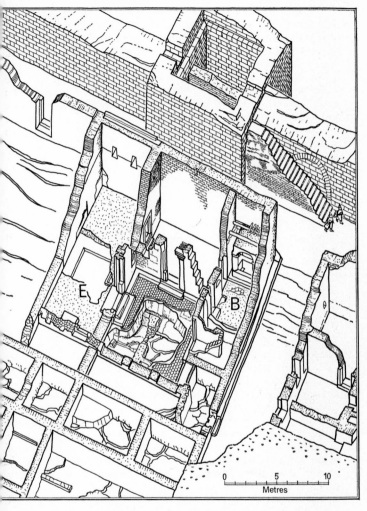

Plan of the Christian Church at Dura-Europos. B marks the baptistery, and E the room where the Eucharist was celebrated, with a step for the altar at one end. The rooms are grouped round a courtyard.

Several scholars have refused to believe that the Jerusalem Church could so readily have accepted this new and (to it) disturbing development, and they reject Luke's statement that Barnabas was sent from Jerusalem. But Paul in his account of his second visit to Jerusalem (Gal. 2$^{1-10}$) does not imply in the least that the leaders of the Jerusalem Church ('pillars' he calls them) were hostile to his evangelizing the Gentiles. The only ones who showed hostility to this were people whom he calls 'false brothers', and who are clearly distinct from the leaders of that Church. He also admits that later Barnabas was influenced by Peter, unduly influenced, he thinks (Gal. 2^{13}), which suggests that Barnabas and he had had previous relations. Again, Paul ends this account by saying that the only stipulation made by these leaders was that Paul and Barnabas should 'remember the poor, which very thing I was eager to do'. What are we to imagine that the leaders of the Jerusalem Church meant by this? That wherever he went Paul should be charitable to those who were needy? They would hardly have wasted time on pious general exhortations such as these. Obviously they meant the poor *in Jerusalem*. It is just as obvious that this has nothing to do with Paul's later collection, because Paul would hardly have failed to make a strong point by mentioning this—'in fact I am now organizing a collection for their benefit'. But he does not say this. If we adopt Paul's own chronology, this visit to Jerusalem must have happened in A.D. 46, 47, or 48. His collection can hardly have been made until about 55 (see above, Introduction, pp. 20–21). His care for the poor in 48 could not possibly have been expressed by a collection made seven years later. It looks very much as if Paul's words in Gal. 2^{10} imply that he did make some contribution towards the poor of Jerusalem in the early period. Certainly it is as reasonable to come to the conclusion that there is genuine historical fact behind Acts 11$^{27-30}$ as it is to conclude that these verses are only a confused recollection of a much later collection, which in fact Luke does later in his narrative mention (Acts 24^{17}), even though he puts it very much in the background.

We may therefore reconstruct the history lying behind Acts 11$^{19-30}$ by assuming that the regular and effective evangelizing of Gentiles began in the Church of Antioch and was carried on by Greek-speaking Jewish Christians, 'Hellenists',

that arose over Stephen traveled as far as Phoenicia and
Cyprus and Antioch, speaking the word to none except
Jews. But there were some of them, men of Cyprus and
Cyrene, who on coming to Antioch spoke to the Greeks[a] also,

a *Other ancient authorities read* Hellenists

---

and that Paul was involved in this activity and was recognized
sooner or later as its chief exponent. He himself tells us that
after his first visit to Jerusalem after his conversion he went
'into the regions of Syria and Cilicia' (Gal. 1[21]), which does not
accord badly with Luke's statement that he came from Tarsus
(Cilicia) to Antioch (Syria) and there spent some time evangelizing (Acts 11[25, 26]). From there he went to Jerusalem on the
mission with Barnabas which he described in Gal. 2[1–10]; and this
mission had, as well as its primary purpose, described in Galatians, a secondary purpose of arranging for relief to be given to
the poor Christians in Jerusalem, probably on a local scale, by
the Christians of Antioch. It would be inaccurate to describe
Luke as giving in Acts 11[27–30] a parallel account of this mission;
this was the mistake of the older scholars, such as Ramsay,
who adopted approximately the view put forward in this Commentary. What Luke is doing is giving the version of this journey which has come down to him. Inevitably it is a damaged and
indistinct version; compared with Paul's first-hand account it
looks very different. He knows nothing about Paul's private
meeting with the leaders of the Jerusalem Church, nothing
about the issue of circumcision having been raised at this visit,
nothing about the presence of Titus (Gal. 2[1–6]), though he is
aware that there was a 'circumcision party' in the Jerusalem
Church (Acts 11[2], 15[1–5]). But there is enough evidence to make
the rejection of Luke's account as sheer invention unreasonable.

Now those who were scattered refers back to 8[4]. Phoenicia is a narrow
strip of territory which runs along the coast of Palestine for about 80
miles north from Mount Carmel, but whose administrative boundaries
varied very much. Antioch was the capital of Syria, and one of the
greatest cities in the Eastern part of the Roman Empire at that time,
second only to Alexandria in size and importance.

Greeks ($"E\lambda\lambda\eta\nu\alpha\varsigma$) is the reading of some MSS. and of Eusebius,
the early Church historian; other MSS. read 'Hellenists' ($'E\lambda\lambda\eta\nu\iota\sigma\tau\dot{\alpha}\varsigma$).

21 preaching the Lord Jesus. And the hand of the Lord was
with them, and a great number that believed turned to the
22 Lord. News of this came to the ears of the church in Jerusa-
23 lem, and they sent Barnabas to Antioch. When he came and
saw the grace of God, he was glad; and he exhorted them all
24 to remain faithful to the Lord with steadfast purpose; for
he was a good man, full of the Holy Spirit and of faith. And
25 a large company was added to the Lord. So Barnabas went
26 to Tarsus to look for Saul; and when he had found him, he
brought him to Antioch. For a whole year they met with*a* the
church, and taught a large company of people; and in
Antioch the disciples were for the first time called Christians.
27 Now in these days prophets came down from Jerusalem

a Or were guests of

Whichever reading we adopt, the word must mean 'heathen', non-
Jews. One early hand in the Codex Sinaiticus reads 'evangelists',
which is probably an emendation from 'Hellenists'.

25 Tarsus was the capital of the province of Cilicia, well known as
a centre of Greek culture, and indeed of philosophy.

26 *met with* could be translated 'were entertained by', but the translation in the text is much preferable. *Christians* is a Latin formation
from Christus, as Herodians (Matt. 22[16]; Mark 3[6], 12[13]) is from
Herodes. This is the name that Suetonius, Pliny, and Tacitus use
to refer to members of the Church. *Were called* is the correct transla-
tion, though the verb ($\chi\rho\eta\mu\alpha\tau\acute{\iota}\sigma\alpha\iota$) is active in form; there is in-
sufficient evidence from writers of this period to justify the translation
'called themselves'. This is a name which outsiders first gave to
Christians and which they eventually adopted themselves. It could
only, of course, have arisen in a Greek-speaking (not an Aramaic-
speaking) *milieu*.

27 That there were people in the early Church whose function was to
act as *prophets* is abundantly clear: 1 Cor. 12[28, 29], 14[29, 32, 37]; Eph.
2[30], 3[5], 4[11]; Rev. 22[9]. There are also references to them in Christian
literature of the second century. They claimed direct inspiration
from the Spirit. We shall meet them again in Acts 13[1], 15[32], 21[10]
(Agabus again). There is no other evidence of prophets travelling in
companies in N.T. times, but the *Didache* (*c.* A.D. 100) mentions
travelling or wandering single prophets.

to Antioch. And one of them named Agabus stood up and foretold by the Spirit that there would be a great famine over all the world; and this took place in the days of Claudius. And the disciples determined, every one according to his ability, to send relief to the brethren who lived in Judea; and they did so, sending it to the elders by the hand of Barnabas and Saul.

ABOUT that time Herod the king laid violent hands upon

There was no world-wide *famine* (i.e. Empire-wide) in the reign of Claudius or of any other Roman Emperor, but there was a series of severe local famines in Claudius' reign. See the Introduction, p. 13. At this verse the 'Western' text prefixes the sentence 'And there was great rejoicing, and as we had been conversing together one of them, Agabus, said . . .'. It has been suggested that this premature insertion of a 'we' passage was done in order to connect Lucius of Cyrene (who will appear in 13¹ as belonging to the prophets at Antioch) with the 'we' who, presumably, denoted a group of whom the author of Acts was a member, or simply in order to connect the author of Acts with Antioch. It may be that this 'Western' reading is the origin of the idea that Luke wrote Acts; or it may be that this tradition was as old as the time of the interpolator, and that he wanted to produce evidence of this from Acts itself. It seems quite likely, on any supposition, that the existence of the 'we' passages as an interesting and significant feature of Acts was observed as early as the time of the interpolator.

The word for *relief* (*diakonia*) is the same word as Paul uses for his collection for the poverty-stricken Christians in Jerusalem (2 Cor. 8⁴, 9¹, ¹², ¹³), but it is a word very generally used and is probably not significant here.

elders is a new way of referring to the authorities of the Church of Jerusalem. It is likely that at a fairly early period, once the Twelve had quitted Jerusalem or for one reason or another left the scene, that Church was governed by James the brother of the Lord and a council of elders; see below, p. 136.

12: 1–25. *Peter's imprisonment and escape, and the fate of Herod Agrippa*

Without taking the angel *au pied de la lettre* we can reasonably see here an imprisonment of Peter from which he managed to

2 some who belonged to the church. He killed James the
3 brother of John with the sword; and when he saw that it
pleased the Jews, he proceeded to arrest Peter also. This was
4 during the days of Unleavened Bread. And when he had
seized him, he put him in prison, and delivered him to four
squads of soldiers to guard him, intending after the Passover

---

escape because of bribery, negligence, or simply a change of
mind on the part of the authorities, all of which are well
evidenced as likely to occur in the ancient world. There is no
necessary connexion between the imprisonment of Peter and
the death of Herod Agrippa. In fact we cannot date this
imprisonment of Peter more closely than between 41 and 44,
during which years Herod Agrippa was King of Judaea. Luke
takes the opportunity of this mention of Herod to relate his
horrible end.

1   Herod the King is Herod Agrippa I, son of Aristobulus, son of
Herod the Great. In A.D. 37 he received the tetrarchy of Philip his
uncle (Trachonitis) and perhaps the tetrarchy of Abilene as well,
from the hands of the Emperor Gaius. In 40 Herod Antipas, another
uncle of his, was deposed and he received this uncle's territory,
Galilee and Peraea, again from the Emperor Gaius. In 41 he gained
the whole of Judaea in addition to his other possessions, and the title
of King from the Emperor Claudius. This was the zenith of his career
and he now ruled an area nearly as large as that which his grandfather
Herod the Great had ruled. As long as he was King there were no
more prefects nor procurators in Judaea. But in 44 he died. Josephus
also regards his death as an example of divine punishment for
arrogance bred by prosperity.

2   *James the brother of John*, son of Zebedee: see Mark 1[19, 29], 3[17], 5[37],
10[35, 41], 13[3], 14[33], and parallels; Acts 1[13]. In view of Mark 10[38-40]
it has been thought that John his brother was martyred at the same
time. But the evidence for this is very weak indeed and the tradition
that John survived a long time and ended his days in Ephesus cannot
lightly be set aside.

3   *the days of Unleavened Bread* covered a whole week after the Passover
festival (which itself occupied only a single day), but in popular usage
the two festivals were confused; cp. Mark 14[1].

4   *Four 'quaternions' of soldiers*, each set to watch during three of the
twelve evening and night hours.

to bring him out to the people. So Peter was kept in prison; but earnest prayer for him was made to God by the church.

The very night when Herod was about to bring him out, Peter was sleeping between two soldiers, bound with two chains, and sentries before the door were guarding the prison; and behold, an angel of the Lord appeared, and a light shone in the cell; and he struck Peter on the side and woke him, saying, 'Get up quickly.' And the chains fell off his hands. And the angel said to him, 'Dress yourself and put on your sandals.' And he did so. And he said to him, 'Wrap your mantle around you and follow me.' And he went out and followed him; he did not know that what was done by the angel was real, but thought he was seeing a vision. When they had passed the first and the second guard, they came to the iron gate leading into the city. It opened to them of its own accord, and they went out and passed on through one street; and immediately the angel left him. And Peter came to himself, and said, 'Now I am sure that the Lord has sent his angel and rescued me from the hand of Herod and from all that the Jewish people were expecting.'

When he realized this, he went to the house of Mary, the mother of John whose other name was Mark, where many

---

The 'Western' text after *they went out* has added 'and they went down the seven steps'. But as there is no indication in the narrative as to where in Jerusalem Peter was imprisoned, and as no 'seven steps' are witnessed to in any ancient authority, we are left entirely in the dark as to the significance of this addition. A reference to Ezek. $40^{22, 26}$ serves only to make obscurity obscurer.

Mark is also mentioned in Acts $15^{37, 39}$; Col. 4^{10}; 2 Tim. 4^{11}; Philemon 24 and 1 Pet. 5^{13}. Whether these all refer to the same Mark, and whether this Mark is the author of the Second Gospel are matters of conjecture.

13 were gathered together and were praying. And when he knocked at the door of the gateway, a maid named Rhoda
14 came to answer. Recognizing Peter's voice, in her joy she did not open the gate but ran in and told that Peter was standing
15 at the gate. They said to her, 'You are mad.' But she insisted
16 that it was so. They said, 'It is his angel!' But Peter continued knocking; and when they opened, they saw him and were
17 amazed. But motioning to them with his hand to be silent, he described to them how the Lord had brought him out of the prison. And he said, 'Tell this to James and to the brethren.' Then he departed and went to another place.

---

13   *the gateway* ($\pi v \lambda \dot{\omega} v$) is the gatehouse separating the main room of the house from the street.

15   His guardian angel is meant, not his ghost; the same word ($\ddot{\alpha}\gamma\gamma\epsilon\lambda os$) is used in 6¹⁵, where Luke certainly had no intention of saying that Stephen looked like a ghost.

17   *Tell this to James and to the brethren* appears to imply that once Peter is out of Jerusalem the affairs of the Church will be in the hands of James and a council of the local Church to assist him. Not only have we had a faint indication of this already (11³⁰), but later we shall find that precisely this is the situation of the Jerusalem Church when Paul visits it for the last time (21¹⁷, ¹⁸). At this point the apostles have, as a separate group, completely disappeared. James is not one of the Twelve, but the brother of the Lord. Paul does not class him with the Twelve but may nevertheless regard him as an apostle (1 Cor. 15³⁻⁸), and he too recognizes him as a leading member of the Jerusalem Church (Gal. 1¹⁹, 2⁹, ¹²). We have independent evidence given us by Eusebius, the early Church historian, of the predominant position occupied by James in this Church. He was probably martyred in A.D. 62. Here Luke is assuming the existence of a situation which certainly obtained later, but probably not as early as 41–44. We shall meet a few more mentions of the apostles at Jerusalem in Chapter 15 (where see Commentary). It should be noticed that Luke, in placing Peter's imprisonment between the famine-relief visit of Paul and Barnabas to Jerusalem and the first account of a missionary journey by the same pair, cannot be relied on as giving us the correct chronological order. If Peter was imprisoned by Herod, and if the famine visit was Paul's second visit to Jerusalem, then the famine visit almost certainly came after the imprisonment. It is clear that

Now when day came, there was no small stir among the soldiers over what had become of Peter. And when Herod had sought for him and could not find him, he examined the sentries and ordered that they should be put to death. Then he went down from Judea to Caesarea, and remained there.

Now Herod was angry with the people of Tyre and Sidon; and they came to him in a body, and having persuaded Blastus, the king's chamberlain, they asked for peace, because their country depended on the king's country for food. On an appointed day Herod put on his royal robes, took his seat upon the throne, and made an oration to them. And the people shouted, 'The voice of a god, and not of man!' Immediately an angel of the Lord smote him, because he did not give God the glory; and he was eaten by worms and died.

But the word of God grew and multiplied.

And Barnabas and Saul returned from[a] Jerusalem when they had fulfilled their mission, bringing with them John whose other name was Mark.

a   *Other ancient authorities read* to

Luke at this point in his narrative is disposing of material which came to him in isolated units, probably of very varied form and value, and that he had to determine the order of it himself. Notice the vagueness of this account of Peter's movements. Evidently Luke had no information about what Peter was doing between his escape from prison and his next appearance in the narrative (in Ch. 15).

There is no doubt that from the standpoint of strict textual criticism we should read 'to Jerusalem' instead of '*from* Jerusalem', but the reading 'to' clearly presents grave difficulties, for any straightforward reading of the narrative of Acts must convince the reader that Paul and Barnabas were in Jerusalem already (11³⁰). Various explanations of the 'to' have been suggested: that it was written by Luke as a kind of bare summary of 11²⁷⁻³⁰, in order to make it clear to the reader that the famine visit took place (as is very likely) after Peter's escape from prison and not before; or that we should translate 'returned, having fulfilled the ministry at Jerusalem' (which is just possible,

13 Now in the church at Antioch there were prophets and teachers, Barnabas, Symeon who was called Niger, Lucius

---

but extremely awkward); or that the whole phrase 'to Jerusalem' is a gloss; or (perhaps the best and simplest solution) that Luke made a slip of the pen here and wrote 'to Jerusalem' instead of 'to Antioch'. The alternative is to do what the RSV has done, and to read 'from Jerusalem'. But not only is this the worse-attested reading, but it is hard to envisage how an original 'from Jerusalem' could have been altered to 'to Jerusalem', and very easy to see how the reverse process could have taken place.

13: 1–14: 28. *First account of a missionary journey*

There are several reasons for thinking that this journey, which some have regarded as an invention by Luke, is historical. In the first place, it is hard to believe that Luke would have allowed an unseemly and unedifying quarrel between two Christian missionaries, Paul and John Mark, whose reconciliation, if it ever occurred, is not recorded in Acts, to figure in an invented story. In the second place, it is difficult to see why Luke should have chosen the route he did for this journey if he was simply allowing his fancy free scope— Cyprus, Pisidian Antioch, Iconium, Lystra, Derbe. These are not particularly famous places, except for Cyprus; they are mentioned in Acts again only at 16[1, 2], and that in a passage connecting Timothy with Derbe and Lystra, a piece of information whose presence is difficult to explain on any theory except that it happened to be true. Except for Cyprus, these places are not mentioned in the O.T. Thirdly, how can we account for the mention of places where nothing particular is recorded as happening—Seleucia, Perga, Attalia? If Luke was inventing freely, he must have had some motive in including these places. But no plausible motive can be discovered. It is more satisfactory to assume that Luke had at his disposal here sources, probably oral sources, which gave him a reasonably reliable outline at least upon which to construct his narrative, and that the journey here described did take place in the order in which he described it. We have not called it the 'First Missionary Journey', the title it has usually borne in the past, because we have no right to assume that it was Paul's first missionary journey; he may have made others before it during

of Cyrene, Manaen a member of the court of Herod the tetrarch, and Saul. While they were worshiping the Lord and fasting, the Holy Spirit said, 'Set apart for me Barnabas and Saul for the work to which I have called them.' Then after fasting and praying they laid their hands on them and sent them off.

---

the years that he spent in 'the regions of Syria and Cilicia' (Gal. 1²¹). It is simply the first missionary journey about which Luke has been able to discover information.

It is startling to find Saul numbered among the *prophets and teachers*. But Luke no doubt regarded Paul as the great teacher of the Gentiles. Except for Paul and Barnabas nobody in this list is known elsewhere. It has been conjectured that *Symeon who was called Niger* (= Black) is Simon of Cyrene (Luke 23²⁶), but this can be no more than conjecture. Clearly Luke did not just invent this list, but received it from some source. Antioch seems to have been particularly connected with prophets: Acts 11¹⁹ff., 27ff.. *The tetrarch* means Herod Antipas.

worshiping, literally, 'liturgizing' (λειτουργούντων), a word which had in the past, in pagan usage, meant the undertaking of a piece of expense on behalf of a town or community, either compulsorily or voluntarily, but which by the first century meant no more than 'holding public office', usually of a minor and expensive nature. In the LXX, however, it had been used to mean the sacrificial cult of the Jewish people (and Hebrews echoes this use: 8⁶, 9²¹). Paul himself uses the verb to describe the action of the Gentile churches in giving relief to the Church of Jerusalem (Rom. 15²⁷), and the noun (λειτουργία) to describe the same subject (2 Cor. 9¹²), and also his own service in the ministry of the gospel, using sacrificial language (Phil. 2¹⁷, ³⁰). Here it clearly means worship (though not liturgical worship). The question arises, who conducted this worship? The syntax and grammar are wholly in favour of the prophets and teachers as the subject of the verb *were worshiping*, rather than a more indefinite 'they', meaning the authorities or the people at large. There is a little support in sub-apostolic literature for prophets and teachers conducting worship in the early Church (*Didache*, xiii. 3, xv. 1).

This laying-on of hands is less likely to be ordination than blessing. It is true that it is during this journey that Paul and Barnabas are called 'apostles' (14⁴, ¹⁴), and nowhere else in Acts. But 'apostles' here could mean no more than 'representatives', i.e., people sent out (of the Church of Antioch), corresponding to the Jewish *shaliach*,

4   So, being sent out by the Holy Spirit, they went down to
5 Seleucia; and from there they sailed to Cyprus. When they
   arrived at Salamis, they proclaimed the word of God in the
   synagogues of the Jews. And they had John to assist them.
6 When they had gone through the whole island as far as
   Paphos, they came upon a certain magician, a Jewish false
7 prophet, named Bar-Jesus. He was with the proconsul,
   Sergius Paulus, a man of intelligence, who summoned
8 Barnabas and Saul and sought to hear the word of God. But
   Elymas the magician (for that is the meaning of his name)
   withstood them, seeking to turn away the proconsul from
9 the faith. But Saul, who is also called Paul, filled with the

---

a use which does occur elsewhere in the N.T. (John 13^{16}; Rom. 16^7;
2 Cor. 8^{23}; Phil. 2^{25}). According to Daube, the *shaliach* was not
appointed by the 'leaning' or laying-on of hands as an act of ordination. Acts differs perceptibly from the Pastoral Epistles in showing no
special interest in the subject of ordination.

4   *Seleucia* was the port of Antioch.
5   *Salamis* is the main harbour of Cyprus in the part facing Syria.
6–8   *Paphos* is in the south-west of the island. A L. Sergius Paullus is
known to have been a Curator of the Banks and Channel of the Tiber,
along with others, in the reign of Claudius. It is quite possible that
he went to be proconsul of Cyprus after holding this position. It is
now no longer thought likely that he is the 'Paulus proconsul' referred
to in an inscription found at Soli in Cyprus (which may refer to an
earlier period). How Luke comes to say that the name *Bar-Jesus*
means, when translated (or rendered differently), *Elymas* is a baffling
problem, for it certainly does not. Various conjectures have been
made to explain this strange statement: that Luke had before him
the story of Elymas in two variant forms, one about somebody called
Elymas and another about somebody called Bar-Jesus; that the
reading of the 'Western' text at this point (v. 8), Hetoimas, points
either to a word behind Bar-Jesus, of which it is a corruption, meaning
'ready' (ἔτοιμος), or to a Jew mentioned by Josephus called Atomos,
who devoted himself to magic; or that there is a corruption here
which makes it impossible to reconstruct the original text; or that
Bar-Jesus was the man's Aramaic name and Elymas or Hetoimas the
name he used in Greek-speaking circles.
9   The change from Saul to Paul here has been remarked upon by

Holy Spirit, looked intently at him and said, 'You son of the devil, you enemy of all righteousness, full of all deceit and villainy, will you not stop making crooked the straight paths of the Lord? And now, behold, the hand of the Lord is upon you, and you shall be blind and unable to see the sun for a time.' Immediately mist and darkness fell upon him and he went about seeking people to lead him by the hand. Then the proconsul believed, when he saw what had occurred, for he was astonished at the teaching of the Lord.

Now Paul and his company set sail from Paphos, and came to Perga in Pamphylia. And John left them and returned to Jerusalem; but they passed on from Perga and came to Antioch of Pisidia. And on the sabbath day they went into

---

many commentators. It was very common for Jews to have two names, one an Aramaic and one a Greek or Latin one, the second often either translating the first or sounding like it. There are several examples in the N.T. (Cephas—Petros; Simon—Niger; John— Marcus) and in the Apocrypha (Menahem—Menelaus; Jesus—Jason); Luke never suggests that Paul only at this point adopted the name Paul. No doubt he introduces the second version of Paul's name here because the mention of another Paulus makes it necessary for him to mention Saul as Paul for people who knew already that Saul had this other name (another slight indication that he is writing for the Roman Church), and because the introduction of Saul's Gentile name appropriately heralds his mission to the Gentiles.

the proconsul believed. Nothing is said about his having been baptized, and it is most unlikely that a man holding an official position like that of Sergius Paulus could have submitted to the abjuration of all forms of pagan religion which baptism, and with it full membership of the Christian Church, then entailed. It is probable that in the original story it was simply recorded that Sergius Paulus was greatly impressed and that in the process of the transmission of the story this was improved into the statement that he believed.

his company suggests more than merely Barnabas and John Mark, but the Greek does not demand more than this number. It may be, however, that there were others as well as these two accompanying Paul on this journey.

Pisidian Antioch was the chief town of the southern part of the

15 the synagogue and sat down. After the reading of the law and the prophets, the rulers of the synagogue sent to them, saying, 'Brethren, if you have any word of exhortation for
16 the people, say it.' So Paul stood up, and motioning with his hand said:

17 'Men of Israel, and you that fear God, listen. The God of this people Israel chose our fathers and made the people great during their stay in the land of Egypt, and with up-
18 lifted arm he led them out of it. And for about forty years he
19 bore with[a] them in the wilderness. And when he had destroyed seven nations in the land of Canaan, he gave them their land as an inheritance, for about four hundred and fifty
20 years. And after that he gave them judges until Samuel the
21 prophet. Then they asked for a king; and God gave them

<hr>

a Other ancient authorities read cared for (Dt. 1. 31)

<hr>

province of Galatia and a Roman colony (Colonia Caesarea). Its Jewish population has been evidenced by an inscription.

15　　*rulers of the synagogue* are a committee who are responsible for the synagogue, bearing a title of honour rather than of office. The title is found in papyri referring to Jewish communities in Ptolemaic Egypt.

16–41　　This speech is addressed both to Jews and to sympathetic Gentiles (*you that fear God*, vv. 16 and 26). But its structure follows the usual pattern of Lukan speeches to Jews. There is more purely Lukan material here than in any kerygmatic speech hitherto, but even here we may detect some earlier materials.

17 ff.　　These verses are meant to lead up to the rule of David and the promise made to him. It is possible that these details about the history of Israel are given because the Gentiles present could not be expected to be well acquainted with it.

19, 20　　The four hundred and fifty years of this account are not directly supported by the Hebrew text of the O.T., but are found in the Armenian and Latin Vulgate versions. Luke may have meant it to refer to the whole period from the Exodus to Samuel. Variations in reproducing the chronology given in the O.T. are to be found in Josephus, and were probably quite common in popular tradition at the time. Modern scholars would regard 450 years as much too long a time to assign to the period of the Judges.

Saul the son of Kish, a man of the tribe of Benjamin, for forty years. And when he had removed him, he raised up David to be their king; of whom he testified and said, "I have found in David the son of Jesse a man after my heart, who will do all my will." Of this man's posterity God has brought to Israel a Savior, Jesus, as he promised. Before his coming John had preached a baptism of repentance to all the people of Israel. And as John was finishing his course, he said, "What do you suppose that I am? I am not he. No, but after me one is coming, the sandals of whose feet I am not worthy to untie."

'Brethren, sons of the family of Abraham, and those among you that fear God, to us has been sent the message of this salvation. For those who live in Jerusalem and their rulers, because they did not recognize him nor understand the utterances of the prophets which are read every sabbath, fulfilled these by condemning him. Though they could charge him with nothing deserving death, yet they asked Pilate to have him killed. And when they had fulfilled all that

---

This conflation of proof-texts (Ps. 89^{20}; 1 Sam. 13^{14}; Isa. 44^{28}) reappears in *1 Clement* (date, about 96). Perhaps Luke here is reproducing an earlier collection of proof-texts.

This (for Luke's speeches) unusual emphasis on John's inferiority to Christ is thought to be directed against circles who claimed that John the Baptist was the Messiah; cp. 18^{25}–19$^{3,\ 4}$. The difference in wording between the disclaimer attributed here to John and his words in Luke 3^{16} have led Dodd to conclude that Luke is here relying on a source different from that which he used in his Gospel (*Historical Tradition in the Fourth Gospel*, pp. 255, 257).

Ignorance is again attributed to those who killed Jesus; here it is not represented as excusable, as it is in 3^{17}. But, in typical Lukan fashion, all the blame is put on the Jewish authorities and none on Pilate.

It is only the condensed style, and not Luke's deliberate intention, that represents the Jews as burying Jesus.

was written of him, they took him down from the tree, and
30, 31 laid him in a tomb. But God raised him from the dead; and
for many days he appeared to those who came up with him
from Galilee to Jerusalem, who are now his witnesses to the
32 people. And we bring you the good news that what God pro-
33 mised to the fathers, this he has fulfilled to us their children
by raising Jesus; as also it is written in the second psalm,

> "Thou art my Son,
> today I have begotten thee."

34 And as for the fact that he raised him from the dead, no
more to return to corruption, he spoke in this way,

> "I will give you the holy and sure blessings of David."

---

31   This statement excludes Paul as a witness to the Resurrection
(which was the claim he made for himself, 1 Cor. 9[1], 15[3-9]). But it
does imply that a larger number than simply the Twelve were
witnesses of the Resurrection.

33   There is uncertainty about the text here. 'This he has fulfilled to
our children' is clearly the best-attested reading, of which the other
readings, 'to their children for us' and 'to their children', are alterations designed to make sense, as the best-attested reading makes no
sense. The translation in the RSV text is a smoothing-out of another
reading ('to the children us') which looks very like an attempt to
elucidate the original reading.

34   *the holy and sure blessings of David* is a smooth translation of a very
rough passage. Literally it runs 'I will give you the holy things of
David the sure things', the last eight words being an exact reproduction of the LXX translation of Isa. 55[3], 'even the sure mercies of
David', and the LXX Greek is as unintelligible as the English literal
translation of it. A recent suggestion is that 'the holy things' means
Christ, as the concrete manifestation of God's holiness, but this
interpretation strains the meaning of the words too far. The best
explanation is that given by Lake and Cadbury in their commentary.
They point out that it was a well-known principle of exegesis among
the Rabbis to explain an obscure passage by means of another one
(in almost any part of the O.T.) like it. This is what the argument of
this speech is doing here. 'I will give you the holy things' (substituting
'I will give', $\delta\acute{\omega}\sigma\omega$, for the LXX 'I will appoint', $\delta\iota\alpha\theta\acute{\eta}\sigma\omega\mu\alpha\iota$) is
explained by Ps. 16[10], 'Thou shalt not give thy Holy One' (the word
'holy' ($\acute{o}\sigma\iota\sigma$) is the same in each passage). The earlier passage, Isa.

Therefore he says also in another psalm,

"Thou wilt not let thy Holy One see corruption."

For David, after he had served the counsel of God in his own generation, fell asleep, and was laid with his fathers, and saw corruption; but he whom God raised up saw no corruption. Let it be known to you therefore, brethren, that through this man forgiveness of sins is proclaimed to you, and by him every one that believes is freed from everything from which you could not be freed by the law of Moses. Beware, therefore, lest there come upon you what is said in the prophets:

"Behold, you scoffers, and wonder, and perish;

for I do a deed in your days,

a deed you will never believe, if one declares it to you."'

As they went out, the people begged that these things might be told them the next sabbath. And when the meeting of the synagogue broke up, many Jews and devout converts

---

55^3, then, must, so the argument runs, refer to the Resurrection, meaning 'I will restore to you the Holy One of David, the faithful one'. Verses 36 and 37 go on to explain that 'the Holy One' could not mean David; it must therefore refer to the Messiah. It should be noted that this argument turns entirely upon the LXX translation, for 'the holy things' does not appear in the Hebrew text of Isa. 55^3. But at the same time it is a thoroughly Rabbinic argument; it is hard to imagine that Luke could have invented it, though it could easily have been born in the fertile, Pharisaic, mind of Paul. No doubt Luke inherited it, and quite possibly from Paul.

Here we meet Pauline language—the believer is given righteousness (*freed* is literally 'justified') which the Law could not give. Luke evidently had some acquaintance with Pauline vocabulary.

These verses are preparing for the rejection of the Jews in favour of the Gentiles. The LXX at Hab. 1^5 translates the Hebrew word 'among the nations' as 'you scorners', and the reading which accounts for this translation is found also in the Hebrew text followed by the author of the Habakkuk Commentary among the literature of the Dead Sea Sect.

devout converts to Judaism disguises an odd phrase, 'devout ones to Judaism followed Paul and Barnabas, who spoke to them and urged them to continue in the grace of God.

44 The next sabbath almost the whole city gathered together
45 to hear the word of God. But when the Jews saw the multitudes, they were filled with jealousy, and contradicted what
46 was spoken by Paul, and reviled him. And Paul and Barnabas spoke out boldly, saying, 'It was necessary that the word of God should be spoken first to you. Since you thrust it from you, and judge yourselves unworthy of eternal life, behold,
47 we turn to the Gentiles. For so the Lord has commanded us, saying,

"I have set you to be a light for the Gentiles,
that you may bring salvation to the uttermost parts of the earth."'

48 And when the Gentiles heard this, they were glad and glorified the word of God; and as many as were ordained to
49 eternal life believed. And the word of the Lord spread
50 throughout all the region. But the Jews incited the devout

---

proselytes'; the 'devout ones' (i.e. Gentiles attracted towards Judaism, who attended the synagogue but could keep little of the Law and the *Halakah*, for they were not circumcised), and the 'proselytes' (i.e. Gentiles who were entirely converted to Judaism, had been circumcised, and kept the whole Law and *Halakah*) were two different classes. We may suspect an original corruption; perhaps an 'and' has fallen out.

44–52   It is possible to envisage this very general summary as referring to the same events as are referred to in a much more direct and first-hand way when Paul in his letter to the Galatians speaks of his first evangelizing among them (Gal. $3^{1, 2}$, $4^{12–17}$). They are Gentiles, but are open to pressure from Jews, and they are acquainted with Barnabas (Gal. $2^{11, 13}$). Lake and Cadbury even suggest that Gal. 4^{14} ('you received me as an angel of God') refers to the identification of Paul with Hermes (Acts 14^{12}).

46   Here the Jews of Asia Minor are warned. Later those in Greece (18^6) and later still the Jews in Rome ($28^{25–28}$) will receive the same warning.

women of high standing and the leading men of the city, and stirred up persecution against Paul and Barnabas, and drove them out of their district. But they shook off the dust from their feet against them, and went to Iconium. And the disciples were filled with joy and with the Holy Spirit.

Now at Iconium they entered together into the Jewish synagogue, and so spoke that a great company believed, both of Jews and of Greeks. But the unbelieving Jews stirred up the Gentiles and poisoned their minds against the brethren. So they remained for a long time, speaking boldly for the Lord, who bore witness to the word of his grace, granting signs and wonders to be done by their hands. But the people of the city were divided; some sided with the Jews, and some with the apostles. When an attempt was made by both Gentiles and Jews, with their rulers, to molest them and to stone them, they learned of it and fled to Lystra and Derbe, cities of Lycaonia, and to the surrounding country; and there they preached the gospel.

Iconium (the modern Konja) was about 95 miles from Antioch. It was a centre of trade and a Roman colony (Colonia Claudiconium), though the date of the establishment of the colony is not certain (the reign either of Claudius, 41–54, or of Hadrian, 118–38). Politically it was in the province of Galatia.

Only here and in v. 14 are Paul and Barnabas called 'apostles' in Acts. In 1 Cor. 9[6] Paul associates Barnabas very closely with his own work as an apostle, without actually calling him an apostle. We have already noticed (see above, on 13[3], pp. 139–40) that 'apostle' can be used as meaning no more than 'representative' in the N.T., and it may be that Luke means the word in this sense in these two passages. But Conzelmann may be right in suspecting a source here.

Lystra (the modern Zoldera) was about 26 miles from Iconium, and was made a Roman colony (Colonia Iulia Felix Gemina Lustra), trial, admits that Apollonius did not deliver it (ibid., viii. 7).

8   Now at Lystra there was a man sitting, who could not use his feet; he was a cripple from birth, who had never walked.

9   He listened to Paul speaking; and Paul, looking intently at

10 him and seeing that he had faith to be made well, said in a loud voice, 'Stand upright on your feet.' And he sprang up

11 and walked. And when the crowds saw what Paul had done, they lifted up their voices, saying in Lycaonian, 'The gods

12 have come down to us in the likeness of men!' Barnabas they called Zeus, and Paul, because he was the chief speaker, they

13 called Hermes. And the priest of Zeus, whose temple was in

---

8–18   It has been suggested that even poor ignorant Lystrans could not have been so much impressed by two wandering Jewish exorcists as to do sacrifice to them. But Lucian, writing of a period about a century later, alleges of the people of Abounoteichos, a little town of Paphlagonia, that their reaction to the arrival of Alexander (the very successful prophet and wonder-worker against whom Lucian is writing) was that they believed him to be 'the god visible' (ἐναργῆ τὸν θεόν) and 'they were astonished, and they began to make prayers to him and to worship him' (ἐτεθήπεσαν καὶ εὔχοντο καὶ προσεκύνουν, *Alexander the False Prophet*, 13). Again, one of the charges made against Apollonius of Tyana, when he was tried before the Emperor Domitian (81–96) was that he allowed himself to be worshipped as a god (Philostratus, *Life of Apollonius of Tyana*, viii. 5). That Philostratus' account of Apollonius' trial before Domitian is historically reliable seems to be shown by the fact that Philostratus, even though he has a speech ready to put into Apollonius' mouth as a defence at this under Augustus.

10   The addition in MSS. CDE 614 and some versions and Fathers of the words 'in the name of the Lord Jesus Christ' to the words *Stand upright on your feet* is no doubt not original, but may reflect an early formula of exorcism.

12   Ovid in his *Metamorphoses* tells a story of a devoted couple, Philemon and Baucis, who lived approximately in this neighbourhood, being visited by Zeus and Hermes, and it is thought by some that this story may have influenced Luke's account here, or that the story may point to the existence of a local cult here of these two gods. But it is likely that the Lycaonians in fact worshipped local, non-Olympian deities, and that these had been vaguely identified with the more cosmopolitan Greek gods—a process which had taken place all over the Roman Empire. Philemon and Baucis are really irrelevant.

front of the city, brought oxen and garlands to the gates and wanted to offer sacrifice with the people. But when the apostles Barnabas and Paul heard of it, they tore their garments and rushed out among the multitude, crying, 'Men, why are you doing this? We also are men, of like nature with you, and bring you good news, that you should turn from these vain things to a living God who made the heaven and the earth and the sea and all that is in them. In past generations he allowed all the nations to walk in their own ways; yet he did not leave himself without witness, for he did good and gave you from heaven rains and fruitful seasons, satisfying

---

It is uncertain whether *the gates* are those of the temple or of the city.

Tearing the garments is a sign of dissociation of the person who does it from blasphemy which others are committing (Mark 14[63]).

This speech is a short one, but it is of peculiar interest. It is the first speech made to a purely pagan audience (for Cornelius and his group can hardly be called purely pagan, 10[34–43]), and it is totally different from any that has occurred hitherto. It represents in fact a new type of Lukan speech, a speech to Gentiles. The structure is quite different from that of the speeches to Jews, and the argument is different. It has only one parallel in Acts, and that is Paul's speech on the Areopagus (17[22–31]). Its argument runs simply: You are worshipping false gods; we bring you news of the true God; in fact he has already brought himself to your notice, if you would recognize him (for a more detailed examination of the origin of this argument, see on 17[22–31], below, pp. 178–83). It is wholly unlikely either that Luke invented this argument, or that he is simply reproducing the propaganda of the Church of his day, though he certainly is clothing the argument in his own words.

Cp. 1 Thess. 1[9] 'you turned to God from idols, to serve a living and true God'.

The ignorance of God shown by the Gentiles is here excusable. Paul in Rom. 1[20ff.] regards it as anything but excusable. But in Rom. 3[25] he speaks of the 'divine forbearance' which had 'passed over former sins'. And we have already seen examples in Luke of ignorance regarded as both excusable and culpable (Acts 3[17], 13[27]).

If there is any biblical justification for holding Harvest Thanksgiving services, it is this verse; but it is worth noting that this verse applies to people who had not yet heard the Christian gospel.

18 your hearts with food and gladness.' With these words they
scarcely restrained the people from offering sacrifice to them.

Acts 15¹¹⁻²¹ᵃ in Codex Bezae in Greek.

19 But Jews came there from Antioch and Iconium; and
having persuaded the people, they stoned Paul and dragged
20 him out of the city, supposing that he was dead. But when

the disciples gathered about him, he rose up and entered the
city; and on the next day he went on with Barnabas to Derbe.

Acts 15[11-21a] in Codex Bezae in Latin.

Derbe was for long unidentified, so small and obscure a place was
it. It has now been identified by an inscription as Kerti Hūyūk, 15
miles NNE. of Karaman-Laranda. The very insignificance of the

21 When they had preached the gospel to that city and had made many disciples, they returned to Lystra and to Iconium and
22 to Antioch, strengthening the souls of the disciples, exhorting them to continue in the faith, and saying that through many
23 tribulations we must enter the kingdom of God. And when they had appointed elders for them in every church, with prayer and fasting, they committed them to the Lord in whom they believed.

24   Then they passed through Pisidia, and came to Pamphylia.
25 And when they had spoken the word in Perga, they went
26 down to Attalia; and from there they sailed to Antioch, where they had been commended to the grace of God for the
27 work which they had fulfilled. And when they arrived, they

---

place argues strongly for the authenticity of its inclusion by Luke in this account.

22   *the faith*, meaning the Christian religion, is a use of the word 'faith' ($\pi i \sigma \tau i s$) which is unknown in Paul's letters, but found in the Pastoral Epistles (cp. 1 Tim. 1[19], 4[1, 6], 5[8], 6[10, 12, 21]; 2 Tim. 3[8], 4[7]; Titus 1[13], 2[2]). But Paul's use of the word in Gal. 1[23], 3[23, 25]; 1 Cor. 15[14, 17], 16[13]; 2 Cor. 13[5]; Phil. 1[27], 2[17] approaches this meaning.

23   The appointment of presbyters or *elders* (there is apparently no question of the laying-on of hands) at this point has been questioned by some commentators. There can be little doubt that by the time Luke was writing presbyters were functioning in a great many churches. But did Paul and Barnabas appoint them as early as this? Paul in his letters never mentions elders. He mentions 'bishops and deacons' (Phil. 1[1]), and 'those who are over you in the Lord' (1 Thess. 5[12]); and in his list of functions performed by Christians as a calling from the Spirit in 1 Cor. 12[28] he mentions 'administrators' ($\kappa v \beta \epsilon \rho v \dot{\eta} \sigma \epsilon \iota s$). Luke seems to equate presbyters and bishops in Acts 20[17, 28]. It is therefore likely that Paul appointed some persons in the churches which he founded to perform the function of oversight, but that he did not call them presbyters, and that Luke, looking back some years later, equates these with presbyters. But this anachronism is not enough to prove Luke totally out of touch with Paul's generation. It is likely that there were elders functioning in the Church of Jerusalem in Paul's lifetime.

27   It is, as we have seen, unlikely that this was in fact Paul's first

gathered the church together and declared all that God had
done with them, and how he had opened a door of faith to
the Gentiles. And they remained no little time with the
disciples.

BUT some men came down from Judea and were teaching
the brethren, 'Unless you are circumcised according to the

---

enterprise in evangelizing Gentiles. But it was the first effort of his in
this direction about which Luke had information.

III. THE CHURCH SPREADS TO THE GENTILES. CHAPTERS 15:1–21:16

15: 1–35. *The Turning-point: the Jerusalem Church recognizes the
mission to the Gentiles*

Scholars have been trying to make the incident described
here conform with Paul's own account of his movements (in
the first two chapters of Galatians) for more than seventy years
now, and it cannot be said that they have achieved any clear
success. If Galatians was written after the Council here
described, why does Galatians make no mention of the
important decisions taken there, and why does Paul say in it
that he had visited Jerusalem only twice since his conversion?
If Galatians was written before the Council described here,
how can we account for the resemblance of Galatians to
Romans, and how can Luke describe Paul's first evangelization of the Galatian churches as taking place directly before
this Council?[1] If Gal. 2^{1-10} corresponds to Acts 15^{1-29} why is
there no mention of Titus and John in Acts? Why does Luke
attribute the demand for universal circumcision, or at least
for the denial of table-fellowship, to a small group of Pharisees
(Acts 15^5), but Paul to the party of James (Gal. 2^{12})? Why does
Paul locate the *no small dissension* in Antioch but Luke in
Jerusalem? Why does Paul give the impression that he had
been evangelizing Gentiles for some considerable time already

[1] This is assuming that the churches addressed in Galatians are South
Galatian and not North Galatian churches. See above, pp. 19, 20.

(Gal. 2²), whereas Luke represents this as the first time the evangelizing of the Gentiles by Paul and Barnabas had been seriously considered by the Jerusalem Church? Finally, how is it that this account represents the very serious dissension about the terms upon which Gentiles were to be admitted to the Church as having been finally and satisfactorily settled at this Council, whereas it is clear from 2 Cor. 10–13 and Phil. 3², ³ (not to mention Romans) that the question of whether Gentile Christians should be circumcised remained a very live issue during the whole period of Paul's ministry that we can follow through his letters?

A very large number of theories have been advanced in the attempt to answer these questions.[1] The more recent of them have tended to abandon the attempt to identify Acts 15¹⁻²⁹ with any incident that could be imagined in Paul's real career, and to relegate the account, in whole or part, to Luke's capacity for literary reconstruction. As Haenchen says, conjectural sources lying behind Acts 15 have faded into the background the more Luke's motives for depicting this scene are appreciated. Scholars who take this line have solid evidence to support their views. The most striking point is that the speech attributed to James (15¹³⁻²¹) contains a quotation from the O.T., part of which is found only in the LXX, and that James's argument rests upon that part. The historical James, brother of the Lord, the acknowledged leader of the Aramaic-speaking Church of Jerusalem, could not conceivably have made a speech like this. Therefore Luke composed it. The important parts of the chapter consist of two speeches, those of Peter and of James. That of James is certainly artificial. Is it not very likely that Peter's speech is artificial too? Then is it not very likely that Luke composed the whole scene? Certainly Acts 15¹⁻³⁰ is largely written in his usual style.

It is not difficult to perceive why Luke wished to paint this particular scene, and indeed to make it the turning-point of the whole plot and strategy of his book. Hitherto the evangelization of the Gentiles had been unplanned, almost accidental, but henceforward the book is to be occupied exclusively with this enterprise. Hitherto the Twelve had been, at least

[1] For an able summary of the more important of them, see C. S. C. Williams's Commentary, pp. 24–33.

nominally, the leaders of the expansion of the Church. Henceforward Paul, and Paul alone, is to occupy the centre of attention. Peter and the apostles disappear from the narrative. Chapter 15 does make, artistically considered, an excellent transition-piece. The Church of Jerusalem, where the apostles still are, gives its blessing to the mission to the Gentiles. Recalling that Peter had begun the process by receiving Cornelius, the apostles hand the initiative to Paul and Barnabas. The controversy about circumcision and the *Halakah* is settled. The Church has burst the swaddling-bands of Judaism.

It seems best to adopt this point of view. The 'Apostolic Council' is an imaginative reconstruction by Luke, designed to serve the purposes of his narrative and the lessons which he wished to convey, useful for effecting a transition between two missionary journeys about both of which he had some solid information. It is a carefully designed water-shed between a period of the Church's expansion about which Luke was often little informed, to reconstruct which he had usually little more than fragmentary material, and a period where his information, though neither complete nor exhaustive, was fuller, more detailed, and more reliable, because it was a period during which he himself had been a member of the Church and in some of whose events he had participated.

But there is one piece of material in Acts 15 which the most radical scholars have found difficult to explain away altogether, and that is the 'decree' and the letter accompanying it (Acts 15$^{20-21, 23-29}$). There are a number of facts which make it very difficult to reject this as just another of Luke's 'reconstructions'. In the first place, there is quite a lot of evidence to suggest that at least two of the four prohibitions in it were still being observed in various parts of the Gentile Church much later—the prohibitions against eating meat offered to idols and the ban on meat with the blood in it.[1] The decree itself is clearly founded on passages in the Pentateuch laying down conditions for the foreigner who lives among the people

[1] Rev. 2$^{14, 20}$; Justin, *Dialogue*, xxxiv. 8; Minucius Felix, *Octavius*, xxx. 6; Eusebius *Hist. Eccl.*, v. i. 26 (referring to the persecution of A.D. 177 in Gaul); Tertullian, *Apology*, ix. 13; Pseudo-Clementine *Homilies*, VII. iv. 2, viii. 1, VIII. 19. One might perhaps add Lucian, *On the Death of Peregrinus*, 16, where Lucian tells us that the Christians broke with Peregrinus because 'he was discovered, I believe, eating one of the things which are forbidden to them'.

of Israel, and in substance cannot have been simply invented by Luke. It obviously is an arrangement whereby the Jewish Christians are making concessions to Gentile Christians, rather than one whereby Gentile Christians are stating the maximum that they are prepared to tolerate in the way of observing Law and *Halakah*; this means that it is composed from the point of view of Jewish Christians who were in a position to lay down minimum requirements for the entry of Gentiles to the Church. This evidence suggests that it must be regarded as an early composition, made well before the Fall of Jerusalem in A.D. 70, and incompatible with the theory that Luke, writing for a mainly Gentile Church, either put it together himself or simply took it over from some contemporary Christian community where it had become established as a working compromise.

Again, there are some points in the letter accompanying it which demand explanation. Why is it addressed *to the brethren who are of the Gentiles in Antioch and Syria and Cilicia* (15^{23})? According to Luke's narrative, it was Gentiles in Galatia or Lycaonia (i.e., in Pisidian Antioch, Iconium, Derbe, and Lystra) whose conversion had necessitated this decree. Antioch, Syria, and Cilicia by no means covered all the field which Paul, or anybody else who had approached the Gentiles, had begun to plough, and indeed Luke had recorded no evangelizing of Gentiles in Cilicia. If this letter was wholly the work of Luke, we should expect a much wider Gentile Christian public to be addressed than this surprisingly narrow and selective one; in fact at Acts 16^4 Luke betrays that he assumes that the decree does apply to Christians beyond the confines of Antioch, Syria, and Cilicia. But we do know from Paul himself that before his second visit to Jerusalem it was in precisely these territories that he had been working: 'Then I went into the regions of Syria and Cilicia' (Gal. 1^{21}). This coincidence suggests that this decree and letter may have been addressed to the very Gentile Christians whom Paul had converted in his labours before his second visit to Jerusalem (Gal. 2^{1-10}), considerably earlier than the period to which Luke assigns it.

Finally, there is the mention of Judas and Silas (15^{27}) as the people entrusted with the carrying of the decree and letter. Luke, of course, includes Paul and Barnabas as well (15^{25}), but the presence of Paul and Barnabas at the whole proceedings has an air of superfluity about it. They make no reported speech. The people whom they have just been evangelizing are not mentioned. If Luke had had no sources but his own imagination for reconstructing this scene, he would certainly have left in Paul and Barnabas and omitted Judas (who has never been heard of before and is never heard of again) and Silas (who does indeed reappear, but, inexplicably, in Antioch (15⁴⁰) when he should have been in Jerusalem (15³⁴), suggesting that the letter comes from a source which Luke has not completely assimilated). This survey leaves a strong impression that though Luke had, of course, worked over the decree and letter, as he worked over all his sources, they nevertheless represent an authentic identifiable source and are not merely the product of his historical imagination.

But how do the decree and letter fit into the whole picture of the history of the admission of Gentiles to the Church? It is not impossible to envisage the circumstances in which it might have been produced. Paul tells us that after the satisfactory meeting which he had with James and Cephas and John during his second visit to Jerusalem after his conversion, in which it was recognized that Gentiles could be admitted to the Church without being circumcised (Gal. 2¹⁻¹⁰), he later had a sharp controversy at Antioch with Peter and with the emissaries of James, and even with Barnabas, over the question of table-fellowship between Jewish and Gentile Christians (2¹¹⁻²¹). He leaves this narrative entirely in the air. As far as his words in Galatians go, Paul might have remained in irreconcilable enmity to all these three persons for the rest of his career. But historical evidence is not lacking to tell us something about his later relations with the Church of Jerusalem and his attitude to the sort of subjects dealt with in the Decree. We know from 1 Corinthians, 2 Corinthians, and Romans that Paul during his last two years of activity on the Aegean littoral was occupied in collecting a contribution from the Gentile churches for the poverty-stricken Church of Jerusalem. To whom are we to imagine that he handed over this collection? There can be only one answer. All the evidence we possess suggests that when Paul reached Jerusalem with this collection, James the brother of the Lord was the dominating figure in the Church of Jerusalem. We are bound by the logic of the facts to conclude that at some point or other the Jerusalem Church came to terms with Paul's demand for table-fellowship between Jews and Gentiles within the Church, and that Paul was reconciled with and recognized by James.

We can trace some hints that he is not unaware of the possibility of people existing within the churches evangelized by him who will make demands or entertain scruples about meat offered to idols and meat with the blood in it (Rom. 14$^{1-4, 13-17}$; 1 Cor. 8$^{1-13}$). He does not indignantly repudiate their ideas. His words at 1 Cor. 5$^{1-13}$ suggest that there are several relationships regarded as legal by the Gentiles which Christians do not tolerate; he may well have in mind marriage within the prohibited degrees, which probably lies behind the word 'unchastity' in the decree. It has even been suggested that his language in Gal. 2^6 betrays the fact that he is aware of the existence of this decree. It is, in view of this evidence, not unreasonable to conclude that the decree and letter of Acts 15 represent an approach to the Gentile churches evangelized by Paul before his second visit to Jerusalem, an approach made by the Church of Jerusalem some time after the controversy between Paul on the one hand and Peter, James (or his representatives), and Barnabas on the other, offering a compromise on the basis of the Levitical laws for ritual observance by the sojourner among Israel, but conceding Paul's main demand, that circumcision was not to be enforced upon Gentile Christians. Whether this compromise was made before or after the writing of Galatians we cannot tell. On the whole it looks as if it was made before Galatians was written. Paul would not openly recognize this decree, because it affected, in his opinion, his right to order his own churches as God's own apostle according to his own ideas. This was the point for which he was contending so strongly in his letter to the Galatians (to whom, anyway, this decree had not been addressed). The decree had not been composed at any council at which he had been a consenting member, but it did not directly contravene the principles which seemed to him so much a matter of life and death, the freedom of Gentile Christians from circumcision and the maintenance of table-fellowship between Jewish and Gentile Christians. He could not openly recognize it; but he could not openly denounce it either.

Lastly, we need not regard Luke as forfeiting the right to

custom of Moses, you cannot be saved.' And when Paul and Barnabas had no small dissension and debate with them, Paul and Barnabas and some of the others were appointed to go

---

the name of historian by the 'reconstruction' which Acts 15[1-29] represents. History cannot be written as it happens, and the letter to the Galatians is not historical writing. It is evidence from which history can be written. Luke knew that there had been a controversy over circumcision; he had already hinted at this in Acts 11[1,2], and stated it more plainly in 15[1-5], and he refers to it again at 21[20ff.]. But he also knew that James and Paul were no longer at variance by the time that Paul was arrested, and that the Church of Jerusalem, in spite of pressure from extreme Judaizers among the Christians, had in the end accepted Gentiles into the Church without demanding circumcision from them. This was, from the point of view of the historian looking at the events in perspective, the outstandingly significant fact. The letter and decree had come into his hands, and he knew that they were relevant to the subject of the controversy. He did not know Galatians, nor the exact number of times Paul had visited Jerusalem after his conversion. He therefore composed this ideal scene, using as its historical core the letter and the decree. No contemporary historian would have blamed him for it. We can at least agree, in the light of the later history of Christianity, that he had got hold of the most significant fact, and that he presented it in a dramatic and effective way.

The 'Western' text has extensive differences here, designed to establish that it was a group from among the Pharisees who came down to Antioch, made their objections about circumcision, urged Paul and Barnabas to go to Jerusalem, and attacked them when they were there. The reasons for this alteration are not clear, but it may be that the interpolator did not want the impression created that the Church of Antioch (traditionally founded by Peter) had sent a deputation to receive instruction from the Church of Jerusalem.

were appointed disguises the fact that the Greek has 'they appointed Paul and Barnabas', and that it is uncertain who is the subject of the verb. It is possible that the sentence is meant to be vague and indefinite, as the RSV translates it. But it is possible too that the men of v. 1, who came down from Judaea, are the subject, as strict syntactical usage demands.

up to Jerusalem to the apostles and the elders about this
3 question. So, being sent on their way by the church, they
passed through both Phoenicia and Samaria, reporting the
conversion of the Gentiles, and they gave great joy to all the
4 brethren. When they came to Jerusalem, they were welcomed by the church and the apostles and the elders, and
5 they declared all that God had done with them. But some
believers who belonged to the party of the Pharisees rose up,
and said, 'It is necessary to circumcise them, and to charge
them to keep the law of Moses.'

6   The apostles and the elders were gathered together to con-
7 sider this matter. And after there had been much debate,
Peter rose and said to them, 'Brethren, you know that in the
early days God made choice among you, that by my mouth
the Gentiles should hear the word of the gospel and believe.
8 And God who knows the heart bore witness to them, giving

---

6   This Council is the last point at which *the apostles* appear in Acts.
No individual member of the Twelve is mentioned again. But Luke
wanted to represent the primitive Church as fully sanctioning Paul's
next great missionary move, so that he included the apostles, as
representing the authority of the primitive Church, with *the elders*,
whom he knew to be the controlling authority in the Church of
Jerusalem, along with James, at a very early period. It is likely that
by this time there were very few of the original Twelve left in
Jerusalem. Writing of an earlier period, Paul only mentions Peter
and John (Gal. 2⁹), unless the dark phrase 'those who were reputed
to be something' (Gal. 2⁶) includes other of the Twelve.
7   By *in the early days* Peter presumably is referring to the episode of the
reception of Cornelius into the Church, which, as we have seen, must
have taken place before A.D. 41. Luke chooses to bring this episode
into prominence, in order to emphasize that the mission to the Gentiles was inaugurated at an early period, by the apostle Peter himself,
and that it had been sanctioned by the Church of Jerusalem. It is
wholly unlikely that this obscure and isolated episode would have had
the prominence and the publicity which Luke attributes to it.
8–11   This is Pauline language, though Paul never speaks of anyone
actually cleansing his heart by faith. It was indeed Paul's conviction

them the Holy Spirit just as he did to us; and he made no distinction between us and them, but cleansed their hearts by faith. Now therefore why do you make trial of God by putting a yoke upon the neck of the disciples which neither our fathers nor we have been able to bear? But we believe that we shall be saved through the grace of the Lord Jesus, just as they will.'

And all the assembly kept silence; and they listened to Barnabas and Paul as they related what signs and wonders God had done through them among the Gentiles. After they finished speaking, James replied, 'Brethren, listen to me. Symeon has related how God first visited the Gentiles, to take out of them a people for his name. And with this the words of the prophets agree, as it is written,

"After this I will return,
and I will rebuild the dwelling of David, which has fallen;
I will rebuild its ruins,
and I will set it up,
that the rest of men may seek the Lord,

---

that it was impossible to keep the whole Law (Rom. 3^{20}, 4^{15}, $5^{13, 20}$, $7^{5, 7, 8}$, 8^3, 9^{31}; Gal. $3^{10, 21}$, 5^3, 6^{13}), though he never expressed it in this way. It is, however, odd to find Peter, the apostle to the Jews, expressing this sentiment.

Symeon is the Aramaic form of Simon, and the most Jewish way of spelling it. Peter (= Cephas) was, of course, only a nickname which Jesus himself had given to Simon bar Jonah (Mark 1^{16}, 3^{16}; Matt. $16^{17, 18}$). No doubt this is a touch of local colour on Luke's part (cp. 2 Peter 1^1). This is the last mention of Peter in Acts, no doubt because Luke had no information about his movements between this period (or a period before it) and his arrival at Rome much later, after the point at which Acts closes.

This verse of Amos (9^{12}) reads in translation of the Hebrew text 'that they (i.e. the people of Israel) may inherit what remains of Edom and of the other nations over which my name is named'. The LXX mistranslates it as 'That the remainder of men may seek out

and all the Gentiles who are called by my name,

18   says the Lord, who has made these things known from of old."

19   Therefore my judgment is that we should not trouble those

20   of the Gentiles who turn to God, but should write to them to abstain from the pollutions of idols and from unchastity

21   and from what is strangled^a and from blood. For from early

---

^a *Other early authorities omit* and from what is strangled

[me] and all the nations (Gentiles) over whom my name is called', thus producing a reference not in the Hebrew to the Gentiles' seeking God, and providing James with the main force of his argument.

18   This verse is either a comment by James or a confused memory of a Scriptural tag or the appearance of an otherwise unknown gloss in the Greek text of Amos. It cannot be satisfactorily identified with any text in the O.T. The suggestion that Luke is here using material from a book of proof-texts used in the early Church is an attractive one.

19   *my judgment* certainly suggests that Luke attributes considerable authority to James, more than to Peter, at least as far as the Jerusalem Church goes. It could be translated 'I decree' (ἐγὼ κρίνω). *Should not trouble* conveys indirectly one of the great purposes of this Decree, that Gentile Christians should be relieved of the necessity of being circumcised.

20   There has been much discussion of the text of the Decree, for the textual tradition is complicated, and the 'Western' text exhibits markedly different readings at this point, at v. 29, and at 21²⁵ where the text of the Decree recurs. The variation can be reduced to three different versions:

   (i) The main tradition of MSS. reads:
     (*a*) the pollution of idols; (*b*) unchastity; (*c*) what is strangled; (*d*) blood.
   (ii) The 'Western' text reads:
     (*a*) the pollution of idols: (*b*) unchastity; (*c*) blood; (*d*) 'and whatsoever they do not wish to happen to themselves not to do to others'.
   (iii) In 𝔓⁴⁵ (a third-century papyrus), in the Ethiopic Version, and in the third-century writer Origen (*Contra Celsum*, viii. 29) the text is as in (i), except that 'unchastity' is left out.

But this complicated situation is not very difficult to interpret. The state of text in (iii) is probably due simply to an early mistake of

generations Moses has had in every city those who preach
him, for he is read every sabbath in the synagogues.'

---

omission and nothing else. The text represented by (i) is no doubt the
original, and is to be interpreted in a ritual rather than a moral sense,
i.e., all these prohibitions are designed to preclude ritual uncleanness
in Gentiles according to the Jewish Law. Contact with idols produced
uncleanness; in fact, the words probably refer to food offered to
idols, for in v. 29 *what has been sacrificed to idols* (εἰδωλοθύτων, the
regular word for food offered to idols) has been substituted for
pollutions of idols. Equally unclean was marriage within the prohibited
degrees (which might be regarded as quite innocent by pagans). *What
is strangled* means animals killed in such a way that the blood was not
drained from them, and *blood* indicates meat which still has the blood
in it, by whatever means it may have been killed; to eat this was to
entail ritual uncleanness. These prohibitions about food derive from
Lev. 17^{10-15}, ritual regulations which apply to the 'sojourner' as well
as to the Israelite. But the 'Western' text, represented by (ii) here, has
chosen to moralize all these prohibitions. For it, idolatry is dis-
obedience to God, unchastity is fornication of any sort, *blood* means
murder, the spilling of blood; and as *what is strangled* cannot be
interpreted in a moralistic rather than a ritual sense, the interpolator
has here substituted a general moral maxim, put in the negative
form. The positive form of this, 'do-as-you-would-be-done-by', is
called the Golden Rule, and is well evidenced in ancient Jewish
ethical teaching. Clearly the interpolator saw no point in Jewish
ritual observances being imposed upon Christians, and decided that
the apostle really meant to give a series of general moral rules for
the Gentiles to observe. The fact that this involved assuming that the
apostles had issued an authoritative decree, after holding a council,
suggesting to Gentile Christians that murder was incompatible with
Christianity shows how far the 'Western' version of the Decree is from
reproducing its original form.

The relevance of this verse to James's argument, or indeed to the
tenor of the whole chapter, is obscure. It could mean: 'It ought by
now to be well known, even among Gentiles, that these prohibitions
are an essential part of Judaism, which Jews cannot allow the Gentile
Christians to forgo'; or that the Jewish-Christians need have no
special care taken of them by this Council, for the synagogue cares
for them already. Ropes has suggested that it refers to the quotation
from Amos in vv. 16 and 17: Amos' reference to the Gentiles' seeking the Lord is fulfilled in the synagogues of the widespread Jewish
communities of the Diaspora, where God's truth has long been proclaimed and where Gentiles have long come to listen to it.

22   Then it seemed good to the apostles and the elders, with the whole church, to choose men from among them and send them to Antioch with Paul and Barnabas. They sent Judas called Barsabbas, and Silas, leading men among the brethren,

23   with the following letter: 'The brethren, both the apostles and the elders, to the brethren who are of the Gentiles in

24   Antioch and Syria and Cilicia, greeting. Since we have heard that some persons from us have troubled you with words, unsettling your minds, although we gave them no instruc-

25   tions, it has seemed good to us in assembly to choose men and send them to you with our beloved Barnabas and Paul,

26   men who have risked their lives for the sake of our Lord

27   Jesus Christ. We have therefore sent Judas and Silas, who themselves will tell you the same things by word of mouth.

28   For it has seemed good to the Holy Spirit and to us to lay upon you no greater burden than these necessary things:

29   that you abstain from what has been sacrificed to idols and

---

22   *Judas called Barsabbas* may have been brother of the Joseph Barsabbas of 1²³. Silas is no doubt the figure of whom we shall hear more in Acts, and who is mentioned in 1 Thess. 1¹ and 2 Thess. 1¹ as writing the letters along with Paul, and in 2 Cor. 1¹⁹ as having preached with Paul in Corinth; in the last three references he is called Silvanus, but it is generally agreed that these are two forms of the same name. He reappears in 1 Pet. 5¹² as Peter's amanuensis in writing the letter.

24–26   Next after the opening sentence of Luke's Gospel (Luke 1¹⁻⁴), this is the most complex and, from a grammatical point of view, most carefully constructed sentence in the whole of Luke's extant work. It is therefore certain that Luke himself composed it, though this does not preclude the possibility of his reproducing here the substance of an earlier letter, as we have argued.

28   Haenchen suggests as a parallel to *it has seemed good to the Holy Spirit and to us* the phrase from a letter from the Roman Emperor (Augustus) 'it seemed good to me and to my council' (Josephus, *Antiquities*, xvi. 163).

from blood and from what is strangled[a] and from unchastity. If you keep yourselves from these, you will do well. Farewell.'

So when they were sent off, they went down to Antioch; and having gathered the congregation together, they delivered the letter. And when they read it, they rejoiced at the exhortation. And Judas and Silas, who were themselves prophets, exhorted the brethren with many words and strengthened them. And after they had spent some time, they were sent off in peace by the brethren to those who had sent them.[b] But Paul and Barnabas remained in Antioch, teaching and preaching the word of the Lord, with many others also.

And after some days Paul said to Barnabas, 'Come, let us return and visit the brethren in every city where we proclaimed the word of the Lord, and see how they are.' And Barnabas wanted to take with them John called Mark. But

[a] *Other early authorities omit* and from what is strangled
[b] *Other ancient authorities insert verse 34,* But it seemed good to Silas to remain there

---

Farewell is a very abrupt ending to a letter, unparalleled in any letter of Christians to Christians in the N.T. (unless we count Jas. 5[20], but James is not really a letter). But *you will do well* (εὖ πράξετε) is the future form of a very well-known greeting in contemporary secular correspondence—'Do well' (i.e., fare well, εὖ πράσσετε), so that the ending may not be as abrupt as it seems to us.

Judas and Silas have been called 'leading men among the brethren' in v. 22. Three passages in Hebrews (13[7, 17, 24]) use the same word (ἡγούμενοι) for leaders in the Church. Here the two are called prophets. We have already seen prophets taking the initiative twice (11[27ff.], 13[1ff.]). Early Christian literature fully supports the conclusion that prophets wielded considerable influence and authority in the early Church, before a stereotyped and well-defined official ministry developed.

This verse consists entirely of an addition by the 'Western' text, designed to eliminate the inconsistency between v. 33 and v. 40.

15: 36–16: 10. *The gospel brought as far as Troas*

Some time before Paul wrote 1 Corinthians, Barnabas and Paul

Paul thought best not to take with them one who had withdrawn from them in Pamphylia, and had not gone with them
39 to the work. And there arose a sharp contention, so that they separated from each other; Barnabas took Mark with him and
40 sailed away to Cyprus, but Paul chose Silas and departed, being commended by the brethren to the grace of the Lord.
41 And he went through Syria and Cilicia, strengthening the churches.

16 And he came also to Derbe and to Lystra. A disciple was there, named Timothy, the son of a Jewish woman who was
2 a believer; but his father was a Greek. He was well spoken

---

were reconciled, for at 1 Cor. 9[6] Paul mentions him as evangelizing in partnership with him in Corinth. Philem. 24 and Col. 4[10] mention Mark (who in the latter passage is described as Barnabas' cousin) as sending greetings with Paul; presumably therefore he too was later reconciled. We do not hear of Barnabas again in Acts.

40   We do not know how Silas reached Antioch; but if the Letter of the last chapter in reality applies to an earlier period there is no difficulty in believing that he was there and did accompany Paul.

41   *Syria and Cilicia* are in fact on the way from Antioch to Derbe and Lystra, but it is likely that Luke inserted this statement because the Letter which he had just given in his account of the Council had been addressed to Christians in Syria and Cilicia.

16: 1–3   Some scholars have found it impossible to believe that Paul could have so far compromised his principles as to circumcise Timothy, adducing particularly Gal. 2[3], where Paul apparently declares emphatically that Titus was not compelled to be circumcised. But it is possible to go too far in emphasizing Paul's rejection of the Law. There is no evidence at all that Paul ever believed that Jews should not be circumcised, and children of mixed marriages (such as Timothy) were counted as Jews by Jewish law, even if it was the mother who was Jewish. In the case of Titus, he was not a Jew; the Greek words at Gal. 2[3] (Ἕλλην ὤν) may mean 'because he was a Greek', not 'though he was a Greek'. Paul himself tells us 'To the Jews I became as a Jew in order to win Jews' (1 Cor. 9[20]). C. F. D. Moule has pointed out that Gal. 5[11] suggests that there were some ultra-radical anti-Semitic Christians to the 'left' even of Paul, who accused

of by the brethren at Lystra and Iconium. Paul wanted
Timothy to accompany him; and he took him and circumcised him because of the Jews that were in those places, for

Head of Christ from the Roman villa at Hinton St. Mary, Dorset, in
a mosaic floor, with the Chi Rho monogram and pomegranates signifying
eternity; date, fourth century.

they all knew that his father was a Greek. As they went on
their way through the cities, they delivered to them for
observance the decisions which had been reached by the
apostles and elders who were at Jerusalem. So the churches
were strengthened in the faith, and they increased in
numbers daily.

---

him of still preaching circumcision, and that Rom. 14 was written in
order to defend the Jewish Christian against the objections of the
Gentile Christians (*The Birth of the New Testament*, pp. 35, 51). We
have seen already that Paul must have come to terms with the wholly
Jewish Church of Jerusalem. Finally, what possible motive can we
attribute to Luke for inventing such an incident as the circumcision
of Timothy?

6   And they went through the region of Phrygia and Galatia,
     having been forbidden by the Holy Spirit to speak the word
7 in Asia. And when they had come opposite Mysia, they
     attempted to go into Bithynia, but the Spirit of Jesus did not
8 allow them; so, passing by Mysia, they went down to Troas.
9 And a vision appeared to Paul in the night: a man of Mace-
     donia was standing beseeching him and saying, 'Come over

---

6–10   This part of the journey is sketched by Luke in terms which are
         vaguer than his usual language when describing journeys. He men-
         tions no names of towns, and the expression *the region of Phrygia and
         Galatia* has given the commentators great trouble. Does it mean
         'Phrygia and the Galatian region', as the Greek would suggest, or
         'the Galatian part of Phrygia', as Ramsay urged? And what is meant
         by *Asia*? Does it mean the Roman province of Asia, which included
         an extensive territory, and which Paul and his companions could
         scarcely have failed to pass through? Or does it mean 'the Aegean
         coast near Ephesus' (C. S. C. Williams), a much smaller extent of
         territory? On the whole it is better to follow Lake (*The Beginnings of
         Christianity*, v, Additional Note XVIII) and conclude that Paul, having
         reached some town like Iconium, wanted to make for the Greek cities
         of the coast of what we now call Asia Minor ('Asia' in its narrower
         sense, as in Acts 2^9 and $19^{10, \, 11}$), but, prevented in that enterprise,
         turned north and, travelling through a part of Phrygia where there
         were several Celtic-speaking communities (who would be called
         Galatian), reached some point east of the mountain range of which
         the Mysian Mount Olympus is the highest point. According to the
         geographer Strabo, Mysia extended eastward as far as this. There
         Paul and his companions could easily have extended their journey
         into Bithynia, but they were prevented as before, turned westward
         instead, and travelled across Mysia to Troas. This would make sense
         of Luke's rather vague directions. If we do not regard these pro-
         hibitions to preach in vv. 6 and 7 as a mere literary device, we must
         put them down to some internal illumination experienced by Paul
         or by other members of the group, or to some combination of circum-
         stances interpreted by them as the guidance of God.

8   *Troas* was then a Roman colony, Colonia Alexandria Troas;
         cp. 20^{6ff}.

9   It has been suggested that the *man of Macedonia* was Luke himself,
         in view of the immediate occurrence of the first 'we' passage. But this
         is mere conjecture.

to Macedonia and help us.' And when he had seen the vision, immediately we sought to go on into Macedonia, concluding that God had called us to preach the gospel to them.

Setting sail therefore from Troas, we made a direct voyage to Samothrace, and the following day to Neapolis, and from there to Philippi, which is the leading city of the district[a]

[a] *The Greek text is uncertain*

Here begins the first 'we' passage. It lasts until v. 17, breaking off in the middle of the episode of the ventriloquist girl. If any ancient historian lapsed in the course of his narrative into the first person he certainly meant to give the reader the impression that he had been present at the events so described. There can be little doubt that this is the impression Luke meant to convey. There is no precedent in ancient history writing for an historian reproducing somebody else's 'we' source without giving notice to the reader and without transposing the first persons into thirds. If this is what Luke is doing here then, it is a unique example of this procedure, and the *onus probandi* is on those who think that he is following it. Presumably in this case he means the reader to conclude that he was present from the departure from Troas until the appearance of the ventriloquist girl, but not at the later episodes. This suggests that he was not a regular companion of Paul, as was Timothy or Silas, but a fellow traveller for part of his way.

16: 11–40. *The adventures of Paul and Silas at Philippi*

Neapolis is 130 miles from Troas as the crow flies, and *Philippi* is 9 miles from Neapolis. The full name was Colonia Iulia Augusta Philippensis. Luke describes it as *the leading city of the district of Macedonia*, literally 'the first of the district (μερίς) of Macedonia city'. The Roman province of Macedonia had the unusual characteristic of being divided into four *regiones*, sub-provinces. The Greek word corresponding to *regio* was μερίς. Each μερίς had a 'leading city' (πρώτη πόλις) as its capital. The verse here does not directly say that Philippi was the πρώτη πόλις of its region, though it comes very near to saying this. A possible analogy is provided in Lucian, who describes a certain Demostratus as 'first of Pontus' (τοῦ Πόντου πρῶτος), presumably meaning 'one of the leading men in the province of Pontus' (*Alexander the False Prophet*, 45). In that case we should perhaps translate the expression here as 'a leading city of the district of Macedonia' (meaning its district, or that district).

of Macedonia, and a Roman colony. We remained in this
13 city some days; and on the sabbath day we went outside the
gate to the riverside, where we supposed there was a place of
prayer; and we sat down and spoke to the women who had
14 come together. One who heard us was a woman named
Lydia, from the city of Thyatira, a seller of purple goods,
who was a worshiper of God. The Lord opened her
15 heart to give heed to what was said by Paul. And when
she was baptized, with her household, she besought us, saying, 'If you have judged me to be faithful to the Lord, come
to my house and stay.' And she prevailed upon us.

16   As we were going to the place of prayer, we were met by
a slave girl who had a spirit of divination and brought her
17 owners much gain by soothsaying. She followed Paul and
us, crying, 'These men are servants of the Most High God,
18 who proclaim to you the way of salvation.' And this she did
for many days. But Paul was annoyed, and turned and said
to the spirit, 'I charge you in the name of Jesus Christ to
come out of her.' And it came out that very hour.

19   But when her owners saw that their hope of gain was gone,
they seized Paul and Silas and dragged them into the market
20 place before the rulers; and when they had brought them

---

13   The river is the Gangites, 1½ miles west of the city. *Place of prayer*
(προσευχή) might be translated 'synagogue'.

14   Thyateira was famous as the centre of the industry connected with
manufacturing and dyeing purple cloth.

15   For other passages in the N.T. referring to Christian hospitality, see
Matt. 10⁴⁰; Rom. 12¹³; 1 Tim. 5¹⁰.

16   *a spirit of divination*, literally 'a spirit Python' (Python was originally
the snake-god who was supposed to supply the priestess at Delphi
with her oracles). No doubt this girl was trained to tell fortunes by
means of ventriloquism practised in a pretended trance.

20–24   The procedure applied to Paul and Silas in their arrest was normal,
on the assumption (which clearly was made by the magistrates) that

to the magistrates they said, 'These men are Jews and they are disturbing our city. They advocate customs which it is not lawful for us Romans to accept or practice.' The crowd joined in attacking them; and the magistrates tore the garments off them and gave orders to beat them with rods. And when they had inflicted many blows upon them, they threw them into prison, charging the jailer to keep them safely. Having received this charge, he put them into the inner prison and fastened their feet in the stocks.

But about midnight Paul and Silas were praying and singing hymns to God, and the prisoners were listening to them,

---

they were not Roman citizens. Private accusers make their charge, the accused (not being locally known to be of good standing) are imprisoned. The next move (which never took place) would have been to bring them for trial before the proconsul governing the province of Macedonia. The terms used for *magistrates, στρατηγοί,* was very widely used throughout the Hellenistic world for local city magistrates. Because Philippi was a Roman colony the term would correspond here to the Latin *duumviri.* Their officers, mentioned in v. 35 (where RSV calls them 'police'), are called ῥαβδοῦχοι in Greek, *lictores* in Latin.

The charge made by the accusers of the two missionaries that they are Jews suggests that Luke did not want to commend Christianity as a new form of Judaism. The serious charge is that of causing civil disturbance (v. 20). Jews had gained a reputation in the Roman Empire for causing disturbances and riots. It may be that it was at that time illegal to convert a Roman citizen to Judaism, but the evidence is not clear. But it certainly would add considerable odium to the charge of riot if it could also be said that the rioters were trying to convert honest citizens to an un-Roman way of life.

It is not difficult to produce parallels to the story of Paul and Silas experiencing the earthquake in prison and escaping as a result of it, ranging from Euripides' *Bacchae* to *The Testaments of the XII Patriarchs,* and certain features of this story are highly improbable, e.g., that a *great* earthquake should have taken place without apparently affecting any other house than the prison; that it should have had the effect of releasing the prisoners from their fetters, and moving the foundations of the prison without bringing the building down on top of them; and that the jailer should really have attempted suicide.

26 and suddenly there was a great earthquake, so that the foundations of the prison were shaken; and immediately all the doors were opened and every one's fetters were un-

27 fastened. When the jailer woke and saw that the prison doors were open, he drew his sword and was about to kill himself,

28 supposing that the prisoners had escaped. But Paul cried with a loud voice, 'Do not harm yourself, for we are all here.'

29 And he called for lights and rushed in, and trembling with

30 fear he fell down before Paul and Silas, and brought them

31 out and said, 'Men, what must I do to be saved?' And they said, 'Believe in the Lord Jesus, and you will be saved, you

32 and your household.' And they spoke the word of the Lord

33 to him and to all that were in his house. And he took them the same hour of the night, and washed their wounds, and

34 he was baptized at once, with all his family. Then he brought them up into his house, and set food before them; and he rejoiced with all his household that he had believed in God.

Fancy has been at work a little in this story. But parallels to the earthquake as a device for rescuing the heroes of a popular story from prison are rare, if not unobtainable, and earth tremors are common enough in that part of the world. The judgement of Lake is a sound one: 'It seems to me quite possible that the jailer, aware that he had with him two distinguished magicians and that they had been singing magic charms all night, released them in the belief that they were responsible for the earthquake. Naturally enough, the direct and indirect result of the earthquake were confused in tradition.'

30, 31   This question and reply may be a stereotyped formula from early Christian catechetical teaching.

33, 34   This baptism was certainly not by total immersion. It was a baptism performed very much on the spur of the moment, with very little preparatory teaching. But we do not know enough about early Christian baptism to deny that it was possible. We can be sure from his letter to the Philippians that Paul left the nucleus of a church in Philippi, where Christian teaching was given.

But when it was day, the magistrates sent the police, saying, 'Let those men go.' And the jailer reported the words to Paul, saying, 'The magistrates have sent to let you go; now therefore come out and go in peace.' But Paul said to them, 'They have beaten us publicly, uncondemned, men who are Roman citizens, and have thrown us into prison; and do they now cast us out secretly? No! let them come themselves and take us out.' The police reported these words to the magistrates, and they were afraid when they heard that they were Roman citizens; so they came and apologized to them. And they took them out and asked them to leave the city. So they went out of the prison, and visited Lydia; and when they had seen the brethren, they exhorted them and departed.

Now when they had passed through Amphipolis and Apollonia, they came to Thessalonica, where there was a synagogue of the Jews. And Paul went in, as was his custom, and for three weeks[a] he argued with them from the scriptures,

[a] Or sabbaths

The 'Western' text, whose interpolator feels that the narrative is not full enough at this point, here prefixes to the verse the sentence, 'The magistrates came together into the market-place and, recalling the earthquake which had taken place, became frightened and sent . . .'.

The magistrates would have had no right to cause Roman citizens to be beaten. Presumably they could always justify the beating of lesser men on the ground that this procedure was necessary in order to discover the truth from them; cp. Acts 22[23-29].

17: 1-15. *Paul at Thessalonica and Beroea*

It was about 33 miles from Philippi to *Amphipolis*, from Amphipolis to *Apollonia* about 30 miles, and from Apollonia to *Thessalonica* about 38 miles.

three weeks seems a short time, in view of the evidence of 1 and 2 Thessalonians and Philippians (see especially Phil. 4[9]) of a very thorough ministry of Paul in this region.

3 explaining and proving that it was necessary for the
Christ to suffer and to rise from the dead, and saying, 'This

4 Jesus, whom I proclaim to you, is the Christ.' And some of
them were persuaded, and joined Paul and Silas; as did a
great many of the devout Greeks and not a few of the leading

5 women. But the Jews were jealous, and taking some wicked
fellows of the rabble, they gathered a crowd, set the city in
an uproar, and attacked the house of Jason, seeking to bring

6 them out to the people. And when they could not find them,
they dragged Jason and some of the brethren before the city
authorities, crying, 'These men who have turned the world

7 upside down have come here also, and Jason has received
them; and they are all acting against the decrees of Caesar,

8 saying that there is another king, Jesus.' And the people and

---

4   *devout Greeks and leading women.* The 'Western' text divides these
into three groups, 'God-fearers, Greeks, and wives of leading men',
perhaps on the (incorrect) assumption that 'God-fearers' were Jews.
Though there is no precise parallel for the phrase *devout Greeks*, the
reading followed by RSV is preferable.

5–9   The action taken here corresponds precisely to what we know of
the internal affairs of Thessalonica at the time. It was a free city, i.e.
it had a great deal of autonomous power over its own affairs without
the necessity of invoking a Roman official. It was governed by
magistrates called 'politarchs', the precise word used by Luke
(vv. 6, 8), and an assembly or parliament, also mentioned by Luke
who calls it *demos* (v. 5, translated *people* in RSV; the word similarly
translated people in v. 8 is a different one, ὄχλος, and means the
whole population of the city generally, enfranchised citizens and
others). The Jews attempted to prosecute Paul and Silas before the
demos, but, failing to find them, prosecuted their host Jason before the
politarchs, who made him give security for the good conduct of his
guests. The procedure for *taking security* (v. 9, λαβεῖν τὸ ἱκανόν
corresponding to Latin *satis dare*) is evidenced as an official and legal
one. The accusation against Paul and Silas is vague; perhaps that is
why the magistrates did not act on the charge. They were not, as
magistrates of a free city, obliged to investigate charges of treason or
acts detrimental to the Emperor. But Luke may not have known the
precise terms of the charge.

the city authorities were disturbed when they heard this.
And when they had taken security from Jason and the rest,
they let them go.

The brethren immediately sent Paul and Silas away by
night to Beroea; and when they arrived they went into the
Jewish synagogue. Now these Jews were more noble than
those in Thessalonica, for they received the word with all
eagerness, examining the scriptures daily to see if these things
were so. Many of them therefore believed, with not a few
Greek women of high standing as well as men. But when the
Jews of Thessalonica learned that the word of God was proclaimed by Paul at Beroea also, they came there too, stirring
up and inciting the crowds. Then the brethren immediately
sent Paul off on his way to the sea, but Silas and Timothy remained there. Those who conducted Paul brought him as
far as Athens; and receiving a command for Silas and
Timothy to come to him as soon as possible, they departed.

Now while Paul was waiting for them at Athens, his spirit

Beroea, modern Verria, is about 50 miles south of Thessalonica on
the Via Egnatia.

Paul's letters, and indeed the whole literature of the N.T., reveal
to us how much early Christian teaching consisted of exposition of
the Scriptures of the O.T. and how great a part proof-texts played in
its doctrine: cp. 9[22], 17[2, 3].

According to this account Paul journeyed on to Athens, leaving
Silas and Timothy behind; they were to join him later. In 1 Thess.
3[1-6] it is made clear that Timothy accompanied Paul to Athens, that
from there he was sent back to Thessalonica, and that Timothy later
returned to him (presumably, but not certainly, at Athens), with
good news of the Christians at Thessalonica. But these are precisely
the small differences which one would expect to find between a
generally reliable account given later to a third party and a letter
written in the very midst of the events themselves.

17: 16–34. *Paul at Athens*

Apollonius of Tyana, a younger contemporary of Paul, remarked,

was provoked within him as he saw that the city was full of
17 idols. So he argued in the synagogue with the Jews and the
devout persons, and in the market place every day with those
18 who chanced to be there. Some also of the Epicurean and
Stoic philosophers met him. And some said, 'What would
this babbler say?' Others said, 'He seems to be a preacher of
foreign divinities'—because he preached Jesus and the resur-
19 rection. And they took hold of him and brought him to the
Areopagus, saying, 'May we know what this new teaching is

according to Philostratus, that the Athenians were 'fond of offering
sacrifice' (φιλοθύτας, *Life of Apollonius of Tyana*, iv. 19).

18   *Epicurean and Stoic philosophers* are mentioned because they were at
the time the most influential, and Luke wanted to show that he knew
this. The Stoics believed in a life after death. The doctrine of the
Resurrection of Christ would have been uncongenial to them, though
they did believe in a regular renewal of the whole world after
periodical destruction by fire. Both life after death and resurrection
would have been quite alien to Epicurean views. *Babbler* (σπερμολόγος)
must have meant originally a man who picks up different ideas as
a bird picks up different seeds, an intellectual magpie. It may well
have been coined first in Athens, though it was certainly used beyond
Athens. By now it must have acquired a more vaguely abusive sense.
It has been suggested that Paul's hearers assumed that he was trying
to induce them to worship a pair of foreign divinities, a male and
a female deity (as so often appeared in the ancient world), Jesus and
Anastasis (Resurrection).

19   *the Areopagus*: the exact location of this has been much disputed. It
could mean the ancient sacred meeting-place on the top of the hill
called (AV) Mars' Hill (Ἄρειος πάγος originally), where there would
have been little room for a crowd of hearers, though they could have
assembled on a high, broad ridge between the Areopagus and the
Acropolis, and presumably within earshot of the Areopagus. Or the
phrase could indicate, not a place, but a judicial court, the court of
the Areopagus, consisting of some of the senior citizens, which is
known to have existed at that time and to have been permitted some
jurisdiction, including the regulation of matters concerning education.
On this interpretation the phrase *in the middle of the Areopagus* would
mean 'at the hearing of the court of the Areopagus', and the speech
would be placed in the Agora, in front of the Stoa Basileios, where
the court met. Ramsay, Cadbury, and Gärtner argue for this,

which you present? For you bring some strange things to
our ears; we wish to know therefore what these things mean.'
Now all the Athenians and the foreigners who lived there
spent their time in nothing except telling or hearing something new.

So Paul, standing in the middle of the Areopagus, said:
'Men of Athens, I perceive that in every way you are very

Dibelius vigorously for the former site. In favour of Dibelius's view is
the fact that there is no sign at all in all Luke's account that Paul is
officially on trial before a court; in favour of the other view is the
distinct impression created by the whole incident that Paul was
speaking to an audience which he wanted to convert, and therefore
probably not a small one. Not very much is known about the powers
of the Areopagus court at this time. It may have had authority to
listen to philosophers expounding their views without formally
putting them on trial.

The second speech addressed to Gentiles who have had no contact
with Judaism, and a much more elaborate and complex one than the
earlier (14[15-17]), though it uses basically the same arguments. It is
pointless to ask the question here whether the speech embodies
a primitive pattern of preaching to Gentiles; there can have been no
such thing, because there were no Gentiles in the primitive Church.
There are, nevertheless, two divergent views on the origins of the
doctrine found in this speech. Norden and Dibelius tend to think that
it is composed almost solely of ideas drawn from contemporary
popular pagan philosophy, and has very little contact with Jewish or
biblical thought. Strong arguments can be produced in favour of this
view. For instance, *he gives to all men life and breath and everything* (v. 25)
and *Yet he is not far from each one of us* (v. 27) are Stoic-sounding sentiments. The Stoics used this word 'breath' ($\pi\nu o\eta$) in their system, and
a tag from Seneca can be quoted—*prope est ad te deus, tecum est, intus
est* (*Letters*, xii. 1). The statement that God *does not live in shrines made
by man* (v. 24) resembles another Senecan sentiment to the effect that
no temple is suitable for God, but *in suo cuique consecrandus est pectore*
(frag., quoted Lactantius *Div. Instit.* vi. 25). And the speech certainly
quotes a pagan poet (v. 28) voicing a rather Stoic idea.

But in a special study devoted to this speech B. Gärtner has
succeeded in making an even stronger case for another view (*The
Areopagus Speech and Natural Revelation*). He believes that the ideas
behind this speech can be shown to be, not reproductions of popular

23 religious. For as I passed along, and observed the objects
   of your worship, I found also an altar with this inscription,
   "To an unknown god". What therefore you worship as un-
24 known, this I proclaim to you. The God who made the
   world and everything in it, being Lord of heaven and earth,

---

philosophy, but thoroughly traditional Old Testament or Jewish ideas
which occasionally clothe themselves in Stoic expression (as will be
shown below). No doubt Conzelmann is correct in concluding that
what we really find in this speech is Jewish Hellenistic ideas, used for
long against pagan religion, and taken over by Christian propaganda
directed towards Gentiles. Whether these ideas are compatible with,
or identical with, Paul's doctrines is a question which will be discussed
in the course of the Commentary.

22   When Paul says that the Athenians are *very religious* ($\delta\epsilon\iota\sigma\iota\delta\alpha\iota\mu\sigma\nu\epsilon$-
$\sigma\tau\epsilon\rho\sigma\nu s$) does he mean this in a good or a bad sense? Does he
mean 'devout' or 'superstitious'? The word could be used in either
meaning. When the noun occurs at 25^{19} it is, rightly, translated *superstition* by RSV. Lucian tells us that the inhabitants of Abounoteichos
were 'superstitious' ($\delta\epsilon\iota\sigma\iota\delta\alpha\iota\mu\sigma\nu\alpha s$), i.e., peculiarly vulnerable to
religious charlatans. The probability is that it is meant in a bad
sense here.

23   No archaeological or other investigations have yielded knowledge
of an inscription in Athens couched in precisely these terms, but it is
certain that there was an inscription in the city 'to gods unknown',
and elsewhere 'to the nameless god' or 'to the appropriate god'. An
inscription in precisely the terms given us by Luke may yet turn up,
but it seems on the whole most likely that Luke altered the well-known
inscription 'to gods unknown' into '*To an unknown god*', in order to
suit the purposes of his argument. For *what therefore you worship as
unknown, this I proclaim to you* cp. 14^{15}, 'we bring you good news that
you should turn from these vain things'.

24   *The God who made the world and everything in it*: cp. 14^{15} 'the living God
who made the heaven and the earth and the sea and all that is in
them'. Though there is not much material to argue from in this
speech and in that of Paul and Barnabas at Lystra, it is probable that
H. P. Owen is correct in saying[1] that Luke is not in either place
presenting the Hellenistic Jewish argument for the existence of God
from the design of his creation (as presented, e.g., in Wisd. 13^{1-5}).
His point is that it is only by his Gospel or by his Word that men can

[1] In his article 'The Scope of Natural Revelation in Romans I and Acts
XVII' (*New Testament Studies*, v (1958), pp. 133–43).

does not live in shrines made by man, nor is he served by
human hands, as though he needed anything, since he himself
gives to all men life and breath and everything. And he
made from one every nation of men to live on all the face
of the earth, having determined allotted periods and the

---

know that God is a creator (Acts 14[15], εὐαγγελιζόμενοι, 'we bring
you good news', 17[23], καταγγέλλω, 'I declare, preach'). The Gentiles
could have known God's creating activity, for he did give them
evidence, but they refused to see it, and now must listen to his Word
or Gospel. That the fact of God's creatorship can only be known by
faith is stated in Heb. 11[3] and Rom. 4[17], and the whole argument is
the theme of Rom. 1[18–23]. *Does not live in shrines made by man* echoes
a well-documented jibe of the Jews against idols: 2 Kings 19[18]; Dan.
(LXX) 5[4]; Wisd.13[10], and also is found in Bel and the Dragon, Jubilees,
Epistle of Jeremy, 1 Enoch, 2 Enoch, and Sibylline Oracles.

as though he needed anything: the Epicureans stressed the self-sufficiency
(ἀταραξία) of the gods, and the Stoics inculcated emotional and
spiritual self-sufficiency and invulnerability in men (αὐταρκεία,
ἀπαθεία). But the self-sufficiency of God is found as a prominent
doctrine in Jewish tradition too—Ps. 50[8–13]; 2 Macc. 14[35]; 3 Macc.
2[9 f.]; Josephus, *Antiquities*, viii. 111; Philo, *De Spec. Leg.* i. 271. *He gives
to all men life and breath and everything* is not difficult to parallel from
the LXX (Gen. 2[7]; Wisd. 1[7, 14]).

These words have given scholars considerable trouble in determining their exact meaning. Does this sentence refer to geographical and
ethnological distinctions or to aeons and periods of world-history predetermined by God, the first Hellenistic and philosophical, the second
Jewish in origin? Dibelius (*Studies*, pp. 30 ff.) opts for the Hellenistic
interpretation. Boundaries (ὁροθεσίας) he thinks refer to an idea well
known in the ancient world, and found especially in Stoic thought
and in Cicero, that the whole earth was divided into five zones, only
two of which were temperate enough to be habitable. This had been
used as a proof of God's providence, on the ground that two zones
had been specially prepared for human habitation. On this interpretation *allotted periods* (καιρούς) would refer to the seasons, and here
Acts 14[17], 'fruitful seasons', supports this view. Gärtner, however,
produces weighty evidence against this opinion (*The Areopagus Speech*,
pp. 147–52). He maintains that Jewish apology and polemic usually
did not attempt to prove God's existence or providence; καιρός by
itself cannot mean 'season' (in 14[17] it does not stand by itself but is
preceded by an adjective 'fruitful'), for the proper term for 'seasons'
is ὧραι; καιροί must mean 'historical epochs'; cp. Acts 1[7]. The verse

27 boundaries of their habitation, that they should seek God,
   in the hope that they might feel after him and find him. Yet
28 he is not far from each one of us, for
       "In him we live and move and have our being";
   as even some of your poets have said,
       "For we are indeed his offspring."

---

means that God has decreed the territories for the dwelling of the
various nations and the times for their predominance. ὁροθεσία
means a boundary or landmark, marking inhabited earth, and cannot apply to zones covering uninhabited territory. The verse conveys
the thought that God determines the bounds of nations in time and
space. The better reading here is *from one* (as in RSV) rather than
'from one blood' ('Western' text). The reference no doubt is to the
origin of the human race from Adam.

27   Against the view that this is an apocalyptic idea, Dibelius says that
in apocalyptic doctrine men do not *seek* God; rather this seeking of
God is a philosophical idea. Gärtner replies that 'to seek' (ζητεῖν)
used absolutely, is a philosophical term meaning 'to speculate about
God'. But the fact that ζητεῖν has an object, God, precludes this
meaning, and the great uncertainty expressed as to whether God
might be found (*in the hope that they might*) is not consistent with the
Stoic confidence that God can easily be inferred from the universe.
'Seeking God' is a well-known O.T. term for serving God piously
and uprightly. The uncertainty expressed corresponds to the typically
Jewish conviction that man in fact would not, chose not to, grope
after God and find him; cp. Wisd. 1¹, 13⁶; also Ps. 14¹, as quoted in
Rom. 3¹⁰ff. ('no one seeks for God'). So Luke means that man was
created for the express purpose of seeking God, but whether he will
find him is rendered uncertain by man's moral weakness. *He is not
far from each one of us* is more readily paralleled by Deut. 4⁷ and Ps.
145¹⁸ than by Stoic maxims.

28   *For we are indeed his offspring* is a quotation from a Greek poet,
Aratus, who lived in the early fourth century B.C. and was influenced
by Stoic thought; the poem was on the subject of astronomy and was
called *Phainomena*; it had been translated into Latin and was widely
popular by Luke's day. It is possible that the phrase *in him we live and
move and have our being* is also a quotation from a poet called Cleanthes,
of the third century B.C., also a Stoic, who may have been quoting an
earlier and much more misty figure called Epimenides. But these are
only conjectures. The Stoic parallels to *in him we live and move and have
our being* are not convincing: 'we are in him' is not the same as 'he is

Being then God's offspring, we ought not to think that the

in us', and the latter is the teaching of Stoicism, with its doctrine of the immanence in man of the divine *Logos* or Word, and its pantheism.

Mosaic of merchant ships in sail from the floor of a shipping office in Ostia. Note the two paddles used as rudders. Neither ship has its topsail spread. In the background is a lighthouse.

The sentiment is better paralleled in the Pauline concept, and perhaps the Johannine too, of our being in Christ. The words *live and move* emphasize the contrast found elsewhere in the speech between living man's kinship with a living God and lifeless idols incapable of motion. Cp. 14¹⁵, 'turn from these vain things to a living God'. It is his life which gives man kinship with a living God (cp. Job 12¹⁰ and Ps. 104²⁹). This is the point of the quotation of the pagan poet, *for we are indeed his offspring*, not the Stoic doctrine that all men, endowed with their own *logos*, can have communion with the supreme *Logos*. The quotation of the poet corresponds in this speech to the *yet he did not leave himself without witness* of 14¹⁷. Pagan poets are quoted in two other passages in the N.T., 1 Cor. 15³³ and Tit. 1¹². There are several examples of both Jewish and Christian apologists' falsifying or mis-interpreting fragments of pagan poets for their own purposes. The poet Aratus himself (*Phainomena*, 1–9) had been used by Aristobulus,

Deity is like gold, or silver, or stone, a representation by the
30 art and imagination of man. The times of ignorance God
overlooked, but now he commands all men everywhere to
31 repent, because he has fixed a day on which he will judge the
world in righteousness by a man whom he has appointed, and
of this he has given assurance to all men by raising him from
the dead.'

---

an Hellenistic-Jewish writer who probably lived in Alexandria in the
second century B.C., to support the biblical account of creation.

29   *The Deity*, literally 'the divine' ($\tau\grave{o}\ \theta\epsilon\hat{\iota}ov$), is an unusual way of
referring to God, conveying a rather remote and impersonal im-
pression. But it is used by Philo, Aristobulus, and Josephus. The
attack on idols is abundantly paralleled in Jewish and Christian
literature: Ps. 115[5f.]; Isa. 37[19], 46[7ff.]; Wisd. 13[16], 15[16] (also in Epistle
of Jeremy vv. 4–73 and Bel and the Dragon vv. 3–22); Rom. 1[22, 23, 25];
1 Cor. 8[4]; 1 Thess. 1[9], and, of course, Acts 14[15–17].

30   *The times of ignorance* are exactly paralleled in 14[16], 'in past generations he allowed all the nations to walk in their own ways'. General
references to the ignorance of the Gentiles are Wisd. 14[22]; Rom.
1[18ff.]; Eph. 4[17ff.]; 1 Pet. 1[14]: particular statements about God's
overlooking ignorance, Wisd. 11[23]; Rom. 2[4], 3[25].

31   An unmistakable reference to the Second Coming, and one which
in the context could not be described as deferring the Second Coming
indefinitely. It means 'there is a limit to God's forbearance; repent
while there is time'. *Assurance* here is a quite un-Pauline use of the
word for 'faith' ($\pi\acute{\iota}\sigma\tau\iota\varsigma$). For this, perhaps intentionally abrupt,
reference to the Resurrection at the end of a speech, cp. 24[21], 26[23].

The contents of this speech, then, are Jewish and Christian in their
affinities rather than borrowed from pagan philosophy. Hellenistic
Judaism, of course, is the matrix from which they spring, for it was
Hellenistic Judaism which addressed the Gentiles. But the type of
Hellenistic Judaism that made great concessions to pagan philosophy
(such as Philo's version of it) is not particularly prominent here. As
Gärtner says (p. 249), the best analogies for the speech are 1 Thess.
1[9f.], Rom. 1[18ff.], and Wisd. 13–15 (a part of that book which many
have thought to lie behind the early chapters of Romans). It must
be pointed out, however, that though the content of the speech is far
from incompatible with Paul's ideas, the language is wholly un-
Pauline. In fact the language is often the language of contemporary
philosophy, deliberately adopted to suit the philosophically minded
audience which Paul is represented as addressing, but clothing ideas

Now when they heard of the resurrection of the dead, some mocked; but others said, 'We will hear you again about this.' So Paul went out from among them. But some men joined him and believed, among them Dionysius the Areopagite and a woman named Damaris and others with them.

AFTER this he left Athens and went to Corinth. And he

---

which are those of the early Gentile Church. The speech was certainly not composed by Paul; it was composed by Luke, and represents the sort of propaganda which the Church was making among the Gentiles when he first came in contact with it. The speech is one of his most elaborate, most brilliant, most effective efforts. The N.T. would be immensely poorer without it. But the doctrine which it conveys is not the product of Luke's fancy, but of the mind of the early Church. In as far as this is true, it may represent in content, though not in expression, the sort of message which Paul used to deliver to Gentile audiences.

the Areopagite presumably means that Dionysius belonged to the council of the Areopagus, and therefore must have been a rich and influential man. Nothing more is reliably known of him, but later legend and forgery busily used his name, attributing to him an immensely popular fifth-century treatise on mystical theology and several letters, and identifying him with St. Denys of Paris.

18: 1–17. *Paul in Corinth*

The ancient Greek city of Corinth, one of the most prominent of the city states during the period of Greek freedom and democracy in the fifth and fourth centuries B.C., had found itself on the wrong side during the period of the break-up of the kingdoms succeeding to Alexander's Empire in the second century B.C., and had been pillaged and destroyed by the Roman general L. Mummius in 146 B.C. It was refounded by Caesar as a Roman colony, Colonia Laus Iulia Corinthiensis, and by 27 B.C. its advantageous commercial position on the isthmus had restored its trade and industries to prosperity. By the time Paul reached it Corinth was the capital of the Roman province of Achaea, which since A.D. 44 had been a senatorial province, governed by a proconsul. Corinth was equally famous in the ancient world for its artistic treasures and for its immorality.

found a Jew named Aquila, a native of Pontus, lately come
from Italy with his wife Priscilla, because Claudius had
commanded all the Jews to leave Rome. And he went to
3 see them; and because he was of the same trade he stayed
with them, and they worked, for by trade they were tent-
4 makers. And he argued in the synagogue every sabbath, and
persuaded Jews and Greeks.

5   When Silas and Timothy arrived from Macedonia, Paul
was occupied with preaching, testifying to the Jews that the
6 Christ was Jesus. And when they opposed and reviled him,
he shook out his garments and said to them, 'Your blood be
upon your heads! I am innocent. From now on I will go to
7 the Gentiles.' And he left there and went to the house of

---

2   Aquila and Priscilla were Christians already, and as they came
direct from Rome to Corinth it is highly likely that the Christian
Church had reached Rome as early as A.D. 52, and probably rather
earlier, independently of either Peter or Paul, whom later tradition
regarded as the founders of that Church. Incidentally, this means
that it is inaccurate to describe Acts as the story of how Christianity
came to Rome, for Christianity had reached it before Paul did, as
Luke admits in his last chapter (28^{15}). This makes it all the more
likely that Acts is written to explain how *Paul* reached Rome, and
written for Christians of Rome. Priscilla is another form of Prisca,
the same person as is mentioned, with her husband, in Rom. 16^3;
1 Cor. 16^{19} (and 2 Tim. 4^{19}).
3   *tent-makers*: cp. 1 Thess. 2^9; 1 Cor. 4^{12}, 9$^{1ff.}$.
6   Paul now testifies to the Jews in Greece that it is their fault that he
leaves them to go to the Gentiles; cp. 13$^{46ff.}$ and 28$^{25-28}$.
7   There were very few detached or semi-detached houses in cities
of the ancient world. Wealthy people lived in villas outside the town
in their own grounds or estates, but the others inhabited what we
should call 'terrace' houses, with no spaces between them. People
of a lower social class, like the majority of people with whom Paul
was associating, and the vast majority of early Christians, lived in
houses of two or more stories, sometimes divided into flats, and often
having shops on the ground floor; they faced outward on to the street,
like modern houses. See Plates pp. 14, 41. The inward-facing house,
like the one Peter went to after his escape from prison (12$^{13, 14}$), was

a man named Titius[a] Justus, a worshiper of God; his house
was next door to the synagogue. Crispus, the ruler of the
synagogue, believed in the Lord, together with all his household; and many of the Corinthians hearing Paul believed and
were baptized. And the Lord said to Paul one night in a
vision, 'Do not be afraid, but speak and do not be silent;
for I am with you, and no man shall attack you to harm you;
for I have many people in this city.' And he stayed a year and
six months, teaching the word of God among them.

But when Gallio was proconsul of Achaia, the Jews made

---

[a] *Other early authorities read* Titus

---

common too and designated its owners as rather better off. The
synagogue would probably be situated in an inward-facing house,
like the one at Dura-Europos. The house of Titius Justus next door
would provide a large room in which the Christians might meet and
worship. *He left there* presumably means that he ceased to frequent the
synagogue where the Jews resisted him, and by Titius Justus' permission set up a centre of worship in his house. It does not necessarily
mean that he ceased to stay with Aquila and Priscilla (v. 3). 1 Cor.
16[19] refers to 'Aquila and Prisca, together with the church that meets
in their house', but the last expression ($\tau\hat{\eta}$ $\kappa\alpha\tau$' $o\hat{\iota}\kappa o\nu$ $\alpha\hat{\upsilon}\tau\hat{\omega}\nu$ $\dot{\epsilon}\kappa\kappa\lambda\eta\sigma\dot{\iota}\alpha$)
need mean no more than the members of the Christian Church who
live in their house, and this verse would, of course, refer to Ephesus,
not Corinth. The 'Western' interpolator thinks that Paul did leave
Aquila's house, and reads 'And removing from there'.

Crispus is mentioned in 1 Cor. 1[14], where Paul tells us that he
baptized him.

Luke records other visions of Paul's (9[12], 16[9], 23[11], 27[23]). Paul
himself tells us that he had experienced visions (2 Cor. 12[1–5]).

This date is a most valuable one for deciding the chronology both
of Paul's career and of the narrative of Acts (see Introduction above,
p. 9). But it must be realized that Luke does not necessarily link it
directly with what goes before nor with what follows after. All he
knows is that during one of Paul's visits to Corinth the Jews attempted
to prosecute him before Gallio and that Gallio would not accept the
case for trial. Gallio was the elder brother of the philosopher Seneca;
his full name was Lucius Junius Gallio Annaeanus. The date is
almost certainly A.D. 51/2. The tribunal (*bema*) has been discovered on
the south side of the *agora* at Corinth.

a united attack upon Paul and brought him before the tri-
13 bunal, saying, 'This man is persuading men to worship God
14 contrary to the law.' But when Paul was about to open his
mouth, Gallio said to the Jews, 'If it were a matter of wrongdoing or vicious crime, I should have reason to bear with
15 you, O Jews; but since it is a matter of questions about
words and names and your own law, see to it yourselves;
16 I refuse to be a judge of these things.' And he drove them
17 from the tribunal. And they all seized Sosthenes, the ruler
of the synagogue, and beat him in front of the tribunal. But
Gallio paid no attention to this.

---

13   The charge which the Jews make is vague. There was no law of
which the Roman authorities would take cognizance which forbade
people to worship any god. Even to prosecute somebody directly for
failing to worship Caesar as god would be wholly unlikely at any time
in the first century, and inconceivable in the reign of Claudius, who
refused to allow the people of Alexandria to erect temples to him, on
the ground that he was a man, not a god. It may be that the Jews
hoped to persuade Gallio to confuse the laws of the SPQR and the
Law of the Old Testament, but with so vague a statement as this we
cannot be certain. If they had accused Paul of preventing Jews from
following their own customs and religion, then Gallio would have had
to take notice.

14   *I should have reason to bear with you*: the words translated 'have reason
to' (κατὰ λόγον) could mean 'according to your wish' or 'naturally',
and the Greek word for *bear with* (ἀνεσχόμην) is a technical legal term
for admitting a case to court.

17   As far as the language goes, Luke could mean that some of the
Greek population of the city, delighted that the Jews had been
rebuffed by the proconsul, beat up a local Jewish synagogue official.
This is the sort of incident that happened quite commonly in the
Roman Empire. But if we identify this Sosthenes with the Sosthenes
mentioned at 1 Cor. 1[1] as greeting the Corinthian Christians, presumably from Ephesus, we must assume that he was a Christian
convert. In that case Paul would have converted two members of
a board of 'rulers of the synagogue' in Corinth, which would be quite
enough to exasperate the Jews. The Jews, piqued at their lack of
success in the law case, would then have avenged themselves on
a prominent Christian convert.

After this Paul stayed many days longer, and then took leave of the brethren and sailed for Syria, and with him Priscilla and Aquila. At Cenchreae he cut his hair, for he had a vow. And they came to Ephesus, and he left them there; but he himself went into the synagogue and argued with the Jews. When they asked him to stay for a longer period, he declined; but on taking leave of them he said, 'I will return to you if God wills', and he set sail from Ephesus.

18: 18–19: 41. *The Church at Ephesus*

The account of Paul's movements here is vague and unsatisfactory. Why should Paul go to Syria via Caesarea and probably Jerusalem (his stopping at Ephesus is understandable enough)? Why did he make the vow? Why are we told that Paul stayed *many days longer*, when we have already been told (v. 11) that he stayed a year and a half in Corinth? When he reached Ephesus, *he left them there*, and went—not on to some other place, but *into the synagogue*, presumably at Ephesus. Had Aquila and Priscilla taken a vow not to enter synagogues? Anyway, why did Paul go to Antioch? We are not told. The move of Aquila and Priscilla to Ephesus is vouched for by 1 Cor. 16¹⁹. There is absolutely no reason why Luke should have invented these movements on the part of Paul. They do not advance his plot or develop his ideas in the least. They are not recounted in his literary reconstruction style. He rather gives the impression of relating some information at third or fourth hand. Perhaps Conzelmann is near the truth in thinking that Luke may here be compressing somebody else's account of this journey in so condensed a manner that it makes sense for him, but not for the reader.

Cenchreae was the port of Corinth, immediately to the south of it. The details of this kind of vow are given in Num. 6¹ff. Josephus (*Jewish War*, ii. 313) tells us that the vow lasted 30 days and involved abstinence from hair-cutting and wine. *He cut his hair* probably means that he did so solemnly, vowing never to do so again till he had fulfilled the vow. Some commentators have objected that Paul would never make as much concession to the Jewish Law as was involved in carrying out a vow like this. But it is clear that Luke did not invent this story, for he does not even trouble to tell us that Paul carried out the vow, leaving us to infer this. He had no reason either, at this stage of the narrative, to emphasize Paul's obedience to the Jewish Law.

22   When he had landed at Caesarea, he went up and greeted
23   the church, and then went down to Antioch. After spending
     some time there he departed and went from place to place
     through the region of Galatia and Phrygia, strengthening all
     the disciples.

24   Now a Jew named Apollos, a native of Alexandria, came to

---

22   *he went up* is almost a technical term for 'he went to Jerusalem', and
        here it can mean nothing else, for a vow such as Paul had made could
        only be discharged in the Temple at Jerusalem.

23   Unless we are to take the statement in 16⁶ that Paul, with others,
        'went through the region of Phrygia and Galatia' as equivalent to
        saying that Paul evangelized them, this is the first information we
        possess from Acts that Paul had congregations to look after in these
        parts.

24–28   This little account of Apollos is a most enigmatic passage. How can
        we envisage him being *instructed in the way of the Lord*, and teaching
        accurately *the things concerning Jesus*, and yet never having received
        Christian baptism? And why, when he has learnt the way from
        Aquila and Priscilla *more accurately*, is no mention made of his Christian
        baptism? Paul mentions Apollos in 1 Corinthians as a fellow worker
        of his, by some mistakenly regarded as a rival, in Corinth, one who
        watered after he had planted. Presumably therefore Apollos worked
        in Corinth after Paul had first worked there, but he was not in
        Corinth when Paul wrote the letter (1 Cor. 1¹², 3⁴⁻⁶, ²², 4⁶, 16¹²).
        Paul never implies that Apollos was not baptized, nor that he had
        affinities with John the Baptist. Conzelmann suggests that from the
        end of 18²⁵, from 'though he knew only the baptism of John' to the end
        of 18²⁶, 'expounded . . . the way of God more accurately', should be
        omitted as a later addition. This would relieve the situation con-
        siderably, for it would mean that Apollos was a Christian from
        Alexandria who later met Paul and worked with him. But there are
        several objections to this suggestion. The 'Western' interpolator reads
        at v. 25 'who was instructed in the way of the Lord in his native
        country'. If he had had before him a text which made no reference
        to John the Baptist nor to Aquila and Priscilla, he would have seen
        no necessity to alter the text in order to suggest that Apollos was a
        Christian already in Alexandria, for it would have been obvious from
        the existing text that he was. Again, it looks very much as if this
        passage and the next (19¹⁻⁷) were put next to each other by Luke
        because they both dealt with people who knew only the baptism of
        John, in which case the reference to John's baptism in Apollos'

Ephesus. He was an eloquent man, well versed in the scriptures. He had been instructed in the way of the Lord; and being fervent in spirit, he spoke and taught accurately the things concerning Jesus, though he knew only the baptism of John. He began to speak boldly in the synagogue; but when Priscilla and Aquila heard him, they took him and expounded to him the way of God more accurately. And when he wished to cross to Achaia, the brethren encouraged him, and wrote to the disciples to receive him. When he arrived, he greatly helped those who through grace had believed, for he powerfully confuted the Jews in public, showing by the scriptures that the Christ was Jesus.

WHILE Apollos was at Corinth, Paul passed through the

---

case must be original. Finally, there is virtually no evidence for the existence of Christianity in Alexandria until a period considerably after this one. The status of Apollos remains a mystery. It is quite likely that there were disciples of John the Baptist who kept his memory alive long after his death. It has often been thought that the first chapter of St. John's Gospel has these in mind (see C. H. Dodd, *Historical Tradition in the Fourth Gospel*, pp. 288–301). But Alexandria is not a likely place to encounter them. It is difficult to avoid the conclusion that Luke has made some sort of mistake here.

Apollos' being called *eloquent* (λόγιος; it could mean 'learned') is probably to be connected with his coming from Alexandria, one of the great homes of learning in the ancient world.

It is worth noting that this verse implies that Christianity had reached Ephesus before Paul arrived there; there were *brethren* there already.

This too is a mysterious episode, disconnected from the preceding one in fact, though associated with it by Luke for the sake of order. Two assumptions seem to underlie it: that 'believing' is something different from being baptized and receiving the Holy Spirit; and that receiving the Holy Spirit is closely linked, as at least a parallel event, with baptism into the Name of Jesus. It echoes the conviction evident in 18[24-26] that a man can know much about Jesus and can even believe in him without being baptized into his Name. It suggests

upper country and came to Ephesus. There he found some
2 disciples. And he said to them, 'Did you receive the Holy
Spirit when you believed?' And they said, 'No, we have never
3 even heard that there is a Holy Spirit.' And he said, 'Into
what then were you baptized?' They said, 'Into John's bap-
4 tism.' And Paul said, 'John baptized with the baptism of
repentance, telling the people to believe in the one who was
5 to come after him, that is, Jesus.' On hearing this, they were

---

that by Luke's day, and no doubt well before it, a good deal of
traditional material had been accumulated to form a body of Christian
instruction. This episode strengthens the impression that there did
exist quite a large body of devotees of John the Baptist for a long
period after his death (by this date about thirty years after it), and
even that these men may not have been personally acquainted with
John, but were, so to speak, second-generation Baptists.

1   *passed through the upper country* is a very vague phrase, indicating in
fact that Luke had no reliable information as to where Paul was at
the time. Paul now begins a long stay at Ephesus, which he must
have made his headquarters for his missionary activity in many directions. Ephesus was a large and prosperous town, the capital of the
Roman province of Asia.

2   *there is a Holy Spirit*: if these were well-instructed disciples of John
the Baptist and if John taught what he is reported by the Synoptic
evangelists as teaching, then they should have known that John had
foretold the advent of One who would baptize in the Holy Spirit
(Matt. 3[11]; Mark 1[8]; Luke 3[16, 17]: cp. Acts 1[5]). But it may be that the
Synoptic evangelists in reporting John's words are modifying them
to suit the Christian claim that Jesus was indeed the One who should
come. Perhaps it is more likely, however, that what John's disciples
here meant was that they did not know that the Holy Spirit was
here now, that the era had arrived in which the Holy Spirit was
abroad, that the eschatological crisis had now broken, of which the
presence of the Holy Spirit would be the great sign; cp. John 7[39],
'for as yet the Spirit had not been given', literally, 'for Spirit was
not yet'.

5, 6   This laying-on of hands is not easy to explain, any more than the
same act at 8[17] was. The suggestion that it was a regular feature of
Christian baptism that, after the ceremony with water, hands should
be laid on, in order to convey or to symbolize the gift of the Spirit
is anachronistic. No such idea can be found until A.D. 200, and

baptized in the name of the Lord Jesus. And when Paul had laid his hands upon them, the Holy Spirit came on them; and they spoke with tongues and prophesied. There were about twelve of them in all.

And he entered the synagogue and for three months spoke boldly, arguing and pleading about the kingdom of God; but when some were stubborn and disbelieved, speaking evil of the Way before the congregation, he withdrew from them, taking the disciples with him, and argued daily in the hall of Tyrannus.[a] This continued for two years, so that all the residents of Asia heard the word of the Lord, both Jews and Greeks.

And God did extraordinary miracles by the hands of Paul, so that handkerchiefs or aprons were carried away from his body to the sick, and diseases left them and the evil spirits

[a] *Other ancient authorities add* from the fifth hour to the tenth

---

even then it is weakly and uncertainly evidenced. 'The Western' interpolator in v. 5 added at the end 'for the remission of sins'. It may be that he took the laying-on of hands to be a sign of forgiveness of sins, and there is some support for this idea in 1 Tim. 5^{22}. The fact that these people had been baptized by John in a *baptism of repentance* (v. 4) would not necessarily exempt them from a baptism into the Name of Christ for the remission of sins. But on the whole it is likely that the laying-on of hands by Paul here was done as a sign that he was claiming for Christ's obedience a special group. Compare the significance of the same gesture at 8^{17}.

Luke again associates glossolalia and prophesying.

The appearance here of *Tyrannus*, not mentioned before and never mentioned again, is one of those pieces of otherwise pointless local information which inspire confidence in Luke's sources. The 'Western' text adds at the end of this verse 'from eleven o'clock to four'. It is wholly unlikely that so trivial a point as this should have come to the interpolator's ears as a genuine piece of information. It is more likely that he wanted to represent Paul as a Christian philosopher lecturing at regular and usual hours to a class, as we can envisage Justin Martyr doing a century later in Rome.

13 came out of them. Then some of the itinerant Jewish
exorcists undertook to pronounce the name of the Lord Jesus
over those who had evil spirits, saying, 'I adjure you by the
14 Jesus whom Paul preaches.' Seven sons of a Jewish high
15 priest named Sceva were doing this. But the evil spirit
answered them, 'Jesus I know, and Paul I know; but who
16 are you?' And the man in whom the evil spirit was leaped
on them, mastered all of them, and overpowered them, so

13-17   Magical papyri from Egypt and other evidence make it clear that,
in spite of prohibitions in the Law against the practice, Jews did
indulge widely in magic; and also that non-Jewish dabblers in the
art used Jewish, and later Christian, holy names to further it.
Exorcism, i.e., the casting out of evil spirits by invoking the name
of God, or of Jesus, was a very well known practice in the early
Church for centuries, so much so that 'exorcist' became one of the
minor orders in the Western Church (first mentioned in the middle
of the third century).

13   *itinerant Jewish exorcists* suggest a Jewish version of the many
Svengali-like figures who are evidenced as haunting the religious
underworld, half sorcerers and half doctors; in the higher forms of
the type claiming to be philosophers, in the lower forms mere
fortune-tellers, hunted from city to city.

14   *sons of a Jewish high priest named Sceva.* Sceva was certainly not an
official high priest of the temple cult who ever functioned in Jerusalem, for we know all the names of high priests covering this period,
and his is not one of them. The name, which is evidenced elsewhere,
is a Latin one. Luke, like Josephus, uses 'high priest' ($\dot{a}\rho\chi\iota\epsilon\rho\epsilon\acute{v}s$) to
mean anyone belonging to a high-priestly family (see above, p. 79),
but it is not at all likely that a member of a high-priestly family
should have descended as low in the social scale as to become a
wandering exorcist. It may well be that Sceva called himself a 'high
priest', as people today sometimes call themselves Judge or Captain
of Professor in order to enhance their status or impress their customers
or victims. He may even have been the high priest of a pagan cult
(there were plenty in all walks of life entitled to call themselves high
priests) who found it lucrative to describe himself as a Jew.

16   *all of them.* The Greek says 'both', which may mean that there
were only two exorcists, or it may be a loose use of the word to
mean 'all'.

Relief of a ship arriving in harbour, from Ostia. The owner and his family are sacrificing in thanksgiving for safe arrival on the deck; a sailor in the bows is probably preparing to lower a buffer to protect the ship when it meets the quay. The topsail and smaller sail are furled but the mainsail is still spread. The man in the boat may be preparing to moor the ship. In the background are statues of gods and a lighthouse.

17 that they fled out of that house naked and wounded. And
this became known to all residents of Ephesus, both Jews
and Greeks; and fear fell upon them all; and the name of the
18 Lord Jesus was extolled. Many also of those who were now
19 believers came, confessing and divulging their practices. And
a number of those who practiced magic arts brought their
books together and burned them in the sight of all; and they
counted the value of them and found it came to fifty thousand
20 pieces of silver. So the word of the Lord grew and prevailed
mightily.
21   Now after these events Paul resolved in the Spirit to pass

---

19   The ancient world was deeply interested in *magic*, a preoccupation
which it had, perhaps, inherited from prehistoric cultures before it.
Ephesian magic documents in particular had a wide reputation
('Εφέσια γράμματα). It demanded as much effort from a man of the
ancient world to disbelieve in magic as it does of a man of today to
disbelieve in the omnicompetence of science or the application of the
theory of evolution to every part of life. The Christian Church from
the beginning officially disbelieved in magic and set its face against it.
    As Luke does not specify what unit of silver he is reckoning by, it is
impossible confidently to estimate what sum he means to relate. If,
with many commentators, we assume that he means a silver drachma,
then the sum might amount to £2,000. One gains the impression that
vv. 11–20 are retailing material which is of not much greater authenticity than the gossip of Ephesus.
21, 22   A final journey through the Roman provinces of Macedonia and
Achaea as a preliminary to going to Jerusalem is indeed what Paul
clearly has in mind when he writes his letters to the Corinthians and
to the Romans; but its purpose in his mind is evidently to make the
last arrangements for his great collection from the Gentile churches
for the poverty-stricken Jewish church at Jerusalem, to gather
together the representatives from each church, and to escort them
to Jerusalem. Luke makes no mention of this purpose of Paul's here,
though Acts 24[17] makes it clear that he knew of it. But the omission
is perfectly understandable. Luke is writing many years later, when
events have fallen into their proper perspective. To him Paul's arrest
in Jerusalem and its sequel have quite overshadowed in importance
the collection that seemed so important to Paul when he wrote his

through Macedonia and Achaia and go to Jerusalem, saying, 'After I have been there, I must also see Rome.' And having sent into Macedonia two of his helpers, Timothy and Erastus, he himself stayed in Asia for a while.

About that time there arose no little stir concerning the Way. For a man named Demetrius, a silversmith, who made silver shrines of Artemis, brought no little business to the craftsmen. These he gathered together, with the workmen of like occupation, and said, 'Men, you know that from this business we have our wealth. And you see and hear that not

---

letters (and to us when we read them, perhaps). What is significant is that Luke betrays the fact that he knows about this collection.

Luke omits many of the movements of Timothy and Titus which we can see reflected in 2 Cor. $2^{12 f.}$, $7^{6 f.}$, $8^{16 f.}$. But 1 Cor. 4^{17} tells us that Paul sent Timothy to Corinth from Ephesus, and Erastus is mentioned in Rom. 16^{23} as sending greetings, presumably from Corinth; he is also mentioned in 2 Tim. 4^{20}.

As far as Paul's movements go, this incident has no support in any other source. On the contrary, 1 Cor. 15^{32} (whose exact meaning is obscure) and 2 Cor. $1^{8 ff.}$ imply that Paul passed through some very grave danger at Ephesus. This tumultuous meeting in the theatre at Ephesus, from which Paul was saved apparently by the intervention of wealthy and influential pagan friends, could hardly be classed as very grave danger. We are constantly reminded of the fragmentariness of Luke's sources of information. But as far as local colour goes, Luke's references to the assembly and the temple of Artemis in Ephesus are abundantly confirmed by other evidence.

A title which literally means 'shrine-maker' (ναοποιός) is known to have been borne by officials who were responsible for maintaining the fabric of the temple of Artemis at Ephesus, and who often had dealings with the town council. It has been suggested that Luke mistook this title borne by Demetrius the silversmith, and assumed that he made silver shrines. Plenty of models of the temple of Artemis have survived in pottery, but none in silver. On the other hand, it is not surprising that no silver shrines have survived, because it is usually the contents of the rubbish dump, and less often the valuable objects, that archaeologists discover. Further, the word ναοποιός is used elsewhere in its ordinary sense of 'temple-builder', and it could mean 'shrine-maker'.

only at Ephesus but almost throughout all Asia this Paul has
persuaded and turned away a considerable company of
27 people, saying that gods made with hands are not gods. And
there is danger not only that this trade of ours may come into
disrepute but also that the temple of the great goddess
Artemis may count for nothing, and that she may even be
deposed from her magnificence, she whom all Asia and the
world worship.'

28   When they heard this they were enraged, and cried out,
29 'Great is Artemis of the Ephesians!' So the city was filled
with the confusion, and they rushed together into the
theater, dragging with them Gaius and Aristarchus, Mace-
30 donians who were Paul's companions in travel. Paul wished
to go in among the crowd, but the disciples would not let
31 him; some of the Asiarchs also, who were friends of his, sent

---

28   Though when they arrived in the theatre Demetrius and his fellow
craftsmen and their friends behaved wildly and even hysterically,
there was nothing incorrect in their holding what could be described
as an extraordinary meeting of the city assembly in the theatre, as the
presence and behaviour of the town clerk suggests.

29   Gaius is mentioned in 1 Cor. 1¹⁴ as baptized at Corinth by Paul
and in Rom. 16²³ as greeting the Roman Church, presumably from
Corinth. He appears again in Acts 20⁴. Aristarchus appears again
in Acts 20⁴ and 27². He is mentioned in Col. 4¹⁰ and Philem. 24. If
Paul had been dragged along with these two the fact might justify
Paul's language at 1 Cor. 15³² and 2 Cor. 1⁸ᶠᶠ·; but Luke does not
say that he was.

31   *Asiarchs* were people who had been or were then presidents of the
annual council (κοινόν) of the province, which transacted business
concerned mainly with ritual affairs, especially the ritual connected
with emperor-worship. In the second century, on more than one
occasion, these councils provided an opportunity for persecuting
Christians. The title was also borne by high priests of the imperial
cult, and by people appointed to represent the town council on the
provincial κοινόν. They would be rich and influential. It was a
peculiarity of towns in the province of Asia that they had more than
one Asiarch. They would, of course, all be pagans.

to him and begged him not to venture into the theater. Now some cried one thing, some another; for the assembly was in confusion, and most of them did not know why they had come together. Some of the crowd prompted Alexander, whom the Jews had put forward. And Alexander motioned with his hand, wishing to make a defense to the people. But when they recognized that he was a Jew, for about two hours they all with one voice cried out, 'Great is Artemis of the Ephesians!' And when the town clerk had quieted the crowd, he said, 'Men of Ephesus, what man is there who does not know that the city of the Ephesians is temple keeper of the great Artemis, and of the sacred stone that fell from the

---

The status and significance of *Alexander* is not clear. An Alexander is mentioned in 1 Tim. 1²⁰ and 2 Tim. 4¹⁴, but we do not know if he is the same man. The wording here taken at its face value should mean that he was a Jew, and perhaps he was put forward by the Jews to explain that they were distinct from the Christians. But the meaning of the Greek word here translated *prompted* is not at all certain. Nearly all Latin versions translate it *detraxerunt*, 'pulled down', and if it could be translated thus it would make rather better sense.

town clerk is the rendering of a Greek word γραμματεύς, literally 'scribe', but in fact secretary to the town council of Ephesus, an influential person with more authority than even a town clerk holds in the city councils of our society. There is plenty of evidence for his functions and importance. A. H. M. Jones (*The Greek City*, p. 181) tells us that 'An inscription of the reign of Claudius reveals how at Ephesus the vast wealth of Artemis found its way, by means of corrupt bargains with the priests appointed, into the hands of the city government.' The town clerk might not relish the thought that this disorderly meeting in the theatre on the subject of the temple of Artemis might lead to a close scrutiny of temple affairs.

temple keeper is expressed in one word in Greek (νεωκόρος). This title had been borne by cities long before. In a rather later period it is attached to Ephesus, on the ground of the city's possessing a temple dedicated to the cult of the emperor. In the past it had also been attached to individuals who actually were caretakers of temples. *That fell from the sky* (διοπετοῦς) is the usual translation, on the reasonable assumption that in the temple of Artemis there was preserved a meteorite stone. There are several examples of such a stone

36 sky?^a Seeing then that these things cannot be contradicted,
37 you ought to be quiet and do nothing rash. For you have
   brought these men here who are neither sacrilegious nor
38 blasphemers of our goddess. If therefore Demetrius and the
   craftsmen with him have a complaint against any one, the
   courts are open, and there are proconsuls; let them bring
39 charges against one another. But if you seek anything
40 further,^b it shall be settled in the regular assembly. For we
   are in danger of being charged with rioting today, there
   being no cause that we can give to justify this commotion.'
41 And when he had said this, he dismissed the assembly.

   ^a *The meaning of the Greek is uncertain*   ^b *Other ancient authorities read*
                        about other matters

being preserved in pagan temples in the ancient world, notably in
the temple of Cybele at Pessinus. There are no references to such
a stone being preserved at Ephesus, but it is very difficult to give
any other meaning to the word διοπετοῦς. The suggestion may well
be correct that this word is used by the town clerk by way of answer
to the Christians' attack on *gods made with hands* (v. 26). This image, he
implies, was not made with hands; it fell from the sky.

37   *sacrilegious* means, in the Greek, literally, 'temple-robbers', but it
could have a more general meaning. Jews were taught that they should
respect pagan temples, in spite of their dislike of idolatry; cp. Rom. 2²².

38   *proconsuls*: in the plural, not because there ever were more than one
proconsul governing the province of Asia (and Luke is, as usual,
correct in assigning a proconsul as governor of this province, and not
a propraetor, prefect, or procurator), but either because he means
'there are such people as proconsuls', or because the plural suits the
plural *courts* just before, or because proconsuls stayed such a short
time (only one year) that it was natural to refer to them in the plural,
meaning 'a succession of proconsuls'.

40   Emperors were always very sensitive upon the subject of gatherings
or societies which might develop into conspiracies, as Pliny's correspondence with Trajan shows.

41   We may not be able to fit this episode readily into Paul's career, or
even to regard it as particularly important in that career, but we
cannot but admire the skill with which Luke depicts the scene. It
almost provides comic relief, while at the same time demonstrating
that all the forces of law and order were in favour of granting justice
to the Christians.

AFTER the uproar ceased, Paul sent for the disciples and having exhorted them took leave of them and departed for Macedonia. When he had gone through these parts and had given them much encouragement, he came to Greece. There he spent three months, and when a plot was made against him by the Jews as he was about to set sail for Syria, he determined to return through Macedonia. Sopater of Beroea, the son of Pyrrhus, accompanied him; and of the

---

20: 1–21: 16. *Paul's journey to Jerusalem*

The journey here described corresponds to Paul's declarations of his intention to visit Jerusalem after a tour spent in organizing the collection (1 Cor. 16³, 2 Cor. 8 and 9). There is a certain confusion in the wording describing the movement of the party of Christians in vv. 1–5, which suggests an unfinished condition in the original. The 'Western' text tries to improve the verses, not very successfully.

The names on this list are all known elsewhere, except for *Sopater* and *Secundus*. *Aristarchus*, Acts 20⁴, 27²; Col. 4¹⁰; Philem. 24; *Tychicus*, Col. 4⁷; *Trophimus*, Acts 21²⁹; 2 Tim. 4²⁰; *Gaius*, Acts 19²⁹; Rom. 16²³; 1 Cor. 1¹⁴ (3 Jn. 1 probably refers to another Gaius). *Thessalonians* means men from the town Thessalonica; they were of course thereby Macedonians (i.e. from the Roman province of Macedonia) also. Tychicus and Trophimus came from the Roman province of Asia. But what about Gaius? The MS. evidence is uncertain about him. Most MSS. have *Derbaios*, meaning 'from the town of Derbe' (Acts 14⁶, ²⁰, ²¹, 16¹). But some MSS. of the 'Western' tradition[1] suggest a reading *Dob(e)rios*, meaning 'from Doberus', a Macedonian town S.W. of Philippi. This is an attractive reading, for it would group him with the Macedonians, and many commentators have adopted it, as the NEB has. But two considerations tell against it: (*a*) The 'Western' variants usually do not suggest that the interpolator had accurate enough knowledge of events to correct the text, but rather that his alterations are done for various motives of his own (though there may be 'Western' readings which are closer to the original than any other). (*b*) It is possible, even likely, that the men accompanying Paul represented various parts of the Gentile Church, some the Church in Asia, some the Church in Macedonia, a special delegation from the Church in Thessalonica. In that case it is likely that Gaius

---

[1] The Greek of Codex Bezae itself, and the Latin of the same MS., and the Latin MS. called *gigas*, of the thirteenth century.

Thessalonians, Aristarchus and Secundus; and Gaius of
Derbe, and Timothy; and the Asians, Tychicus and Tro-
5 phimus. These went on and were waiting for us at Troas,
6 but we sailed away from Philippi after the days of Unleavened Bread, and in five days we came to them at Troas,
where we stayed for seven days.

7   On the first day of the week, when we were gathered
together to break bread, Paul talked with them, intending
to depart on the morrow; and he prolonged his speech until
8 midnight. There were many lights in the upper chamber

---

would be linked with Timothy, whom we know to have originated in
Lystra or Iconium (16[1, 2]), as coming from Derbe, and therefore
representing the Church in what Paul would probably call Galatia
(but not Luke, who would probably call it Lycaonia). It is better
therefore to keep the RSV translation, *Gaius of Derbe*.

5, 6   The second 'we' passage begins when the main party leaves
Philippi. The last 'we' passage left off in the middle of the first visit
of Paul and Silas to Philippi (16[17]). This does not mean that the
author of the 'we' passage had spent the whole of the intervening
period at Philippi, but it does seem to connect him with that town.

7   The indication of time here could mean either Saturday night or
Sunday night. But clearly this is a meal and a sermon or discourse.
Was it also a celebration of the Eucharist? The accounts which we
have of this service in 1 Cor. 10 and 11 suggest that in Paul's time it
was held in the evening, and during a meal. By the time of Pliny
(*c.* 115) it is likely that the Eucharist was held in the early morning,
and it is possible that Ignatius (perhaps a little earlier than Pliny)
witnesses to the separation of the meal proper (now called an Agape
or Love-Feast) from the Eucharist. The scene here described, therefore, may represent a Eucharist-with-Agape, at which Paul gave
a long discourse.

8, 9   The reason for the mention of the lamps has puzzled several commentators. Some have suggested that Luke is countering contemporary anti-Christian propaganda, which accused the Christians
of indulging in frightful orgies in darkness at their sacred meals.
But Acts was written too early for Luke to be aware of these accusations, and anyway the libels usually accused the Christians of putting
out the lights rather than of holding their services in the dark. Much
the most likely explanation is that a great many lamps, especially
oil lamps, would tend to make the air in the room close, and this

where we were gathered. And a young man named Eutychus was sitting in the window. He sank into a deep sleep as Paul talked still longer; and being overcome by sleep, he fell down from the third story and was taken up dead. But Paul went down and bent over him, and embracing him said, 'Do not be alarmed, for his life is in him.' And when Paul had gone up and had broken bread and eaten, he conversed with them a long while, until daybreak, and so departed. And they took the lad away alive, and were not a little comforted.

But going ahead to the ship, we set sail for Assos, intending to take Paul aboard there; for so he had arranged, intending himself to go by land. And when he met us at Assos, we took him on board and came to Mitylene. And sailing from there we came the following day opposite Chios; the next day we touched at Samos; and*a* the day after that we came to

a Other ancient authorities add after remaining at Trogyllium

---

would make for sleepiness in those who were in the room. The 'Western' text reads ὑπολαμπάδες, which probably, but not certainly, means 'small windows'. But it is not necessary to adopt this reading. Why should Luke say that there were *many* windows? One was quite enough for Eutychus to fall through. The house in which Paul is speaking is probably a three-story house fronting directly on the street. Eutychus is sitting in the window, which has, of course, no glass in it, and falls into the street. We may even venture to regard the reference to lamps as a verification of the fact that the narrator was an eyewitness. Notice that the Christians meet in a large room on the third story of an ordinary house in a not very grand part of the town.

they took the lad away: the Greek simply says 'they brought' (ἤγαγον). It could mean that they brought him in from the street or that they brought him up to the upper room again, or (perhaps most likely) that they brought him to his own house, which was not the one where Paul had been speaking.

From Troas to Assos is about 20 miles. Paul preferred to go on foot rather than by boat for this part of the journey. We do not know why, but it is incomprehensible why anyone should have wanted to invent this detail.

The addition 'after remaining at Trogyllium' introduced by the

16 Miletus. For Paul had decided to sail past Ephesus, so that
    he might not have to spend time in Asia; for he was hastening
    to be at Jerusalem, if possible, on the day of Pentecost.

'Western' text after the words *we touched at Samos, and* . . . is an interesting one. Trogyllium is a town among foothills opposite Samos; it
breaks conveniently the otherwise long journey between Samos and
Miletus. It is difficult to conceive why the 'Western' interpolator
should have inserted this clause, and it may well be that Ropes is
right in deciding that here the 'Western' text has preserved an
original reading which had dropped out of the great uncials apart
from D.

16   Conzelmann conjectures that Luke is here representing Paul as
hastening to reach Jerusalem before Pentecost in order to explain
why he did not touch at Ephesus, and that the real reason why he
did not go to Ephesus, but chose to interview the elders of Ephesus
at Miletus, was that he had made Ephesus too hot for himself, and
had been forbidden to enter it again after the disturbances his
activities there had caused (1 Cor. 15^{32}; 2 Cor. 1$^{8ff.}$). This is an
attractive suggestion, for it would not have suited Luke's purpose in
maintaining that both imperial and civic authorities regarded
Christianity as harmless had he admitted that his hero had been
expelled from Ephesus for causing disturbances there. But if this is
so, it shows that Luke had reliable knowledge of Paul's movements
and vicissitudes at this period, though he chose to suppress part of it.

17   Once again, Luke assumes that Paul has entrusted his churches to
the care of elders; see above, on 14^{23}.

18–35   This is the only elaborate speech that occurs in a 'we' passage in
Acts, and this fact has led some commentators to seek to detect in it
signs of originality, i.e., to argue that here we can recover or approximate to Paul's *ipsissima verba* on this occasion. But probability is
strongly against this suggestion, for Luke has used this occasion
to diversify his narrative (we have not had a speech since Chapter 17)
with a speech of exceptional significance, for which there is no parallel
in Acts. Most of the speeches given have been 'type' speeches, i.e.,
speeches whose basic structure consists of a recognizable pattern,
either 'kerygma-to-Jews' or 'kerygma-to-Gentiles'—a fact which
itself suggests that Luke was working on some traditional material
in composing them. But this is no 'type'-speech. It is composed by
Luke to fit the occasion; it fits the occasion in a dramatic and literary
sense, that is, not in an historical one. Paul is virtually taking farewell
of his missionary activities round the Aegean littoral and commend-
ing his flocks there to the care of God, for he himself will not hence-
forth be able to exercise personal pastoral oversight over them. He

And from Miletus he sent to Ephesus and called to him the elders of the church. And when they came to him, he said to them:

'You yourselves know how I lived among you all the time from the first day that I set foot in Asia, serving the Lord with all humility and with tears and with trials which befell me through the plots of the Jews; how I did not shrink from declaring to you anything that was profitable, and teaching you in public and from house to house, testifying both to Jews and to Greeks of repentance to God and of faith in our Lord Jesus Christ. And now, behold, I am going to Jerusalem, bound in the Spirit, not knowing what shall befall me there; except that the Holy Spirit testifies to me in every city that imprisonment and afflictions await me. But I do not

---

looks back over his years of missionary activity among these churches, and forward to the destiny that lies before him. This does not mean, of course, that the author of the speech knew nothing of Paul. We shall find some surprisingly Pauline language here. But this speech is still intended to mark the end of the third great division of the book of Acts. It is in effect his last words before he takes the road to Rome.

It certainly is unlike Paul to point out his own virtues. In 2 Corinthians, where he does this (Chs. 10–12) he only does so under great provocation, and calling himself a 'fool' the whole time. On the other hand, we can trace in Paul's letters language very like some of the language used here. He can recall the past, as the Paul of this speech does (Phil. 1⁵; Col. 1⁶). He can speak of his ministry in terms of slavery, which is the literal meaning of *serving* (δουλεύων: 1 Thess. 1⁹ᶠ·; Col. 3²⁴). He can refer to his *tears* (2 Cor. 2⁴). He can protest his innocence (1 Thess. 2¹ᶠᶠ·; 2 Cor. 7²).

in public and from house to house. Some commentators detect here a desire to contrast Christian doctrine with secret Gnostic doctrine. It is more probable that Luke intends a contrast, meaning publicly (as at Athens) and privately (as at Troas).

bound in the Spirit means, as the NEB puts it, 'under the constraint of the Spirit', or under an inner compulsion. There is no reference in this phrase to imprisonment.

These verses leave the strong impression that their author knew of

account my life of any value nor as precious to myself, if only I may accomplish my course and the ministry which I received from the Lord Jesus, to testify to the gospel of the
25 grace of God. And now, behold, I know that all you among whom I have gone about preaching the kingdom will see my
26 face no more. Therefore I testify to you this day that I am
27 innocent of the blood of all of you, for I did not shrink from
28 declaring to you the whole counsel of God. Take heed to yourselves and to all the flock, in which the Holy Spirit has made you guardians, to feed the church of the Lord^a which
29 he obtained with his own blood.^b   I know that after my

---

a Other ancient authorities read of God   *b Or* with the blood of his Own

---

Paul's death. They are full of Pauline, or near-Pauline language. Paul more than once uses the figure of running in a race (1 Cor. $9^{24, 25}$; Phil. $3^{13, 14}$). He uses the word *ministry* ($\delta\iota\alpha\kappa\upsilon\acute{\iota}\alpha$) of his own missionary activity frequently. He uses the word *gospel* and the word *grace* over and over again, though never in the exact combination *gospel of the grace*. The impression left by these verses is that their author is not Paul, but that he knew the sort of language Paul used.

28   Here Luke identifies presbyters (i.e. *elders*, v. 17) with bishops ($\dot{\epsilon}\pi\iota\sigma\kappa\acute{o}\pi\upsilon\varsigma$, RSV *guardians*). Paul probably appointed bishops (literally 'overseers') in the churches. This identification is found also in the Pastoral Epistles, in *1 Clement*, the *Didache*, and *The Shepherd* of Hermas. It is possible that in Luke's day titles of Christian officials were fluid enough for this identification to be no very serious anachronism. Bishops in this sense must be distinguished from the 'monarchical 'bishops (i.e. the bishop who is the only one in his local church), who only emerge early in the second century. *The church of the Lord which he obtained with his own blood*, as it stands in the RSV text must mean the Church of Christ and presents no difficulty. But the words *the Lord* ($\tau o\hat{\upsilon}$ $K\upsilon\rho\acute{\iota}o\upsilon$) are not supported by full MSS. evidence. Textual authority quite as impressive as that which supports *of the Lord* can be found for the reading *of God* ($\tau o\hat{\upsilon}$ $\Theta\epsilon o\hat{\upsilon}$).[1] Further, the expression *the church of the Lord* is very seldom found elsewhere. It is difficult to imagine any early Christian, deeply imbued as he must have been with the thought of the Old Testament and of

---

[1] $\tau o\hat{\upsilon}$ $K\upsilon\rho\acute{\iota}o\upsilon$ AC*DE d gig sy^{h(mg)} sah (which include most of the witnesses for the 'Western' text); $\tau o\hat{\upsilon}$ $\Theta\epsilon o\hat{\upsilon}$ $\aleph$B 614 lat.

departure fierce wolves will come in among you, not sparing the flock; and from among your own selves will arise men speaking perverse things, to draw away the disciples after them. Therefore be alert, remembering that for three years I did not cease night or day to admonish every one with tears. And now I commend you to God and to the word of his grace, which is able to build you up and to give you the inheritance among all those who are sanctified. I coveted no one's silver or gold or apparel. You yourselves know that these hands ministered to my necessities, and to those who were with me. In all things I have shown you that by so

---

ancient Judaism, speaking of the blood of God. On the other hand, it is very difficult to see how an original *church of the Lord* could have been altered or corrupted into *church of God*, and the RSV reading (which is also followed in the NEB) looks too much like an evasion of the difficulty. Another question is whether we should adopt the reading 'his blood, his own blood' (τοῦ αἵματος τοῦ ἰδίου), which can also be rendered 'the blood of his Own One', or the variant *his own blood* (τοῦ ἰδίου αἵματος, the reading adopted by the NEB translators). The weighty MSS. evidence is here heavily in favour of the first reading, however we render it. On the whole it looks as if we ought to read 'to feed the Church of God which he obtained for himself with'—τοῦ αἵματος τοῦ ἰδίου. There is no exact parallel for Christ's being called 'the Own One' (but cp. Rom. 8³¹ᶠ· and Gen. 22¹⁶, and the use in Eph. 1⁶ and in early Christian literature of the title 'the Beloved'). Perhaps it is best to adopt Conzelmann's suggestion that the expression 'he obtained with his own blood' is a traditional one, taken over by Luke, and always used with Christ as subject, and that therefore we must assume that Christ is the subject of *obtained* here too, in spite of appearances. It should be noted that this is the second example in Acts of the word 'church' being used to mean the whole Church (cp. 11²²).

This is the only place in Acts in which Christians are warned against false teaching.

This verse too is full of phrases reminiscent of Pauline vocabulary: *the word of his grace* (λόγος, word; χάρις, grace); *build up* (οἰκοδομεῖν, a word often used by Paul); *inheritance* (κληρονομία, Gal. 3¹⁸; Col. 3²⁴, and cp. Col. 1¹², 'the inheritance (κλῆρος) of the saints').

Cp. 1 Thess. 2⁹, 4¹¹.

toiling one must help the weak, remembering the words of the Lord Jesus, how he said, "It is more blessed to give than to receive."'

36 And when he had spoken thus, he knelt down and prayed
37 with them all. And they all wept and embraced Paul and
38 kissed him, sorrowing most of all because of the word he had spoken, that they should see his face no more. And they brought him to the ship.

21 AND when we had parted from them and set sail, we came by a straight course to Cos, and the next day to Rhodes, and
2 from there to Patara.*a* And having found a ship crossing to

a Other ancient authorities add and Myra

---

35 This saying is not attributed to Jesus in any of the four Gospels, though this fact does not preclude its being genuine, for many genuine sayings of Jesus which never found their way into the canonical Gospels could have been circulating in Luke's time. It is, however, curious that Luke did not include it somewhere in his own Gospel if he thought it a word of the Lord. It is very well paralleled indeed in pagan literature. Pericles, in the famous funeral speech in which he commemorated the Athenian dead, is reported by Thucydides as saying 'we make friends by doing good to others, not by receiving good from them' (II. xcvii. 4, tr. R. Warner), and it appears in another form in Plutarch. It appears in *1 Clement* and in the *Didache*, and in Hermas' *Shepherd* too. As we shall see, Luke later ascribes the words of a well-known Greek proverb to the Risen Jesus seen in a vision (Acts 26¹⁴). But there is no reason why Jesus should not have quoted a well-known proverb, especially this proverb, and in this form, for *blessed* is a Jewish rather than Greek way of expressing the thought. He quoted at least one other proverb in his sayings (Mark 6⁴ and parallels). *The Gospel of Thomas* even ascribes to him a reference to one of Aesop's fables (Logos 102, ed. Guillaumont, Puech *et al.*).

36 Prayer on the knees was prayer of a peculiarly solemn sort in the early Church. Standing was the more usual posture for prayer.

21: 1 After *to Patara* the 'Western' text adds 'and Myra'. Myra is a town further to the East on the coast of Lycia. It is difficult to see why anyone should desire gratuitously to insert a reference to Myra here. Perhaps we may agree with Ropes that this is another example of

Unloading a ship (the right-hand side of the relief shown opposite p. 193).
A man carries an amphora of wine along a gangway. The ship is moored by
a strong hawser. The large eye depicted above is to avoid ill-luck.

3 Phoenicia, we went aboard, and set sail. When we had come
in sight of Cyprus, leaving it on the left we sailed to Syria,
and landed at Tyre; for there the ship was to unload its
4 cargo. And having sought out the disciples, we stayed there
for seven days. Through the Spirit they told Paul not to go
5 on to Jerusalem. And when our days there were ended, we
departed and went on our journey; and they all, with wives
and children, brought us on our way till we were outside the
city; and kneeling down on the beach we prayed and bade
6 one another farewell. Then we went on board the ship, and
they returned home.

7   When we had finished the voyage from Tyre, we arrived
at Ptolemais; and we greeted the brethren and stayed with
8 them for one day. On the morrow we departed and came to
Caesarea; and we entered the house of Philip the evangelist,
9 who was one of the seven, and stayed with him. And he had
10 four unmarried daughters, who prophesied. While we were

---

the 'Western' text having preserved words which have dropped out
in most of the great uncials. The town is referred to again at 27⁵, but
this supplies no reason why it should have been inserted here. It is
at this verse that the third 'we' passage begins.

3   *come in sight of* (ἀναφάναντες) is a sailors' technical term, meaning to
'sight' land.

4   *Through the Spirit* suggests that some of the disciples were prophets.
But it may mean no more than a judgement about circumstances
exercised by responsible Christians; cp. 1 Cor. 7⁴⁰.

5   *the beach* at Tyre can still be identified. Is not this the vivid touch
of an eyewitness?

7   *When we had finished*; the verb (διανύσαντες) normally means 'finish',
but there is some support in Greek usage for the meaning 'set out' on
a journey, which would make better sense here.

8, 9   What could be the point of referring to the *four unmarried daughters,
who prophesied*, except that in fact the narrator of the 'we' passage had
been there and had met them? They did not even prophesy that Paul
would meet trouble in Jerusalem, apparently. It is these details
which give the 'we' passages their air of authenticity. We have not
met Philip the evangelist since 6⁵ and 8⁴⁻⁴⁰.

staying for some days, a prophet named Agabus came down from Judea. And coming to us he took Paul's girdle and bound his own feet and hands, and said, 'Thus says the Holy Spirit, "So shall the Jews at Jerusalem bind the man who owns this girdle and deliver him into the hands of the Gentiles."' When we heard this, we and the people there begged him not to go up to Jerusalem. Then Paul answered, 'What are you doing, weeping and breaking my heart? For I am ready not only to be imprisoned but even to die at Jerusalem for the name of the Lord Jesus.' And when he would not be persuaded, we ceased and said, 'The will of the Lord be done.'

After these days we made ready and went up to Jerusalem. And some of the disciples from Caesarea went with us, bringing us to the house of Mnason of Cyprus, an early disciple, with whom we should lodge.

We have encountered *Agabus* already at 11^{28}.

As the text translated in the RSV stands, the party go from Caesarea to Jerusalem direct, without a break, a distance of about 67 miles. As Acts 23^{32} (where the same journey in reverse direction is undertaken, but is broken at Antipatris) reveals, Luke knows that the distance between the two towns is more than one day's journey. The 'Western' text realizes this, and rearranges the verse to read 'they brought us to the people with whom we were to spend the night. And when we reached a certain village we lodged with a man called Naso', etc. It has been thought that this betrays special knowledge of Palestine on the part of the interpolator, but he could have got this knowledge from Acts 23^{32}. If we follow the text translated in the RSV we shall have to conclude that Mnason, with whom the party lodged, lived in Jerusalem. But it is more likely that Luke has expressed himself clumsily here, and that he meant that the party spent the night at Mnason's house in some place intermediate between Caesarea and Jerusalem, whose name he had forgotten, or did not know. Mnason may have accompanied the party from Caesarea.

17   When we had come to Jerusalem, the brethren received
18   us gladly. On the following day Paul went in with us to
19   James; and all the elders were present. After greeting them,
     he related one by one the things that God had done among
20   the Gentiles through his ministry. And when they heard it,
     they glorified God. And they said to him, 'You see, brother,
     how many thousands there are among the Jews of those who
21   have believed; they are all zealous for the law, and they have
     been told about you that you teach all the Jews who are
     among the Gentiles to forsake Moses, telling them not to
22   circumcise their children or observe the customs. What then
     is to be done? They will certainly hear that you have come.
23   Do therefore what we tell you. We have four men who are

IV. PAUL'S ROAD TO ROME. CHAPTERS 21:17–28: 31

21: 17–36. *Paul is arrested*

17, 18   *the brethren* and *James* reflect the constitution of the Church of
         Jerusalem as it was in the years leading up to the Jewish revolt that
         started in 66. But it is highly probable that by the time Paul paid
         his last visit to Jerusalem this state of affairs had been reached. At
         v. 18 the third 'we' passage ends.

20–28   This speech is clearly only a convention used in order to advance
         the story.

21   We have no evidence whatever that Paul at any point taught that
         Jews should abandon circumcision, though he was adamant in his
         conviction that it must not be forced upon Gentiles. Rom. 10⁴,
         'Christ is the end of the law, that everyone who has faith may be
         justified', has been cited to prove that he believed that Jews as well
         as Gentiles should abandon the law, but here 'end' (τέλος) means
         quite as much 'objective, fulfilment' as it does 'stop, finish', and while
         he certainly held that the Law was not God's last word, his language
         never compels us to conclude that he contemplated the Herculean
         task of persuading Jews to throw away the Jewish Law. *Observe the
         customs* means keep the *Halakah*; cp. 6¹⁴, 26³, 28¹⁷.

23 ff.   It is very likely that the *vow* was the vow of a Nazarite, cp. Num.
         6¹³⁻²⁰; Jud. 13⁷. It was permissible and customary for Jews to take
         on Nazarite vows which were not lifelong, but temporary, lasting
         a month, and sometimes rich and pious Jews paid the considerable

under a vow; take these men and purify yourself along with them and pay their expenses, so that they may shave their heads. Thus all will know that there is nothing in what they have been told about you but that you yourself live in observance of the law. But as for the Gentiles who have believed, we have sent a letter with our judgment that they should abstain from what has been sacrificed to idols and from blood and from what is strangled*a* and from unchastity.' Then Paul took the men, and the next day he purified himself with them and went into the temple, to give notice when the days of purification would be fulfilled and the offering presented for every one of them.

When the seven days were almost completed, the Jews from Asia, who had seen him in the temple, stirred up all the crowd, and laid hands on him, crying out, 'Men of Israel,

---

a Other early authorities omit and from what is strangled

---

expenses of discharging these vows in the Temple. The beginning of the thirty days' period was marked by the devotee's shaving his head. Paul could not possibly have taken a Nazarite vow on himself in seven days (v. 27). The expression *purify yourself along with them* must therefore either mean that Paul was to purify himself ritually from having been living in an unclean land (which a strict observance of the Law would demand) while the men discharged their vows, or that these four men had all contracted ritual defilement accidentally during the period of their Nazarite vows, and that Paul was to pay the expenses of the process of purification from that defilement (the period lasting seven days) and undergo the purification ceremonies with them. Or it may simply be that Luke is not well conversant with the Jewish Law and did not understand precisely what process of purification Paul undertook.

The same textual variations attend this account of the decree as appeared in 15²⁰, ²⁹. It seems distinctly odd that the Jerusalem Christians should have had to remind Paul of this decree, if he himself, as Ch. 15 relates, had been present when it was composed and had later circulated it (16⁴).

Part of the barrier which divided the very large Court of the

help! This is the man who is teaching men everywhere against the people and the law and this place; moreover he also brought Greeks into the temple, and he has defiled this

29 holy place.' For they had previously seen Trophimus the Ephesian with him in the city, and they supposed that Paul

30 had brought him into the temple. Then all the city was aroused, and the people ran together; they seized Paul and dragged him out of the temple, and at once the gates were

31 shut. And as they were trying to kill him, word came to the

32 tribune of the cohort that all Jerusalem was in confusion. He at once took soldiers and centurions, and ran down to them; and when they saw the tribune and the soldiers, they stopped

33 beating Paul. Then the tribune came up and arrested him, and ordered him to be bound with two chains. He inquired

34 who he was and what he had done. Some in the crowd

Gentiles from the inner courts open only to Jews has been recovered, and with it an inscription, written in Greek, warning any foreigner that if he went inside this barrier he would himself be responsible for his resulting death. It is possible that Luke's language here reflects an over-simplified conception of the interior arrangement of the Temple-space, but this is not a necessary conclusion.

29   The Asian Jews would have known what Trophimus, who came from the capital of their province, looked like, and known that he was not a Jew.

30–32   Paul was presumably dragged out of the Court of the Women into the Court of the Gentiles. At the north-west corner of the Temple area was a very strong fort, called the Antonia, where any foreign power occupying Jerusalem (the Seleucid kings, when they could, Herod, and the Romans) kept a strong garrison. It was connected with the Court of the Gentiles by a staircase (v. 35). The soldiers clearly ran down this into the crowd and rescued Paul and brought him back into the barracks in the fort. The garrison of Jerusalem consisted of one cohort of auxiliaries, whose full complement was 760 infantry and 240 cavalry. *Centurions* suggests that between 100 and 200 men were called out for this operation.

33   *two chains* is usually taken to mean that he was attached to a soldier on each side of him; cp. 12[6].

shouted one thing, some another; and as he could not learn the facts because of the uproar, he ordered him to be brought into the barracks. And when he came to the steps, he was actually carried by the soldiers because of the violence of the crowd; for the mob of the people followed, crying, 'Away with him!'

As Paul was about to be brought into the barracks, he said to the tribune, 'May I say something to you?' And he said, 'Do you know Greek? Are you not the Egyptian, then, who recently stirred up a revolt and led the four thousand men of the Assassins out into the wilderness?' Paul replied, 'I am a Jew, from Tarsus in Cilicia, a citizen of no mean city; I beg you, let me speak to the people.' And when he had

---

21: 37–22: 29. *Paul speaks to the mob*

The Assassins suggests rather luridly a secret society bound by oaths to murder. But in fact Luke means no more than terrorists or bandits of any sort, operating singly or in bands. Not long after this time individual murders by terrorists armed with daggers, operating when their victims were in the middle of a large crowd, increased greatly in number (Josephus, *Jewish War*, ii. 254–7).

Originally it had been illegal to hold Roman citizenship along with citizenship of a man's native city, or some other, but by the reign of Claudius, at the latest, this prohibition no longer applied. Pride in one's native city was still at this point a noticeable feature of city life in the Roman Empire, because cities throughout the whole Empire still for the most part enjoyed an independent existence with room for the expression of local tastes and traditions. City life had not yet been stifled and rendered colourless by the twin evils of despotism and bureaucracy which afflicted the later Roman Empire. Many commentators have pointed out that Paul has apparently more pride in being a Tarsian citizen than in being a Roman one. He only introduces his Roman citizenship at the last minute, mainly in order to embarrass officials, as in 16[37].

Even though Paul is represented as addressing the mob in Aramaic (for this is what the words *Hebrew language* mean) the speech itself shows no sign of translation from Aramaic, and is clearly a free composition of Luke. It is suitable to its context in a literary but not

given him leave, Paul, standing on the steps, motioned with his hand to the people; and when there was a great hush, he spoke to them in the Hebrew language, saying:

22 'BRETHREN and fathers, hear the defense which I now make before you.'

2 And when they heard that he addressed them in the Hebrew language, they were the more quiet. And he said:

3 'I am a Jew, born at Tarsus in Cilicia, but brought up in this city at the feet of Gamaliel, educated according to the

---

historical sense; that is to say, it is suitable to Luke's purpose that Paul should here defend himself against the hostility of the Jews by recounting his conversion, but it does not say a word to vindicate him against the charge either of violating the Temple or starting a riot, for which he is presumably in custody. This is not to say that the historical details about Paul's career given in it are necessarily false.

22: 3   The punctuation of this verse is a matter of debate, but it is unlikely that the punctuation adopted in the RSV is correct. The NEB rendering, 'I was brought up in this city, and as a pupil of Gamaliel I was thoroughly trained in every point of our ancestral law', is preferable. The phrase *brought up* ($\dot{a}\nu a\tau\epsilon\theta\rho a\mu\mu\acute{\epsilon}\nu o\varsigma$) has a definite meaning, distinct from that of the word 'educated' ($\pi\epsilon\pi a\iota\delta\epsilon\upsilon\mu\acute{\epsilon}\nu o\varsigma$), as van Unnik has shown in an interesting monograph.[1] *Brought up* means 'nurtured from infancy until the age when the child begins formal education', and the scheme 'born . . . brought up . . . educated' was a very well known one in Hellenistic literature, including Hellenistic Jewish literature (e.g. Philo and Josephus): cp. Acts 7[20, 21], where *Moses was born . . . was brought up . . .* was instructed. As it is inconceivable that Paul should have been *brought up* in this sense at the feet of Gamaliel, it is necessary to punctuate the sentence so that the clause *at the feet of Gamaliel* is referred only to the participle *educated* and not to *brought up*. This makes good Greek, if we understand, as we well may, that emphasis is being laid upon the fact that it was Gamaliel with whom Paul had been educated. This means that though Paul was born in Tarsus he must have come to Jerusalem as a baby and spent his youth from very early days there.

[1] W. C. van Unnik, *Tarsus or Jerusalem, the city of Paul's youth* (tr. G. Ogg).

strict manner of the law of our fathers, being zealous for
God as you all are this day. I persecuted this Way to the
death, binding and delivering to prison both men and
women, as the high priest and the whole council of elders
bear me witness. From them I received letters to the brethren,

---

It may of course be said that Luke's information must be incorrect,
in view of Paul's perfect acquaintance with the Greek language and
his constant use of the LXX. But this is really to beg the question,
i.e., to assume that one who had been brought up in Jerusalem could
not have absorbed so much Hellenistic Jewish culture, whereas in
fact Paul might be regarded as one of our strongest witnesses to the
fact that there were circles in Jerusalem open to this culture. We cannot possibly discredit Luke's words by such a tenuous theory. There
is no strong reason for doubting his statement that Paul spent virtually
all his youth in Jerusalem, and that Tarsus had virtually no direct
influence upon his early years. It could, of course, be argued that
even if we accept Luke's statement we could assume that Paul picked
up his Hellenistic Jewish culture during the years after his conversion
about which we know almost nothing, except that he was in 'the
regions of Syria and Cilicia' (Gal. 1²¹). But this seems very unlikely.
There is in fact nothing intrinsically improbable in Paul's having
picked up his acquaintance with Hellenistic Jewish culture, or at
least in his having laid the foundations for it, during his youth in
Jerusalem, especially if his family, as seems likely, retained its connexions with Tarsus. Acts itself tells us that there was a synagogue
(probably only one, but possibly more) for Jews from Cyrene,
Alexandria, Cilicia, and Asia, in Jerusalem (6⁹). And there certainly
was a continual flow of Greek-speaking Jews from the Dispersion into
Jerusalem. This conclusion would suggest that a rigid distinction of
the sources of early Christianity into Semitic or Aramaic-speaking
sources, which are early, and Hellenistic or Greek-speaking sources,
which are late (or later), is a precarious one.

It is curious that Paul here calls the high priest to witness to his
earlier anti-Christian activities, whereas in a very short time (23⁵) he
fails to recognize the high priest. But it is quite certain that the high
priest who had years before (perhaps fifteen or eighteen years)
encouraged Paul the persecutor was a quite different person from the
high priest who in this part of the narrative confronts Paul the
Christian. Paul may therefore be simply appealing to the man who
had at the time of his persecuting been high priest. Or the phrase may
simply be a rhetorical device, meaning, 'It is a matter of common
knowledge in high ecclesiastical circles.'

and I journeyed to Damascus to take those also who were
there and bring them in bonds to Jerusalem to be punished.

6　'As I made my journey and drew near to Damascus, about
noon a great light from heaven suddenly shone about me.

7　And I fell to the ground and heard a voice saying to me,

8　"Saul, Saul, why do you persecute me?" And I answered,
"Who are you, Lord?" And he said to me, "I am Jesus of

9　Nazareth whom you are persecuting." Now those who were
with me saw the light but did not hear the voice of the one who

10　was speaking to me. And I said, "What shall I do, Lord?"
And the Lord said to me, "Rise, and go into Damascus,

---

6 ff.　　The second description of Paul's conversion differs in a number of
points from both the first (9^{1-9}) and the third (26^{12-18}). Almost all
the variations can be accounted for by the fact that in the second and
third descriptions a different audience is being addressed; there is
no need to call in a theory of different sources. Each account retains
unchanged the detail that Paul was thrown to the ground on the
way to Damascus, that a heavenly light appeared, and that the words
'Saul, Saul, why do you persecute me?' and 'I am Jesus whom you are
persecuting', were heard; and in all three accounts it is made clear
that this was not a subjective vision confined to Paul's inner experience, but that in some way it affected his companions, though
the details of how it affected them differ in each version. At 9^7 his
companions hear a voice but see nothing; at 22^9 they see the light
but do not hear the voice; at 26^{14} nothing is said of their reactions
except that they fell to the ground. In the first description a detailed
account of Ananias and the vision he had is given. In the second
description the fact is emphasized that Ananias was a pious Jew,
because the audience consists of fanatical Jews, many of them
Pharisees, but nothing is said of Ananias' vision; and here the name
of Jesus is not mentioned, except in the words 'I am Jesus, whom you
are persecuting', even when Paul's vision in the Temple is mentioned
(22^{18}). This vision, incidentally, is omitted in the first description.
The third description leaves Ananias out altogether, and with him
the blinding and the healing of Paul, because neither Agrippa nor
Festus would be interested in an obscure Jewish Christian; but they
would be impressed by the account of a direct divine command to
Paul (26^{19}). The last description is clearly much compressed in
comparison with the other two.

and there you will be told all that is appointed for you to do."
And when I could not see because of the brightness of that
light, I was led by the hand by those who were with me, and
came into Damascus.

'And one Ananias, a devout man according to the law,
well spoken of by all the Jews who lived there, came to me,
and standing by me said to me, "Brother Saul, receive your
sight." And in that very hour I received my sight and saw
him. And he said, "The God of our fathers appointed you
to know his will, to see the Just One and to hear a voice from
his mouth; for you will be a witness for him to all men of
what you have seen and heard. And now why do you wait?
Rise and be baptized, and wash away your sins, calling on
his name."

'When I had returned to Jerusalem and was praying in the
temple, I fell into a trance and saw him saying to me, "Make

---

saw him. In fact the *him* (εἰς αὐτόν) is scarcely justified as a translation. The word *saw* (ἀνέβλεψα) means 'I received my sight, I was able
to see again', and the *him* is difficult grammatically. 𝔓⁴¹, an eighth-
or ninth-century papyrus, omits it, and it may have crept in as a gloss.

witness. This is, for Luke, Paul's primary function; he is to witness
to Christ among the Gentiles (Acts 1²¹), and, in Luke's scheme, to be
the link between apostolic and post-apostolic times.

This vision is an incident of which we have not heard before, and
we are given no concrete information as to where in Paul's life it
should be fitted in; it would not be impossible to place it during his
first, very brief, visit to Jerusalem after his conversion. We know that
Paul had visions, not only from their mention in Acts (see above, on
18⁹), but because he virtually tells us so himself, when he says (2 Cor.
12¹), 'I will go on to visions and revelations of the Lord', for his
argument at this stage of his letter is that he can match the claims of
his opponents at every point, and they are clearly claiming to have
experienced visions and revelations. Whether the particular vision
alluded to in 2 Cor. 12²⁻⁴ refers to this vision of Paul's we cannot know;
that these verses do refer to Paul's experiences, in spite of his apparent
disavowal of this, is highly likely.

saw him. We are left to understand that *him* means Jesus.

haste and get quickly out of Jerusalem, because they will not
19 accept your testimony about me." And I said, "Lord, they
themselves know that in every synagogue I imprisoned and
20 beat those who believed in thee. And when the blood of
Stephen thy witness was shed, I also was standing by and
approving, and keeping the garments of those who killed
21 him." And he said to me, "Depart; for I will send you far
away to the Gentiles."'

22 Up to this word they listened to him; then they lifted up
their voices and said, 'Away with such a fellow from the
23 earth! For he ought not to live.' And as they cried out and
24 waved their garments and threw dust into the air, the tribune
commanded him to be brought into the barracks, and ordered
him to be examined by scourging, to find out why they
25 shouted thus against him. But when they had tied him up
with the thongs, Paul said to the centurion who was standing
by, 'Is it lawful for you to scourge a man who is a Roman
26 citizen, and uncondemned?' When the centurion heard that,

Conzelmann may be right in guessing that for this incident Luke is using some source, and that this incoherence reveals it.

20 *witness* again, and this time in a sense much more like our modern word 'martyr', which is in fact derived from the Greek word for 'witness' (μάρτυς). But we should be cautious about giving the full sense of 'martyr', meaning 'one who witnesses to his convictions by his death', here, for even as late as Tertullian (*c.* 200) the word has not reached this exclusive meaning in Christian use.

24 *scourging* was not a punishment, but was used as the most direct way of extracting information from suspected persons. It was a recognized way of examining slaves and other unprotected persons.

25 *tied him up with the thongs* could be translated 'stretched him out for the thongs'.

26–29 It was a very grave crime to scourge a Roman citizen or to load him with chains as a punishment, though it would have been regarded as legitimate for a guard to handcuff his prisoner to prevent his escaping when on a journey or in the open. Haenchen quotes Cicero, *In Verrem*, II. v. 66, § 170, *facinus est vincire civem Romanum, scelus verberare,*

he went to the tribune and said to him, 'What are you about to do? For this man is a Roman citizen.' So the tribune came and said to him, 'Tell me, are you a Roman citizen?' And he said, 'Yes.' The tribune answered, 'I bought this citizenship for a large sum.' Paul said, 'But I was born a citizen.' So those who were about to examine him withdrew from him instantly; and the tribune also was afraid, for he realized that Paul was a Roman citizen and that he had bound him.

But on the morrow, desiring to know the real reason why the Jews accused him, he unbound him, and commanded the chief priests and all the council to meet, and he brought Paul down and set him before them.

---

prope parricidium necare. At the same time, as in many other matters under the control of the Roman government, there was often a great gap between law and enforcement of law, and there are several known examples of Roman citizens ill-treated by officials in spite of the law.

The tribune does not mean that the official fee for securing Roman citizenship was a large one, but that he had to spend a lot of money in bribing the appropriate officials. See above, Introduction, p. 10.

he had bound him means that he had chained him to two soldiers, 21³³.

22: 30–23: 11. *Paul before the Sanhedrin*

The statement *he unbound him* has caused a good deal of trouble to commentators. Does it imply that the tribune, in spite of his trepidation of the night before, had left him all night in chains? It is probably because of this difficulty that some MSS. (probably representing the 'Western' text, but D is deficient at this point) add to v. 29 'and immediately he unbound him'. In fact Luke does not say that Paul was removed even from the thongs, but leaves us to assume this. We can take it that we are also to assume, without being told so by Luke, that Paul was not again chained to soldiers. In that case *he unbound him* would either mean 'he set him at liberty', so that he could be entirely free to converse with his accusers, or 'he removed the handcuffs', which he would have worn as long as he was not actually behind bars. It is more difficult to understand how the tribune could have been in a position to order the Sanhedrin, including the High Priest, to attend. It

23 AND Paul, looking intently at the council, said, 'Brethren,
    I have lived before God in all good conscience up to this
  2 day.' And the high priest Ananias commanded those who
  3 stood by him to strike him on the mouth. Then Paul said
    to him, 'God shall strike you, you whitewashed wall! Are you
    sitting to judge me according to the law, and yet contrary
  4 to the law you order me to be struck?' Those who stood by
  5 said, 'Would you revile God's high priest?' And Paul said,

---

should be remembered, however, that this could not have been, and
is not represented by Luke as, an official meeting of the Sanhedrin.
No agenda is drawn up, no decision taken, no general discussion
takes place. *The chief priests and all the council* is a vague phrase. This
may be a Lukan way of saying that the tribune asked the chief priests,
including the high priest, as people responsible for the good behaviour of those who frequented the Temple, to explain to him
the riot of the day before, since he had been unable to examine the
prisoner in the way which he generally used. It is likely that the
chief priests would be anxious to come, in order to shift the blame
for the riot on to Paul and to see that one whom they regarded as
a dangerous enemy of the Temple and its cult was not allowed to
escape punishment. The charge of causing a riot was a very serious
one, and could have very grave consequences if it came to the
procurator's ears. Neither the tribune nor the Temple authorities
could afford to treat it lightly.

23: 1–5   This incident reflects little credit on Paul. He loses his temper under
provocation (unlike Jesus himself) and his quotation of Scripture
(Exod. 22[28], quoted in v. 5), which some have thought to be inserted
in order to put Paul in a good light, only serves to bring out more
clearly that what he did was wrong. Luke is of course relating the
incident in his own words; it is wholly unlikely that he invented it, or
that anybody before him invented it.

  2   *the high priest Ananias*: see above, Introduction, p. 8.
  3   The exact significance of *whitewashed wall* has so far eluded commentators. Matt. 23[27] springs to mind as a comparison. The tomb
appears fair outside but is rotten within. But why should a wall be
like this, unless it be the wall of a tomb? It has been suggested that
the words *God shall strike you* were put down by Luke because he
recalled that this Ananias had met his end by being murdered by
a terrorist. This is quite probable.

'I did not know, brethren, that he was the high priest; for it is written, "You shall not speak evil of a ruler of your people."'

But when Paul perceived that one part were Sadducees and the other Pharisees, he cried out in the council, 'Brethren, I am a Pharisee, a son of Pharisees; with respect to the hope and the resurrection of the dead I am on trial.' And when he had said this, a dissension arose between the Pharisees and the Sadducees; and the assembly was divided. For the Sadducees say that there is no resurrection, nor angel, nor spirit; but the Pharisees acknowledge them all. Then a great clamor arose; and some of the scribes of the Pharisees' party stood up and contended, 'We find nothing wrong in this man. What if a spirit or an angel spoke to him?' And when the

---

The fact that the Sadducees were convinced that the doctrines of Judaism should be confined to what the Pentateuch contained, with as little elaboration as possible, while the Pharisees were ready to develop an elaborate *Halakah*, welcomed apocalyptic ideas, and nurtured beliefs about a future life and a general resurrection is well evidenced by Josephus and by Rabbinic literature (cp. Mark 12[18] and parallels). No other authority speaks of the Sadducees' denying the existence of angels or spirits. That Paul, even when he had become a Christian, was still in many respects a Pharisee, with a Pharisee's conception of religion and revelation and law, is undeniable (such a book as W. D. Davies's *St. Paul and Rabbinic Judaism* makes this quite clear). Nor do Paul's letters suggest that he could not have taken an opportunist's argument in order to divide his opponents at a critical moment.

the hope and the resurrection is almost a hendiadys, i.e., an expression in which two things are equivalent to one—the hope of the resurrection of the dead. Paul does not mention the Resurrection of Jesus, but of course for Paul, as for all Christians, the hope of resurrection was based on the fact of Christ's Resurrection.

spirit or angel are almost synonymous here. It is not impossible that the meaning 'ghost or angel' is intended. The Pharisees probably refer to Paul's vision on the Damascus road, rather than his vision in the Temple (22[17-21]).

dissension became violent, the tribune, afraid that Paul would be torn in pieces by them, commanded the soldiers to go down and take him by force from among them and bring him into the barracks.

11   The following night the Lord stood by him and said, 'Take courage, for as you have testified about me at Jerusalem, so you must bear witness also at Rome.'

12   When it was day, the Jews made a plot and bound them-selves by an oath neither to eat nor drink till they had killed

13 Paul. There were more than forty who made this conspiracy.

14 And they went to the chief priests and elders, and said, 'We have strictly bound ourselves by an oath to taste no food till

15 we have killed Paul. You therefore, along with the council, give notice now to the tribune to bring him down to you, as though you were going to determine his case more exactly. And we are ready to kill him before he comes near.'

---

11   This indication to Paul that in spite of this apparent set-back he is destined to visit Rome sustains the theme of the fourth section of Acts, and keeps the readers' eyes fixed upon his final destination, at a point when several incidents which do not immediately contribute to it are to be related.

23: 12–35. *Paul is removed to Caesarea*

12–22   The sudden appearance of Paul's nephew tells very little, only that his sister was a married woman living in Jerusalem and that he kept in touch with her. The references to the nephew (νεανίαν, v. 17, νεανίσκον, v. 18) suggest that he was a teenager. It does, however, perhaps faintly support the view that Paul had been brought up in Jerusalem.

12 ff.   A violent oath of this sort is characteristic of the fanaticism allied with terrorist tactics which was becoming more and more a feature of life in Jerusalem at the time, and which was shortly to lead to the outbreak of the Jewish revolt against the Romans and the wresting of leadership of the Jewish nation out of the hands of both Sadducees and Pharisees by men inspired with this fanaticism.

Now the son of Paul's sister heard of their ambush; so he went and entered the barracks and told Paul. And Paul called one of the centurions and said, 'Bring this young man to the tribune; for he has something to tell him.' So he took him and brought him to the tribune and said, 'Paul the prisoner called me and asked me to bring this young man to you, as he has something to say to you.' The tribune took him by the hand, and going aside asked him privately, 'What is it that you have to tell me?' And he said, 'The Jews have agreed to ask you to bring Paul down to the council tomorrow, as though they were going to inquire somewhat more closely about him. But do not yield to them; for more than forty of their men lie in ambush for him, having bound themselves by an oath neither to eat nor drink till they have killed him; and now they are ready, waiting for the promise from you.' So the tribune dismissed the young man, charging him, 'Tell no one that you have informed me of this.'

Then he called two of the centurions and said, 'At the third hour of the night get ready two hundred soldiers with

---

It has been objected that the escort given to Paul here is impossibly large; about half the garrison appears to be sent to escort one man. Further, 45 miles (the distance between Jerusalem and Antipatris) is much too far for a night's march for infantry, and too far even for a night's ride for cavalry. And nobody has ever been able to discover what the word translated *spearmen* (δεξιολάβους) means. The 'Western' text rewrites the whole passage, making it tidier, more intelligible, and more probable, but for that very reason cannot be accepted as original. It is probable that there is some early corruption here. But it is also likely that Luke has got the facts wrong. Lake (in *The Beginnings of Christianity*) conjectures that δεξιολάβοι are 'led horses', that the figures for the escorting party should be reduced, and that they only escorted the prisoner and some of the horsemen a certain way outside the city. The failure of Claudius Lysias to try Paul then and there is explained by the fact that he had no power to do so (Sherwin-White, *Roman Society and Roman Law*, p. 54).

seventy horsemen and two hundred spearmen to go as far as
24 Caesarea. Also provide mounts for Paul to ride, and bring
25 him safely to Felix the governor.' And he wrote a letter to
this effect:

26   'Claudius Lysias to his Excellency the governor Felix,
27 greeting. This man was seized by the Jews, and was about
to be killed by them, when I came upon them with the
soldiers and rescued him, having learned that he was a Roman
28 citizen. And desiring to know the charge on which they
29 accused him, I brought him down to their council. I found
that he was accused about questions of their law, but charged
30 with nothing deserving death or imprisonment. And when
it was disclosed to me that there would be a plot against the
man, I sent him to you at once, ordering his accusers also to
state before you what they have against him.'

31   So the soldiers, according to their instructions, took Paul
32 and brought him by night to Antipatris. And on the morrow
they returned to the barracks, leaving the horsemen to go on
33 with him. When they came to Caesarea and delivered the
letter to the governor, they presented Paul also before him.
34 On reading the letter, he asked to what province he belonged.
35 When he learned that he was from Cilicia he said, 'I will

---

26   *his Excellency* is the translation of the epithet applied to Theophilus
in Luke 1[3]. In an inscription of the time of Nero it is used of a prefect.
The letter is, of course, the composition of Luke, for it is most unlikely
that he could have found a copy of the original letter. Claudius
Antonius *Felix*, a freedman, was brother of Pallas, at this time in high
favour with the Emperor Nero; they had both been given equestrian
rank as an unusual mark of the Emperor's patronage; this fact alone
would tend to render them unpopular with the ruling class of the
Roman Empire. For the dates of Felix's procuratorship, see above,
Introduction, pp. 20–21.
34   On this query about the province of Paul's origin, see above,
Introduction, p. 9.

hear you when your accusers arrive.' And he commanded
him to be guarded in Herod's praetorium.

AND after five days the high priest Ananias came down with

24: 1–27. *Paul's encounters with Felix*

Paul's experiences in Roman law courts have caused commentators much research and conjecture, but not many
concrete conclusions have been reached. This is mainly because
in fact ancient historians have very little information at their
disposal about Roman legal processes in the first century A.D.;
most of their ideas have to be derived either from the statements of writers in the first century B.C. (mainly Cicero) or
from the utterances of great jurists of the later Roman Empire,
the earliest of whom dates from the third decade of the third
century. One result of this paucity of evidence is that it is
unscientific and unscholarly to conclude that in any of his
references to Paul's case Luke could not be correct, unless we
have very strong evidence to support such a conclusion.

Many questions have been raised by those who have studied
the account in Acts of Paul's trials. Why did Felix defer the
trial? Was it really true that if Paul had not appealed to
Caesar he would have been set free (26[32])? Had Festus power
to free him? Could only Roman citizens appeal to Caesar, or
could anyone, and was the appeal customarily lodged before
sentence or after sentence? An answer to some of these questions has been attempted in the Introduction (see above,
p. 6). But one important point has been made recently by
one of the latest authorities on the subject, a point which may
throw light on some of the uncertainties involved in Paul's
trials. Sherwin-White (*Roman Society and Roman Law*, pp. 1–23,
49–51, 53) reminds us how informal and how much subject
to the whim or arbitrament of the official holding *imperium* (in
this case the procurator of Judaea) were trials in the provinces
in the period covered by Paul's life. The initiative in presenting
a case against anyone must be taken by an individual, and
a very wide licence was allowed to the speeches both for the
prosecution and for the defence. The use of a *consilium* (assessors) by the presiding official is attested too, and this could be

A ship being towed into harbour, near a lighthouse (left), and (right) the passengers celebrate their arrival in an inn (relief from Ostia).

composed of any persons. Festus, for instance, could, if he liked, have called in the Sanhedrin as his *consilium* in Paul's case (25^{9-12}) and it is possibly because he feared this move that Paul made his appeal to Caesar.

Many commentators have complained of the vagueness of the charges made against Paul, and it is true that one finds a difficulty when one inquires of Acts what were the precise charges made against him. But owing to the wide range of the *imperium* wielded by the procurator in these circumstances it was not necessary for the accusers to make one of a traditional list of charges, but only to invite the judge to consider the facts alleged and to see whether they deserved punishment. The accusations of Tertullus, for instance (24^5), make no reference to any points of Jewish law (though these were no doubt handled in the accusations made by the Jews afterwards), but concentrate on what would alarm the procurator. We have already noted the close similarity between Tertullus' accusation and the conduct attributed to Jews by Claudius in his *Letter to the People of Alexandria* (see above, p. 10). There is plenty of precedent for Felix's adjourning the trial. He could, if he liked, have dismissed the whole case and let

some elders and a spokesman, one Tertullus. They laid
before the governor their case against Paul; and when he was
called, Tertullus began to accuse him, saying:

'Since through you we enjoy much peace, and since by
your provision, most excellent Felix, reforms are introduced
on behalf of this nation, in every way and everywhere we
accept this with all gratitude. But, to detain you no further,

---

Paul go free when he was giving up his procuratorship; or if
at any point during his tenure of office he found the list of cases
to be tried a long one he could have simply cut the list in
half by this method. Lucian says that when, in the middle
of the next century, Peregrinus was awaiting trial, on a charge
connected with his being a Christian, he was discharged scot-
free in this manner by the governor of Syria (Lucian, *On the
Death of Peregrinus*, 14).

Tertullus' speech is only a short summary of a conventional
orator's speech in a law court, including a flattering opening (a well-
known gambit, called the *captatio benevolentiae*), and a piece of gross
exaggeration when he describes Paul as *an agitator among all the Jews
throughout the world*. The speech is almost a humorous caricature, like
the account of the behaviour of the mob in the temple at Ephesus
(19²³⁻⁴¹). Vv. 6*b*, 7, and 8*a* are omitted by the RSV. They appear in
MSS. of the 'Western' tradition, and some others as well. These words
finish off Tertullus' speech better than the last words in the existing
text, and they appear to be supported by 24²³. Some scholars, including Lake (in *The Beginnings of Christianity*) have been inclined to
accept them as one more example of a 'Western' retention of an
original reading. But there are some serious objections to taking this
view. It would mean that the words *by examining him* (v. 8) would
have to mean 'by Felix examining Lysias', which would be strange,
considering that Lysias is not present. By *him* Tertullus must mean
Paul, because the second *him* in the sentence certainly means Paul.
It is not certain that the Jews could have claimed that they might
have *tried* Paul themselves, though it is possible that in view of the
prohibition against bringing non-Jews past the barrier they might
have *lynched* him themselves (and the notice referred to at 21²⁸, ²⁹
suggests a lynching rather than a trial). And the words can be explained as a characteristic piece of 'Western' smoothing and sup-
plementing.

5 I beg you in your kindness to hear us briefly. For we have found this man a pestilent fellow, an agitator among all the Jews throughout the world, and a ringleader of the sect of the Nazarenes. He even tried to profane the temple, but we

6 seized him.[a] By examining him yourself you will be able to

8 learn from him about everything of which we accuse him.'

The Jews also joined in the charge, affirming that all this

9 was so.

And when the governor had motioned to him to speak,

10 Paul replied:

'Realizing that for many years you have been judge over this nation, I cheerfully make my defense. As you may

11 ascertain, it is not more than twelve days since I went up to worship at Jerusalem; and they did not find me disputing

12 with any one or stirring up a crowd, either in the temple or in the synagogues, or in the city. Neither can they prove to

13 you what they now bring up against me. But this I admit to

14 you, that according to the Way, which they call a sect,

a *Other ancient authorities add* and we would have judged him according to our law. [7]But the chief captain Lysias came and with great violence took him out of our hands, [8]commanding his accusers to come before you.

10–23   This is an exact and effective answer to the charges made against him on the part of Paul; the speech, one feels, which he would have made at the examination in the presence of the Sanhedrin, had he not been interrupted.

10   *for many years* is an inaccurate description of the length of Felix's tenure of office, for he had been procurator at this point for probably no more than two years. But miscalculations for the sake of creating goodwill were not uncommon in public statements at that time. The Emperor Claudius in his *Letter to the People of Alexandria* states that he had had goodwill towards the citizens 'for a long time', though he had not been Emperor for a year when he wrote the letter.

14   Paul prefers the description *Way* for Christianity; its opponents call it a *sect.* The Greek for the last word is αἵρεσις, from which the word 'heresy' is derived. It is the word used, in no particularly bad

I worship the God of our fathers, believing everything laid
down by the law or written in the prophets, having a hope in
God which these themselves accept, that there will be a
resurrection of both the just and the unjust. So I always take
pains to have a clear conscience toward God and toward
men. Now after some years I came to bring to my nation
alms and offerings. As I was doing this, they found me purified in the temple, without any crowd or tumult. But some
Jews from Asia—they ought to be here before you and to
make an accusation, if they have anything against me. Or
else let these men themselves say what wrongdoing they
found when I stood before the council, except this one thing
which I cried out while standing among them, "With respect
to the resurrection of the dead I am on trial before you this
day."'

But Felix, having a rather accurate knowledge of the Way,

---

sense, for the 'party' of the Pharisees at 15⁵. In the present passage,
of course, the word has a bad sense. It does not mean 'heresy', for
this sense only appears in the second century. But it does convey the
quarrelsomeness and wilful preference for its own opinion characteristic of some among the supporters of the various schools of Greek
philosophy. Paul says that he believes *everything laid down by the law
or written in the prophets*, not meaning to imply a meticulous observance
by him of the precepts and ordinances of the Pentateuch, but that he
is convinced that the proper fulfilment and meaning given to books
of the Old Testament, legal and historical and prophetical (the last
two categories covered by the *prophets*), is to be found in Christ.

Another allusion to the coming Judgement, for the resurrection of
both the good and the bad would be for judgement: cp. Dan. 12², ³;
Rev. 20¹¹⁻¹⁵.

As has been mentioned already (see above, on 19²¹ and 21²³) Luke
here betrays that he knows that Paul was making a collection for the
poor Christians in Jerusalem on his last journey before his arrest.

Luke may feel justified in describing Felix as *having a rather accurate
knowledge of the Way* because (as v. 24 tells us) he was married to
a Jewess, Drusilla, the youngest daughter of Herod Agrippa I and

put them off saying, 'When Lysias the tribune comes down,
23 I will decide your case.' Then he gave orders to the centurion
that he should be kept in custody but should have some
liberty, and that none of his friends should be prevented from
attending to his needs.

24   After some days Felix came with his wife Drusilla, who
was a Jewess; and he sent for Paul and heard him speak upon
25 faith in Christ Jesus. And as he argued about justice and self-
control and future judgment, Felix was alarmed and said
'Go away for the present; when I have an opportunity I will
26 summon you.' At the same time he hoped that money would
be given him by Paul. So he sent for him often and conversed
27 with him. But when two years had elapsed, Felix was succeeded by Porcius Festus; and desiring to do the Jews a
favor, Felix left Paul in prison.

---

therefore the sister of Herod Agrippa II, who is the 'Agrippa the
king' of Chs. 25 and 26. *Put them off* (ἀνεβάλετο) may be a technical
term, meaning 'prorogued the hearing'.
24   For the 'Western' reading here see on v. 27.
25   Yet another reference to future judgement, which by the nature
of the argument could not be regarded as indefinitely postponed.
26   Both Josephus and Tacitus accuse Felix of a readiness to be bribed.
27   Does the expression *when two years had elapsed* mean that Paul had
next spent two years in captivity in Caesarea? This is the meaning
usually given to it. But the Greek could just as well mean 'when his
tenure of office of two years' duration had elapsed, Felix was succeeded by Porcius Festus'. This is quite as likely a translation as the
other, and if it were adopted would fit in best with the supposition
that Felix gave up office in A.D. 55. This rather vague phrase does
not, however, imply that Felix was recalled immediately after the
last mentioned incident. In fact it is likely that some time elapsed
between Felix's adjournment of Paul's case and his departure.
     At v. 24 the 'Western' tradition (if we can regard it as adequately
represented by the margin of the Harklean Syriac version alone,
D being deficient here) added after *Drusilla who was a Jewess* the
words 'who was anxious to see Paul and to hear him speaking;
therefore, desiring to please her, he sent . . .'. At the end of v. 27 the

Now when Festus had come into his province, after three

'Western' tradition (614, 2147, Sy[h(mg)]) reads 'but he left Paul in custody because of Drusilla'. Felix had enticed Drusilla away from her first husband, Aziz, King of Emesa. It may be that the interpolator assumed that Paul's discourse about self-control (v. 25) came too near the bone in the case of Drusilla, and that she revenged herself for his plain speaking by persuading Felix to leave Paul in custody. It argues a surprising knowledge of the family of the Herods in the interpolator.

25: 1–12. *Paul appeals to Caesar*

To understand Paul's situation we must realize that, to put it technically, Acts assumes the operation of *provocatio* but not of *appellatio*. Acts assumes the early procedure whereby the case, on appeal to Rome, is taken out of the hands of the judge in the provinces (proconsul or proconsular legate or imperial legate), perhaps after a preliminary investigation, before the verdict has been given in the first court, for trial and sentence and everything else in the Emperor's court in Rome. The later system, *appellatio*, whereby *after* sentence by the judge in the provinces the convicted person appeals to the Emperor, was only in its infancy in the time of the Antonines (i.e., no earlier than A.D. 140 and probably later). This means that Paul must have appealed before sentence.

The reason why Festus allowed a serious crime akin to treason to be made the subject of appeal by the accused person is probably that he had no choice. The original *Lex Julia de Vi Publica* (passed somewhere between 50 and 30 B.C.) forbade any official vested with *imperium* or *potestas* to kill, scourge, torture, condemn, or put in heavy chains, a Roman citizen who appealed to the people (converted about 30 B.C. into an appeal to the *princeps*), or to prevent a defendant from presenting himself at Rome within a certain time. Some provincial governors were vested with a particularly wide authority called *merum imperium* (absolute power), and they could try citizens on charges covered by statutory laws (i.e., on a list of conventional crimes such as murder, adultery, fraud), without appeal. From the exercise of *coercitio extra ordinem* (i.e., the judicial process, described above, on 24[1], whereby the accuser stated the facts and asked the judge to decide whether the actions complained

2 days he went up to Jerusalem from Caesarea. And the chief priests and the principal men of the Jews informed him
3 against Paul; and they urged him, asking as a favor to have the man sent to Jerusalem, planning an ambush to kill him
4 on the way. Festus replied that Paul was being kept at Caesarea, and that he himself intended to go there shortly.
5 'So,' said he, 'let the men of authority among you go down with me, and if there is anything wrong about the man, let them accuse him.'

---

of were punishable, a very wide discretion in defining guilt being left to the judge) the right of *provocatio* before sentence did apply, at least for Roman citizens (see A. H. M. Jones, *Studies in Roman Government and Law*, pp. 53–65).[1]

The question why Festus proposed to Paul an adjournment to Jerusalem cannot be answered. We do not know Festus' motive in doing this, though apparently Paul did, or thought he did, and took counter-measures against it. Jones (*Studies in Roman Government*, p. 53) prudently remarks that there can hardly be enough evidence available to say that any feature of the judicial process described by Luke could not have happened.

[1] Among ancient authorities *Porcius Festus* is only mentioned here in Acts, and twice in Josephus, so that very little is known about him. He probably acceded to the procuratorship A.D. 55/6 (see the very useful discussion of this date in Haenchen, pp. 63–69). He died in 62. In the interval between his death and the arrival of a successor

---

[1] There are some examples of Roman officials' ignoring an appeal, and this may be because they held this *merum imperium*. In at least one example, however, a legate of Lower Germany in A.D. 68/9, Fonteius Capito, who refused, or virtually refused, a prisoner's appeal and executed him, was punished with death by the Emperor Galba for this act (Dio Cassius, VIII. xiii. 2). It is unlikely that anybody as insignificant as a procurator of Judaea would have been vested with *merum imperium*; and it is likely that the crime Paul was charged with was *extra ordinem*. It is true that Florus, a later procurator of Judaea, flogged and crucified even Jews who were knights, and therefore certainly Roman citizens (Josephus, *Jewish War*, ii. 308), but this was probably because he thought that in the circumstances he could do so with impunity.

When he had stayed among them not more than eight or ten days, he went down to Caesarea; and the next day he took his seat on the tribunal and ordered Paul to be brought. And when he had come, the Jews who had gone down from Jerusalem stood about him, bringing against him many serious charges which they could not prove. Paul said in his defense, 'Neither against the law of the Jews, not against the temple, nor against Caesar have I offended at all.' But Festus, wishing to do the Jews a favor, said to Paul, 'Do you wish to go up to Jerusalem, and there be tried on these charges before me?' But Paul said, 'I am standing before Caesar's tribunal, where I ought to be tried; to the Jews I have done no wrong, as you know very well. If then I am a wrongdoer and have committed anything for which I deserve to die, I do not seek to escape death; but if there is nothing in their

---

(Albinus) the High Priest Ananus (a different man from the Ananias of Acts 23²) had James the brother of the Lord murdered.

nor against Caesar does not by any means necessarily imply that Paul was accused of a crime against Caesar. The most serious crime that he could presumably have been charged with was that of starting a riot in the Temple area, and this could at a pinch be construed into the accusation of rebellion against Caesar's authority. But this construction seems far-fetched, and there had been no hint hitherto that Paul was accused of a crime against Caesar. Starting a riot in itself, however, was a grave charge.

It is most unlikely that the suggestion of some commentators is correct that Festus was offering Paul the alternative of being tried in Jerusalem by a local court, viz. the Sanhedrin. Quite apart from the words *before me*, it is most doubtful if the Sanhedrin was at any point allowed by the Romans to inflict judicial punishment of a serious sort for grave crimes, nor to put people to death. Festus may have been attempting a compromise: when he was in Jerusalem he would not please the Jews by sending for Paul against his will; but he might persuade Paul to come to be tried in Jerusalem of his own free will.

This verse certainly appears to imply that the charges upon which Paul was being tried could carry the death penalty. In the procedure of *coercitio extra ordinem* few possibilities could be ruled out.

charges against me, no one can give me up to them. I appeal
12 to Caesar.' Then Festus, when he had conferred with his
council, answered, 'You have appealed to Caesar; to Caesar
you shall go.'

13   Now when some days had passed, Agrippa the king and

---

12   It is interesting to observe that Festus *conferred with his council*
before allowing Paul's appeal. These were his assessors, friends, and
legal experts brought in by the presiding official to assist him. It is
unlikely that there was a legal obligation upon Festus to consult his
council. He probably was not, being a new and inexperienced procurator, very well versed in law. He may have wanted assurance from
his legal experts that he was obliged to allow the appeal, or that he
would be well advised to do so.

25: 13–26: 32. *Paul meets King Agrippa*

13   This king is Agrippa II, son of Herod Agrippa of Acts 12[1–23] (who
was himself son of Aristobulus, son of Herod the Great). Agrippa II
had been brought up in Rome; he was brother of Drusilla, Felix's
wife. He reigned *c.* 50–100 over a kingdom which steadily increased
in extent during his lifetime. He was a consistent and lifelong sup-
porter of the Roman government. Berenice is the correct form of
Bernice, a vulgar form used by Luke; it is a Macedonian form of the
name Pherenice, which appears in one Latin form as Veronica. She
was Agrippa's and Drusilla's sister, and had been married first to
a commoner called Marcus, son of Alexander, and then to her uncle,
another Herod, King of Chalcis. He had died in A.D. 48 and she was
now living as a widow with a rather lurid reputation at her brother's
court. Later she had a short trial marriage with Polemo, ruler of a very
small principality which entitled him to call himself King of Cilicia,
but soon returned to her brother's court. Later still she had a romantic
and well-publicized love-affair with Titus, son of the Emperor Vespasian (69–79), who was himself Emperor from 79 to 81. Luke
assumes that all his readers would know who Agrippa and Berenice
were. This certainly suggests that Acts was written after 69, when
Vespasian and his son first came into the limelight, and probably
later. The more important kings of the Herod family would probably
be known to a Roman public because they all had close connexions
with Rome. Incidentally, it is no mean feat of synchronization on
Luke's part which has correctly placed Felix and Drusilla, Agrippa
and Berenice, within a short span of time in the same area (see above,
Introduction, p. 8).

13–22 The conversation between Festus and Agrippa is, of course, a piece

Bernice arrived at Caesarea to welcome Festus. And as they stayed there many days, Festus laid Paul's case before the king, saying, 'There is a man left prisoner by Felix; and when I was at Jerusalem, the chief priests and the elders of the Jews gave information about him, asking for sentence against him. I answered them that it was not the custom of the Romans to give up any one before the accused met the accusers face to face, and had opportunity to make his defense concerning the charge laid against him. When therefore they came together here, I made no delay, but on the next day took my seat on the tribunal and ordered the man to be brought in. When the accusers stood up, they brought no charge in his case of such evils as I supposed; but they had certain points of dispute with him about their own superstition and about one Jesus, who was dead, but whom Paul asserted to be alive. Being at a loss how to investigate these questions, I asked whether he wished to go to Jerusalem and be tried there regarding them. But when Paul had appealed to be kept in custody for the decision of the emperor, I commanded him to be held until I could send him to Caesar.' And Agrippa said to Festus, 'I should like to hear the man myself.' 'Tomorrow,' said he, 'you shall hear him.'

---

of imaginative writing by Luke, in which Festus is careful to present as unimpeachable his motives in offering Paul the chance of being tried in Jerusalem (v. 20). He also (v. 16) gives utterance to a fine sentiment about the impartiality of Roman justice, which supports Luke's claim that the Roman authorities have acted with equity towards Christianity and found no reason to regard it as harmful. He does, however, as presented by Luke, speak as if the alternative of handing Paul over (v. 16, *give up any one*) to the Sanhedrin for trial had been open. We have already seen that it is very unlikely, though not entirely impossible, that the Romans would have allowed the Sanhedrin to try and execute people on capital charges. John 18[31] certainly implies that they had not.

23   So on the morrow Agrippa and Bernice came with great
pomp, and they entered the audience hall with the military
tribunes and the prominent men of the city. Then by com-
24 mand of Festus Paul was brought in. And Festus said, 'King
Agrippa and all who are present with us, you see this man
about whom the whole Jewish people petitioned me, both
at Jerusalem and here, shouting that he ought not to live any
25 longer. But I found that he had done nothing deserving
death; and as he himself appealed to the emperor, I decided
26 to send him. But I have nothing definite to write to my lord
about him. Therefore I have brought him before you, and
especially before you, King Agrippa, that, after we have
27 examined him, I may have something to write. For it seems
to me unreasonable, in sending a prisoner, not to indicate
the charges against him.'

26 AGRIPPA said to Paul, 'You have permission to speak for yourself.' Then Paul stretched out his hand and made his defense:
2   'I think myself fortunate that it is before you, King

24, 25   These verses again imply that whatever it was that the Jews were
accusing Paul of could carry the death penalty.
26   This is the first example in ancient literature of the use of the
expression *my lord* (NEB 'our Sovereign' τῷ κυρίῳ) to denote the
Emperor, unaccompanied by any name or title. But it is paralleled
in literature of about the same period.
27   We cannot, of course, insist that we have here the very words of
Festus and of Agrippa. Luke is constructing the conversation imagi-
natively. But there is no reason why Paul should not have been brought
before King Agrippa II, not in a trial scene nor an official examination, but as an interesting case upon which Agrippa, as a prominent
Jew very well versed in Jewish religion and Jewish ways, might give
advice or make useful comments. And we can sympathize with
Festus' difficulty in obtaining concrete facts and suitable material to
put into the dossier which he was obliged to send with Paul.
26: 2   Paul, as interpreted by Luke (who plainly has composed this

Agrippa, I am to make my defense today against all the accusations of the Jews, because you are especially familiar with all customs and controversies of the Jews; therefore I beg you to listen to me patiently.

'My manner of life from my youth, spent from the beginning among my own nation and at Jerusalem, is known by all the Jews. They have known for a long time, if they are willing to testify, that according to the strictest party of our religion I have lived as a Pharisee. And now I stand here on trial for hope in the promise made by God to our fathers, to which our twelve tribes hope to attain, as they earnestly

---

speech too) can begin a speech with a *captatio benevolentiae* as nicely calculated as that of Tertullus (24², ³).

among my own nation and at Jerusalem. Does this mean 'in the Jewish community in Tarsus and at Jerusalem'? If it does, then it might suggest that Paul spent more than his earliest infancy in Tarsus. The word for *nation* (ἔθνος) is used by Luke for the Jews more than once (24¹⁰, 28¹⁹), and F. F. Bruce (on 24¹⁰) thinks that it means Jews living as an organized community, among Gentiles, and so here it would refer to the Jewish community in Tarsus. Against this van Unnik (*Tarsus or Jerusalem*, pp. 46–48) argues that it would be pointless in Paul to appeal confidently to *all the Jews* as people who had known his life in Jerusalem, if he had come to Jerusalem only when he was fifteen or so, having spent his life up to then in Tarsus. Further, the word for *and* (τε), which is a favourite one with Luke, and particularly in Acts, could mean 'yes, indeed' (as it may at 6⁷, 11²¹, and 15³⁹), so conveying merely a closer definition of the concept *among my own nation* rather than adding a parallel clause to it. We are not therefore compelled by this verse to modify the view we took at 22³.

party is again αἵρεσις; see above, on 24¹⁴.

Paul means that the whole nation of the Jews (which in spite of the loss of ten tribes at the exile in 721 B.C. had in some way which is still obscure divided itself again into twelve tribes, cp. Luke 2³⁶), by maintaining the cult of the Unnamable God in the Temple all round the twenty-four hours of the day, hoped to attain eventually to the resurrection from the dead. The word *Jews* is emphatic. They were the last people who should persecute somebody for believing in the resurrection from the dead.

worship night and day. And for this hope I am accused by
8 Jews, O king! Why is it thought incredible by any of you
that God raises the dead?

9 'I myself was convinced that I ought to do many things in
10 opposing the name of Jesus of Nazareth. And I did so in
Jerusalem; I not only shut up many of the saints in prison
by authority from the chief priests, but when they were put
11 to death I cast my vote against them. And I punished them
often in all the synagogues and tried to make them blas-
pheme; and in raging fury against them, I persecuted them
even to foreign cities.

12 'Thus I journeyed to Damascus with the authority and
13 commission of the chief priests. At midday, O king, I saw
on the way a light from heaven, brighter than the sun,
14 shining round me and those who journeyed with me. And
when we had all fallen to the ground, I heard a voice saying

---

10   Once again it seems that Luke believed the Sanhedrin had the
power to inflict the death penalty.

11   Luke is not representing Paul as using exaggerated language
here. One can point to Paul's own experiences at the hands of Jews
(13^{50}, 14^{19}); and we have his own words, 'five times received I of the
Jews the forty lashes less one' (2 Cor. 11^{24}). Officially or unofficially,
determined Jews could do a great deal of harm to those with whom
they disagreed.

12-18   The last and concisest account of Paul's conversion. (For the others,
see above, on 22^6.) It is also in many ways the one most modified by
later experience; vv. 16–18 represent an elaboration of the original
message of the Voice, designed to indicate clearly to the readers of
Acts what was Paul's precise role in God's design. Many details
present in the first two accounts (including Paul's baptism and the
whole episode of Ananias) have been suppressed in order to make way
for this explanation.

14   *It hurts you to kick against the goads*, an expression which does not
appear in either of the first two accounts, is a well-known Greek
proverb. It appears in its fullest form in Euripides, *Bacchae*, 794 f.,
but also in Aeschylus, *Agamemnon*, 1624. In these authors it means
that it is no use struggling against one's destiny. It is wholly unlikely

to me in the Hebrew language, "Saul, Saul, why do you persecute me? It hurts you to kick against the goads." And I said, "Who are you, Lord?" And the Lord said, "I am Jesus whom you are persecuting. But rise and stand upon your feet; for I have appeared to you for this purpose, to appoint you to serve and bear witness to the things in which you have seen me and to those in which I will appear to you, delivering you from the people and from the Gentiles—to whom I send you to open their eyes, that they may turn from darkness to light and from the power of Satan to God, that they may receive forgiveness of sins and a place among those who are sanctified by faith in me."

'Wherefore, O King Agrippa, I was not disobedient to the heavenly vision, but declared first to those at Damascus, then at Jerusalem and throughout all the country of Judea, and also to the Gentiles, that they should repent and turn to God and perform deeds worthy of their repentance. For this reason the Jews seized me in the temple and tried to kill me. To this day I have had the help that comes from God, and

---

that Luke copied it from Euripides. He threw in a popular saying to make his narrative more effective at this point.

Paul's language, as he describes his own destiny ordained by God, becomes more biblical. He quotes Ezek. 2¹; Jer. 1⁷; and Isa. 35⁵, 42⁷, ¹⁶.

A considerable difficulty is here encountered in the phrase *throughout all the country of Judaea*, for not only does it correspond to no known evangelizing activity of Paul, either referred to in his letters (in fact Gal. 1²² almost contradicts it) or recorded in Acts, but grammatically it is very difficult to fit into the sentence. The only representative of the 'Western' tradition at this point, ℘²⁹, smooths over this difficulty. It may be simply that at this point Luke's attention relaxed long enough for him to admit for the sake of oratorical effect a phrase which was both careless and inaccurate; or the words may be an early interpolation.

This is what the Jews should have paid attention to instead of maintaining the Temple cult (v. 7); understanding the Law and the

so I stand here testifying both to small and great, saying
nothing but what the prophets and Moses said would come
23 to pass: that the Christ must suffer, and that, by being the
first to rise from the dead, he would proclaim light both to
the people and to the Gentiles.'

24   And as he thus made his defense, Festus said with a loud
voice, 'Paul, you are mad; your great learning is turning
25 you mad.' But Paul said, 'I am not mad, most excellent
26 Festus, but I am speaking the sober truth. For the king
knows about these things, and to him I speak freely; for
I am persuaded that none of these things has escaped his
27 notice, for this was not done in a corner. King Agrippa, do
you believe the prophets? I know that you believe.' And
28 Agrippa said to Paul, 'In a short time you think to make me

---

Prophets. If they had, they would have realized that the Christ must
suffer and would rise from the dead.

    Literally, 'if the Christ must suffer . . . if he would proclaim light',
23 an unusual construction but not an impossible one. It was suggested
by Rendel Harris that these clauses are expressed in this way because they were part of a list of subjects in debate between Jews
and Christians, and perhaps had been taken from a book of proof-
texts.

28   This reply of King Agrippa, in what is one of the most effective
dialogues in Acts, and indeed in the whole New Testament, is
a famous one, but its exact meaning is not quite certain. It could
mean 'you are not far from converting me' (said either seriously or
sarcastically); so the AV, with its 'almost thou persuadest me to be
a Christian'. Or it could mean 'you are expecting to convert me in
a very short time, or with very little effort'; so the RV, with its cumbrous and gratuitously archaic 'with but little persuasion thou
wouldest fain make me a Christian', and the RSV here. The NEB
'you think it will not take much to win me over and make a Christian
of me' characteristically gives us such full measure in translation that
we wonder where all this meaning came from, but it seems to incline
to the second translation. There is a question of an alternative reading
too, 'to be a Christian' or 'to profess Christianity' (literally 'to make
a Christian'), of which the second is preferable (and is preferred by

a Christian!' And Paul said, 'Whether short or long, I would

both RSV and NEB). Lake (in *The Beginnings of Christianity*) translates colloquially 'you make short work of turning me into a missionary',

A bust of the Emperor Nero, from Barking Hall, Suffolk.

taking 'make a Christian' to mean 'play the Christian', and no doubt this is the best sense. Agrippa is sneering, not sympathizing.

Whether short or long picks up Agrippa's words, though not in a very exact sense, for *short and long* is clearly a common expression.

to God that not only you but also all who hear me this day might become such as I am—except for these chains.'

30   Then the king rose, and the governor and Bernice and
31   those who were sitting with them; and when they had withdrawn, they said to one another, 'This man is doing nothing
32   to deserve death or imprisonment.' And Agrippa said to
Festus, 'This man could have been set free if he had not
appealed to Caesar.'

27   AND when it was decided that we should sail for Italy, they

---

31, 32   It is unlikely that Luke could have discovered what Festus or
Agrippa or his court could have said to each other after this scene.
These verses express his own opinion of what they must have thought
and of what was the true state of Paul's case. Paul need not have been
fettered during the hearing; but there is good evidence for the practice
of Roman citizens' being fettered on a journey to a court.

27: 1–44. *Paul reaches Malta*

The account of Paul's journey towards Rome and his shipwreck at Malta has attracted the attention of many. The
majority of twentieth-century critics have till recently accepted
the account of the voyage as a reliable piece of narrative given
by, or reproduced from, the pen of someone who accompanied
Paul. The fourth and last 'we' passage begins at 27[1] and does
not end till 28[16]. The voyage, to say the least, has no in-
trinsic improbability in it. If Paul did at some point travel
to Rome from Palestine, presumably he could have done so in
this way. But recently Haenchen and Conzelmann, while not
denying that the story describes a real voyage, have expressed
doubts whether it was the voyage of St. Paul. They point out
that Paul's part in the story, as far, at least, as Malta, can be
easily detached from the rest. They point to the existence of
several stories of sea voyage and shipwreck in literature
roughly contemporary with Luke, or belonging to a period not
long after his. Conzelmann in an Appendix to his Commentary
reproduces parts of a few of these by way of comparison.
They suggest that Luke has used a popular contemporary

delivered Paul and some other prisoners to a centurion of
the Augustan Cohort, named Julius. And embarking in a ship
of Adramyttium, which was about to sail to the ports along
the coast of Asia, we put to sea, accompanied by Aristarchus,

---

story of a shipwreck in order to lend interest and excitement,
and has rather clumsily inserted some fictitious anecdotes
about Paul in order to connect it with the rest of his narrative.

One point can be made without fear of contradiction. The
account of the voyage from Sidon to Malta (vv. 3–44) is the
account of a real voyage, not an imaginary one. The places,
distances, times, winds, and weather conditions are remarkably
and most impressively consistent. The manœuvres of the ship,
as far as we can understand them, are appropriate and
reasonable. Anybody who has read the monograph devoted
to Paul's voyage and shipwreck by the Scotsman James Smith
more than a century ago, or the magisterial commentary upon
this chapter in *The Beginnings of Christianity*, vol. iv, cannot
avoid this conclusion. There are no miracles, no legendary
traits. The question is whether this was a voyage made *by Paul*,
or by somebody else whose narrative Luke used after he had
inserted into it some material introducing Paul. Hitherto the
impression that their author accompanied Paul on the
journeys described has been much stronger in the 'we'
passages than in any other parts of Luke's narratives. The use
of the first person plural undoubtedly implies that the narrator, where he uses it, intends the reader to think that he was
there, and the first two 'we' passages do not remove this
impression. Why should the fourth 'we' passage be an exception? According to the theory of Conzelmann, Luke, having
no information as to how Paul reached Rome from Palestine,
searched till he found a story of someone going in the same
direction and used it. But what a coincidence! A story,
unknown to any other writer of antiquity, describing a voyage
in the same direction, and describing it with an attention to
detail unparalleled in the accounts given by Conzelmann in
his Appendix. What a fortunate discovery!

Augustan (Σεβαστῆς) is an honorary title bestowed sometimes on
auxiliary troops, well attested in inscriptions.

Aristarchus was last met with at 20[4]; cp. 19[29]. If we are to take

3 a Macedonian from Thessalonica. The next day we put in at
Sidon; and Julius treated Paul kindly, and gave him leave to
4 go to his friends and be cared for. And putting to sea from
there we sailed under the lee of Cyprus, because the winds
5 were against us. And when we had sailed across the sea
which is off Cilicia and Pamphylia, we came to Myra in
6 Lycia. There the centurion found a ship of Alexandria sailing
7 for Italy, and put us on board. We sailed slowly for a number
of days, and arrived with difficulty off Cnidus, and as the

Philem. 24 and Col. 4¹⁰ as written by Paul from prison in Rome, he
probably accompanied Paul all the way. But he may have been
travelling only a part of it, perhaps towards his native Thessalonica,
for Luke never mentions him without also mentioning that he came
from Thessalonica in Macedonia. Adramyttium is a rather obscure
city on the coast of Mysia, south of Troas.

3 From Caesarea to Sidon is a distance of about 47 miles. This
sympathetic treatment of a prisoner on a journey is not unparalleled.
About fifty years later Ignatius of Antioch, while he was being
escorted in much less propitious circumstances by five soldiers to
Rome—for he was a criminal condemned on a capital charge and
was not a Roman citizen—was allowed to see groups of his friends in
the cities through which he passed, receive letters from them, and
send letters to them.

4, 5 *sailed under the lee of Cyprus* means keeping Cyprus between them
and the prevailing wind. As this tactic brought them to the coast of
Cilicia and Pamphylia it is likely that they sailed to the *east* of Cyprus,
the wind being westerly, and there, assisted by a local wind, which
blows from the east parallel to the southern shore of Asia Minor,
and by a current, sailed westward along the coast to Myra. In
v. 5, after *when we had sailed across the sea*, the 'Western' text adds 'in
fourteen days'. Lake (*The Beginnings of Christianity*) was so much
impressed by the correspondence of this period to the time likely to
have been spent in a voyage of this sort in a sailing-boat of the ancient
world that he accepted it as genuine.

7 This course is perfectly understandable. Finding themselves now
faced by an open sea with no protection from the prevailing (west)
wind, they could not sail directly into the wind but had to tack, and
chose to make southwards for Crete. To have made this move sooner
than when they were off *Cnidus* would have meant sailing with the

wind did not allow us to go on, we sailed under the lee of
Crete off Salmone. Coasting along it with difficulty, we came
to a place called Fair Havens, near which was the city of
Lasea.

As much time had been lost, and the voyage was already
dangerous because the fast had already gone by, Paul
advised them, saying, 'Sirs, I perceive that the voyage will
be with injury and much loss, not only of the cargo and the
ship, but also of our lives.' But the centurion paid more
attention to the captain and to the owner of the ship than
to what Paul said. And because the harbor was not suitable
to winter in, the majority advised to put to sea from there,
on the chance that somehow they could reach Phoenix,

---

shore of Rhodes to the east of them dangerously near, and with a west
wind blowing them on to it.

Fair Havens may be a place called Calolomonia, of which the name
Fair Havens (Καλοὶ Λιμένες) is a corruption or adaptation.

The fast means the Day of Atonement, on the tenth of the Jewish
month of Tishri, which occurred in part of September and part of
October. Jews usually reckoned that sailing after this day was
dangerous, and the sea can have been regarded as open only for
about another fortnight. Sailing during the winter season was
unusual, though not completely unknown (for instance Herod the
Great sailed from Rhodes to Brundisium and back again from
Brundisium to Ptolemais during the winter months of the year
40/39 B.C.). Paul may have celebrated the Day of Atonement on ship-
board before the party disembarked at Fair Havens, or there may have
been a synagogue at Lasea where he could celebrate it.

The centurion, as a soldier charged with important state business,
is consulted about the question of whether it is safe to sail. The captain
is responsible for the navigation. The owner hires the captain, but,
as he is on board, naturally has a say in the ship's movements. He
may have been a private contractor for the transport of publicly
owned corn (see Plate p. 181). It is unlikely that this was a government
ship. It looks as if there was some discussion of the question among
the passengers also; Paul may have been the spokesman for the
passengers' opinions.

a harbor of Crete, looking northeast and southeast,[a] and winter there.

13 And when the south wind blew gently, supposing that they had obtained their purpose, they weighed anchor and 14 sailed along Crete, close inshore. But soon a tempestuous wind, called the northeaster, struck down from the land; 15 and when the ship was caught and could not face the wind, 16 we gave way to it and were driven. And running under the lee of a small island called Cauda,[b] we managed with difficulty

---

[a] *Or* southwest and northwest
[b] *Other ancient authorities read* Clauda

---

12 The directions of the winds named here (κατὰ λίβα and κατὰ χῶρον) are not quite clear. But it is much more likely that they mean 'northwest' and 'south-west' than that they mean 'north-east' and 'southeast'. Phoenix has generally been identified with a place called Lutro, which is one of the best harbours on the south coast of Crete; it is because Lutro faces south-east that the winds are interpreted as they are in the RSV. But just west of Lutro, separated by the narrow neck of land of the peninsula called Muros, is a place called Phineka, which faces north-west and south-west. The name certainly suggests Phoenix, and the harbour of Phineka may have been larger and more convenient nearly two thousand years ago. It seems therefore reasonable to identify Phoenix with this place.

13 *their purpose,* either of making Phoenix or of reaching Italy before the storms began.

14 *the northeaster* is a guess, but a likely guess. The Greek word is Εὐρακύλων, with some MSS. reading Εὐροκλύδων. Neither name is known elsewhere, but the *euro*-compound certainly implies an easterly direction, and if it was a *south*-easterly wind the later information about the navigation of the ship would make no sense. Lake thinks that a violent gust from one of the valleys of the mountainous part of Crete off which they were sailing blew them out into the more open sea, where they met a steady gale from which the shelter of Crete itself had hitherto protected them.

15 *face the wind,* i.e., shorten sail, put the ship's bow into the wind and try by very short tacks to make a little headway against it; ancient ships were apparently not well constructed for doing this. Alternatively, it may be that the ship's hull was not strong enough to face heavy seas head on. The 'Western' text adds that they furled the sails, apparently anxious to elaborate the phrase *gave way to it.*

16 The island *Cauda* (some MSS. Clauda), modern Gozzo (Cretan

to secure the boat; after hoisting it up, they took measures[a]
to undergird the ship; then, fearing that they should run on
the Syrtis, they lowered the gear, and so were driven. As we
were violently storm-tossed, they began next day to throw

a *Greek* helps

Gozzo, not the Maltese one) is some distance off the coast of Crete,
27 miles SW. They must have sailed south of it to come under its lee
with a NE. wind blowing. *Secure the boat,* i.e., clear it of the water with
which it was probably filling and haul it up on board.

measures are literally 'helps' (see RSV note). It may refer to some
part of a ship's equipment unknown to us (NEB 'made use of tackle',
which sounds impressively technical but does not add much to the
meaning). But it is rather more likely that the RSV translation is right
and that the expression simply means 'took measures', did whatever
was necessary. *Undergird the ship* is a translation indeed, but neither
translators nor readers can know exactly what it means. The expression is found in other writers on nautical matters, but none of them
throws light on what its precise significance was. At first sight one
would think that it might mean passing ropes round the outside of
the ship's hull. This device was occasionally used in the days of
wooden ships in order to strengthen the ship against the waves, and
was known as 'frapping', according to James Smith; but it is very
uncertainly attested in the ancient world. The most likely conjecture
is that it refers to the fastening of a strong rope, or a pair of ropes
twisted together, from the bow of the ship to the stern, inside the ship,
passing the rope over the deck and supporting it by props so as to
keep the tension taut. This operation is known to have been done in
ancient ships. It protected them against breaking their backs, a misfortune to which ancient ships were apparently particularly prone.
Syrtis (NEB 'the shallows of the Syrtis'), a shoal west of Cyrene, called
the *Syrtis maior,* one of two shoals of that part of the north coast of
Africa famous in antiquity for the danger they held for ships. A north-
east wind would have blown the ship on to them eventually if no
measures to avoid this had been taken. *Lowered the gear* is another
conjectural translation. Nobody knows what exactly the Greek word
for 'gear' (a very common one, used in a diversity of meanings,
σκεῦος) means in this context. The RSV translation is impressive,
but vague. What gear? The nautically minded James Smith thought
that it meant the fair-weather sails, in this case 'the yard with the
sail attached to it' (p. 70). The NEB 'lowered the mainsail', though
equally conjectural, has at least a definite meaning. Notice that the

19 the cargo overboard; and the third day they cast out with
20 their own hands the tackle of the ship. And when neither
sun nor stars appeared for many a day, and no small tempest
lay on us, all hope of our being saved was at last abandoned.

21   As they had been long without food, Paul then came forward among them and said, 'Men, you should have listened
to me, and should not have set sail from Crete and incurred
22 this injury and loss. I now bid you take heart; for there
23 will be no loss of life among you, but only of the ship. For
this very night there stood by me an angel of the God to
24 whom I belong and whom I worship, and he said, "Do not
be afraid, Paul; you must stand before Caesar; and lo, God
25 has granted you all those who sail with you." So take heart,
men, for I have faith in God that it will be exactly as I have
26 been told. But we shall have to run on some island.'

27   When the fourteenth night had come, as we were drifting
across the sea of Adria, about midnight the sailors suspected

---

first person plural lapses for one verse here, perhaps because Luke is
describing from the point of view of a passenger what the sailors were
doing.

19   *tackle of the ship*; a different Greek word (σκευή) from the one used
for *gear* in v. 17 (σκεῦος). Lake suggests that this word means 'spare
sails and tackle'; but we cannot be sure.

20   If neither sun nor stars were visible the navigator in the ancient
world had no means of plotting his course or knowing where he was,
possessing neither compass nor sextant. James Smith thought that
all hope of our being saved was at last abandoned because the ship was
leaking.

21–26   The absence of food is not, of course, to be attributed to the lack
of food aboard ship, but to the passengers' being unable to eat owing
to sea-sickness and panic.

27   *Adria* is the name given in the ancient world to the sea which
surrounds Sicily. The distance from Cauda to Malta as the crow flies
is about 310 miles. If the ship was drifting before the wind, with very
little sail, set on the starboard tack (i.e., attempting to make headway
towards the north), and the wind was north-easterly, Lake reckons

that they were nearing land. So they sounded and found twenty fathoms; a little farther on they sounded again and found fifteen fathoms. And fearing that we might run on the rocks, they let out four anchors from the stern, and prayed for day to come. And as the sailors were seeking to escape from the ship, and had lowered the boat into the sea, under pretense of laying out anchors from the bow, Paul said to the centurion and the soldiers, 'Unless these men stay in the ship, you cannot be saved.' Then the soldiers cut away the ropes of the boat, and let it go.

As day was about to dawn, Paul urged them all to take some food, saying, 'Today is the fourteenth day that you have continued in suspense and without food, having taken nothing. Therefore I urge you to take some food; it will give

---

that she would be very likely in about the fortnight mentioned to cover this distance, in a course which was an elliptical curve with the hollow of the curve to the south. He thinks that we must make the very reasonable assumption that by the time she approached Malta the wind must have moderated. *Nearing* (προσάγειν) has been thought by some to be a correction of προσαχειν (read by B), which might be a corruption of προσηχεῖν, and this last (meaning 'roar') would mean that the sailors thought that they could hear waves breaking on a shore.

Those who are skilled in nautical affairs are confident that the move of the sailors in taking to the dinghy need not have been a mere pretext for escape. In the first place, it is not very likely that all the crew would have fitted into the dinghy; in the second place, it would have been very unwise to attempt to make an unknown shore in the dark through a rough sea in a very frail boat; they would have done better to remain on board, had they consulted their safety. In the third place, the reason they alleged may have been a perfectly sound one. It may be, therefore, that Paul and Julius, by precipitately rushing to a false conclusion, were responsible for the loss of the dinghy. Had it been retained, the whole crew and passengers might have rowed themselves by instalments peacefully to the shore when day broke; the ship and its contents might have been preserved, and everybody saved from a wetting and the loss of baggage.

you strength, since not a hair is to perish from the head of
35 any of you.' And when he had said this, he took bread, and
giving thanks to God in the presence of all he broke it and
36 began to eat. Then they all were encouraged and ate some
37 food themselves. (We were in all two hundred and seventy-
38 six*a* persons in the ship.) And when they had eaten enough,
they lightened the ship, throwing out the wheat into the sea.

39   Now when it was day, they did not recognize the land, but
they noticed a bay with a beach, on which they planned if
40 possible to bring the ship ashore. So they cast off the anchors
and left them in the sea, at the same time loosening the ropes
that tied the rudders; then hoisting the foresail to the wind

---

a Other ancient authorites read seventy-six *or* about seventy-six

---

35   *he took bread, and giving thanks to God*: the words are the same as those
used in 1 Cor. 11²³, ²⁴, where Paul describes the institution of the
Eucharist by Jesus ('took bread, and when he had given thanks . . .').
It is not impossible that Paul celebrated the Eucharist on shipboard;
during the persecutions of the first three centuries, it had to be
celebrated in circumstances no less incongruous than these.¹ But, as
the words could refer to an ordinary meal, at which any Jew would
give thanks to God anyway, perhaps they should be taken as so
referring.

37   The number 276 (though there are MS. variations drastically
reducing this number) is not impossible, and is paralleled in other
accounts of the capacity of ships in antiquity. It is likely that there
were 276 people on board and that this is the matter-of-fact statement
of one of them.

38   The cargo had already been jettisoned (v. 18). But as we are
told only that *they began to throw the cargo overboard* (a meaning inferred
from the imperfect tense used, ἐποιοῦντο), presumably they here
completed the process, with the intention of enabling the ship to run
aground in as shallow water as possible.

40   *foresail*, a small sail, attached to the foremast, which was placed
very far forward in an ancient ship. See Plate p. 181.

¹ For instance, early in the fourth century the friends of the martyr
Lucian of Antioch celebrated the Eucharist with him in the darkness of
a prison, when he could not even stand upright (see Bidez's ed. of Philo-
storgius' *Church History*, p. 195 (14)).

they made for the beach. But striking a shoal[a] they ran the vessel aground; the bow stuck and remained immovable, and the stern was broken up by the surf. The soldiers' plan was to kill the prisoners, lest any should swim away and escape; but the centurion, wishing to save Paul, kept them from carrying out their purpose. He ordered those who could swim to throw themselves overboard first and make for the land, and the rest on planks or on pieces of the ship. And so it was that all escaped to land.

AFTER we had escaped, we then learned that the island was

a *Greek* place of two seas

---

a shoal: διθάλασσον. It could mean either a sandbank or a tongue of land or shallows, or indeed (except that this rendering would be meaningless here) a place where two seas meet, as the RV literally but ineptly renders it. The NEB rationalizes this into 'between cross-currents', the last point from which 276 passengers were likely to get safely to land.

pieces of the ship is a possible translation, but from the point of view of strict Greek usage we should render it 'persons from the ship' (τινων without a noun being more usually applied to persons than things), and this may well be the right translation. The sailors were able to carry some of the passengers to safety. On the whole it is likely that St. Paul's Bay, about eight miles NW. of Valletta, the traditional site of the shipwreck, is the correct one.

28: 1–15. *From Malta to Rome*

It is noticeable that during the whole of the rest of the journey until Rome is reached there is no mention of Paul's being a prisoner. The narrative becomes less detailed and more summary, though the 'we' passage continues until v. 16. After the exciting account of the shipwreck, interest in the day-to-day movements of Paul naturally slackens, and it may well be that the centurion (who seems to have been impressed by Paul's judgement and character, 27[3, 31, 43]) allowed him

2 called Malta. And the natives showed us unusual kindness, for they kindled a fire and welcomed us all, because it had
3 begun to rain and was cold. Paul had gathered a bundle of sticks and put them on the fire, when a viper came out be-
4 cause of the heat and fastened on his hand. When the natives saw the creature hanging from his hand, they said to one another, 'No doubt this man is a murderer. Though he has escaped from the sea, justice has not allowed him to live.'
5 He, however, shook off the creature into the fire and suffered
6 no harm. They waited, expecting him to swell up or suddenly fall down dead; but when they had waited a long time and saw no misfortune come to him, they changed their minds and said that he was a god.

7 Now in the neighborhood of that place were lands be-longing to the chief man of the island, named Publius, who
8 received us and entertained us hospitably for three days. It happened that the father of Publius lay sick with fever and dysentry; and Paul visited him and prayed, and putting his
9 hands on him healed him. And when this had taken place,

---

considerable freedom, on the ground that escape from an island like Malta, in winter, for somebody as much in the public eye as Paul, would have been impracticable, even had Paul desired it. The details of winds and durations of journeys and halts during journeys, which impress by their verisimili-tude, however, continue (28¹¹⁻¹⁵).

2-6   This incident is not one modelled on the sort of experience which the 'god-like man' (θεῖος ἀνήρ) of the Hellenistic biography, such as Philostratus' *Life of Apollonius of Tyana*, would be likely to encounter. The Maltese do indeed hail Paul as a god (v. 6), but neither Paul nor Luke would accept this (14¹¹⁻¹⁵). Luke no doubt records this as an example of the unstable superstition of pagans; there may even be a touch of humour in it.

7   The title *chief man of the island* (πρῶτος τῆς νήσου) has been verified by the discovery of an inscription including it.

the rest of the people on the island who had diseases also came and were cured. They presented many gifts to us;[a] and when we sailed, they put on board whatever we needed.

After three months we set sail in a ship which had wintered in the island, a ship of Alexandria, with the Twin Brothers as figurehead. Putting in at Syracuse, we stayed there for three days. And from there we made a circuit and arrived at Rhegium; and after one day a south wind sprang up, and on the second day we came to Puteoli. There we found brethren, and were invited to stay with them for seven days. And so we came to Rome. And the brethren there, when they heard of us, came as far as the Forum of Appius and Three Taverns to meet us. On seeing them Paul thanked God and took courage. And when we came into Rome, Paul was allowed to stay by himself, with the soldier that guarded him.

[a] *Or* honored us with many honors

---

the *Twin Brothers* were a well-known pair of minor Greek deities, Castor and Pollux. *Figurehead* is probably the correct rendering of the Greek (παρασῆμον), though it could refer to a picture prominently displayed. Ships in the ancient world usually took their names from their figureheads.

From *Rhegium* to *Puteoli* is about 230 miles; on the figures indicated in the text the ship must have sailed at about five knots, which is a perfectly possible rate.

Why should a centurion and a party of soldiers in charge of several prisoners permit one at least of them to stay for seven days in Puteoli? One can imagine possible reasons. The centurion may have had to go ahead to Rome to report the arrival of his party and receive instructions about where they were to be bestowed, and then return to take charge of them again. Some latitude in staying with friends had already been permitted (27³). Puteoli was at that time the most important port which served Rome; it was here that the grain-ships coming from Alexandria put in. The route from Puteoli to Rome was by the Via Campana to Capua, and from there by the Via Appia to Rome.

the *Forum of Appius* is 43 miles from Rome, *Three Taverns* 33 miles.

28: 16–31. *Conclusion*

It is known from Ulpian (an eminent Roman jurist of the first

17 After three days he called together the local leaders of the Jews; and when they had gathered, he said to them, 'Brethren, though I had done nothing against the people or the customs of our fathers, yet I was delivered prisoner from Jerusalem 18 into the hands of the Romans. When they had examined me, they wished to set me at liberty, because there was no reason 19 for the death penalty in my case. But when the Jews objected, I was compelled to appeal to Caesar—though I had no charge 20 to bring against my nation. For this reason therefore I have asked to see you and speak with you, since it is because of 21 the hope of Israel that I am bound with this chain.' And they said to him, 'We have received no letters from Judea about you, and none of the brethren coming here has reported or 22 spoken any evil about you. But we desire to hear from you what your views are; for with regard to this sect we know that everywhere it is spoken against.'

---

half of the third century) that a prisoner awaiting trial was allowed to pursue his trade; and it was not forbidden either that he should live in a hired lodging. At this point the 'Western' interpolation adds 'the centurion handed over the prisoners to the στρατοπεδάρχης; but Paul was allowed . . .'. The στρατοπεδάρχης is probably not (as has been suggested) the praetorian prefect himself, i.e., the commander of the main body of picked troops stationed near the city (who would be too exalted an official to take charge of Paul), nor the *praefectus urbi*, the official in charge of policing Rome itself, whose responsibilities would be too local to apply to Paul. He is probably the *princeps castrorum* (or, as he was called up to about 120, *princeps praetorii*), 'the head administrator of the *officium* of the Praetorian Guard' (Sherwin-White, *Roman Society and Roman Law*, p. 110). This shows a remarkable knowledge of police administration in Rome and is the strongest piece of evidence that the 'Western' interpolator lived in Rome.

17–22 This gathering together of *the local leaders of the Jews* and the summary account of Paul's judicial experiences is very vague. The 'we' passage has ceased at v. 16. The actual account here of his trials hitherto is so much condensed as to be inaccurate. It looks like a piece of Lukan 'reconstruction'.

When they had appointed a day for him, they came to him at his lodging in great numbers. And he expounded the matter to them from morning till evening, testifying to the kingdom of God and trying to convince them about Jesus both from the law of Moses and from the prophets. And some were convinced by what he said, while others disbelieved. So, as they disagreed among themselves, they departed, after Paul had made one statement: 'The Holy Spirit was right in saying to your fathers through Isaiah the prophet:

> "Go to this people, and say,
> You shall indeed hear but never understand,
> and you shall indeed see but never perceive.
> For this people's heart has grown dull,
> and their ears are heavy of hearing,
> and their eyes they have closed;
> lest they should perceive with their eyes,
> and hear with their ears,
> and understand with their heart,
> and turn for me to heal them."

Let it be known to you then that this salvation of God has been sent to the Gentiles; they will listen.'[a]

a *Other ancient authorities add verse 29,* And when he had said these words, the
   Jews departed, holding much dispute among themselves

---

lodging (ξενίαν) could mean an inn (see Plate p. 28); or it could mean what we should call lodgings. As Paul's stay was to be an extended one, the latter meaning is the more likely.

Paul's final witness against the Jews' unbelief, this time to the Jews in Rome; see above, on 13⁴⁶ and 18⁶. The passage from Isa. (6⁹⁻¹⁰) was a well-known proof-text in the early Church; it appears at Matt. 13¹⁴⁻¹⁵; Mark 4¹²; and John 12⁴⁰.

A fine summary, in a sentence, of the main message of Acts.

This verse is simply a product of the 'Western' text, and as such is relegated to the margin in the RSV.

30   And he lived there two whole years at his own expense,[a]
31   and welcomed all who came to him, preaching the kingdom
      of God and teaching about the Lord Jesus Christ quite
      openly and unhindered.

                    [a] Or in his own hired dwelling

---

30   *at his own expense* is the correct translation of the Greek expression
      (ἐν ἰδίῳ μισθώματι). The only alternative translation is 'on his own
      earnings' (so *The Beginnings of Christianity*), and this, no doubt, though
      not the preferable rendering, does explain how Paul could afford to
      live at his own expense. The RV (and the RSV margin) 'in his own
      hired lodging' is an impossible translation.

31   For reasons why Luke should not have satisfied natural curiosity
      about the outcome of Paul's trial and the end of his career, see above,
      Introduction, pp. 28–35. The book ends with a good Greek sentence
      terminating in an effective rhythmical phrase. From a dramatic and
      literary point of view, this is a perfectly good ending. As the story of
      how the Christian Church began, how Christianity spread to the
      Gentiles, and how the great apostle of the Gentiles, Paul, came to
      Rome, the book appropriately ends here.

TABLE OF RELEVANT DATES

B.C.	4	Death of Herod the Great.
A.D.	6	Rebellion of Judas at the time of the census.
	14	Death of Augustus. Accession of Tiberius.
	26	Pontius Pilate procurator of Judaea. Caiaphas high priest.
	36	Pilate leaves Judaea.
	37	Death of Tiberius. Accession of Gaius. Caiaphas deposed. Herod Agrippa I made tetrarch of Judaea.
	39	Aretas IV of Nabataea dies.
	41	Murder of Gaius. Accession of Claudius. Herod Agrippa I made King of Judaea.
	44	Death of Herod Agrippa I. Judaea reverts to government by procurators.
	?48	Ananias high priest.
	52	Gallio proconsul of Achaea.
	?53	Felix procurator of Judaea.
	54	Death of Claudius. Accession of Nero.
	?55	Ananias murdered. Felix leaves Judaea.
	?56	Festus procurator of Judaea.
	?62	Festus dies as procurator.
	64	Fire of Rome. Persecution of Christians.
	66	Outbreak of Jewish rebellion.
	68	Nero commits suicide.
	68/9	Year of anarchy.
	69	Vespasian Emperor.
	70	Jerusalem falls to Romans.
	79	Vespasian dies. Accession of Titus.
	81	Death of Titus. Accession of Domitian.
	96	Murder of Domitian. Accession of Nerva.
	98	Death of Nerva. Accession of Trajan.
	?115	Pliny Governor of Bithynia.
	118	Death of Trajan.

INDEX

(names mentioned in the text of Acts are not included here)

PRINTED IN GREAT BRITAIN
AT THE UNIVERSITY PRESS, OXFORD
BY VIVIAN RIDLER
PRINTER TO THE UNIVERSITY